D1598003

Artisans IN THE North Carolina Backcountry

Artisans IN THE North Carolina Backcountry

JOHANNA MILLER LEWIS

THE UNIVERSITY PRESS OF KENTUCKY

Scholarly publisher for the Commonwealth,
serving Bellarmine College, Berea College, Centre
College of Kentucky, Eastern Kentucky University,
The Filson Club, Georgetown College, Kentucky
Historical Society, Kentucky State University,
Morehead State University, Murray State University,
Northern Kentucky University, Transylvania University,
University of Kentucky, University of Louisville,
and Western Kentucky University.

Editorial and Sales Offices: Lexington, Kentucky 40508-4008

Library of Congress Cataloging-in-Publication Data

Lewis, Johanna Miller, 1961—

Artisans in the North Carolina backcountry / Johanna Miller Lewis.
p. cm.
Includes bibliographical references and index.
ISBN 0-8131-1908-1 :
1. Material culture—North Carolina—Rowan County—History—18th century. 2. Artisans—North Carolina—Rowan County—History—18th century. 3. Rowan County (N.C.)—Social life and customs.
I. Title.
F262.R8L44 1995
975.6'71—dc20 94-43855

This book is printed on acid-free recycled paper meeting
the requirements of the American National Standard
for Permanence of Paper for Printed Library Materials.

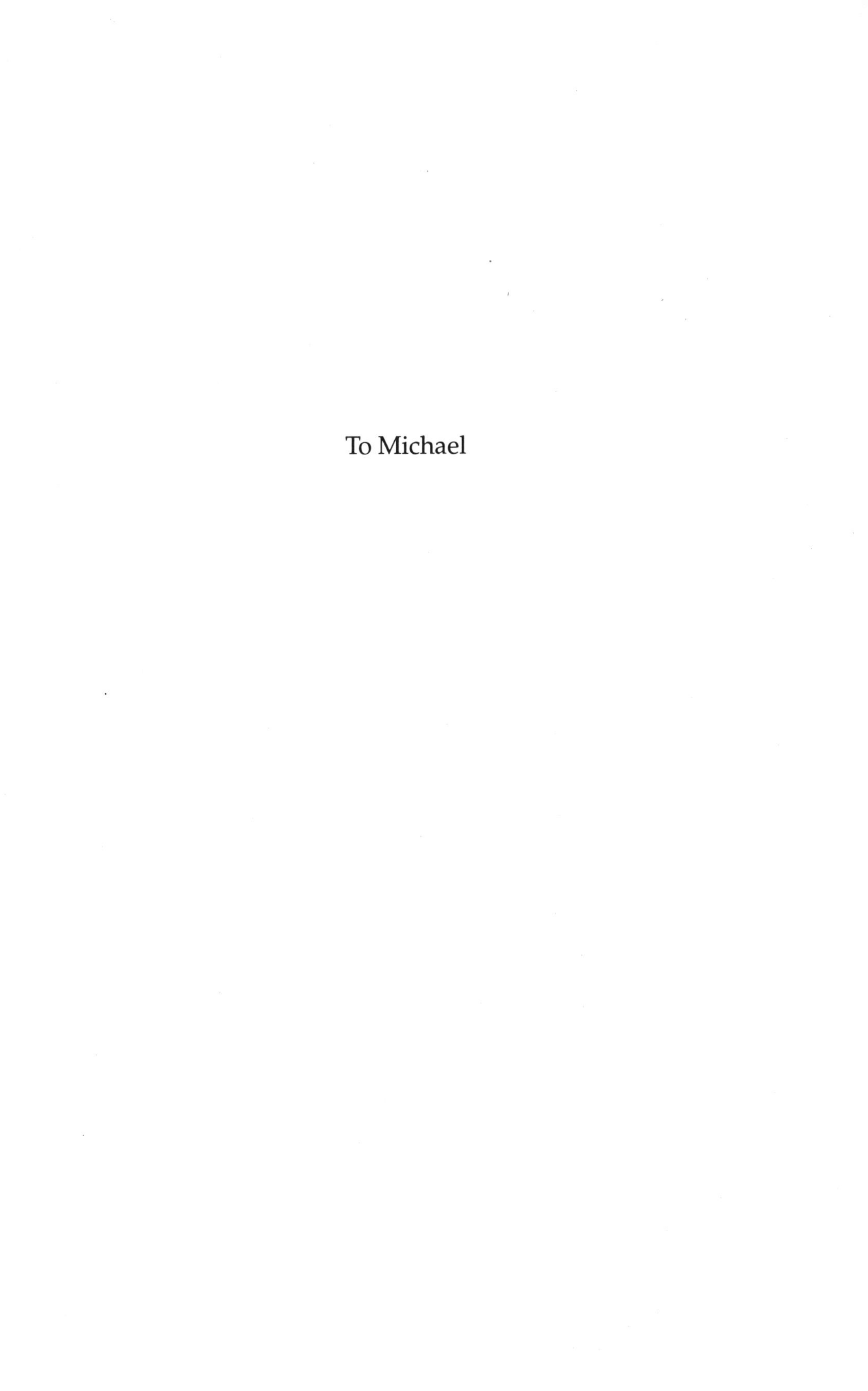

To Michael

Contents

Tables

Acknowledgments

There may be only one author's name on this book, but its creation was really a collaborative effort. Researching and writing can be a lonely experience, but colleagues, family, and friends supported me for the duration. In this instance, duration means almost a decade over which Rowan County artisans began as a paper, turned into a dissertation and then a few articles and papers, and finally evolved into this book.

The majority of research for the dissertation and the book was supported by grants from the Early American Industries Association, the Society of the Cincinnati in the State of Virginia, the Commonwealth Center for the Study of American Culture, the History Department at the College of William and Mary, Old Salem, Inc., and an Archie K. Davis Fellowship from the North Caroliniana Society. That financial support (along with gifts from my parents and in-laws) made it possible for me to do research at the North Carolina Division of Archives and History in Raleigh; the Southern Historical Collection and the North Caroliniana Room in the Wilson Library in Chapel Hill; the Moravian Archives, Southern Province, the Siewers Room of Gramley Library at Salem College, Old Salem, Inc., and the Museum of Early Southern Decorative Arts in Winston-Salem; and the McCubbins Collection in the Local History Room of the Salisbury Public Library. I thank the staff at all of those institutions for their assistance.

For feeding me and giving me a place to stay during my innumerable trips to North Carolina, I want to thank Norvell and Mary Miller, Helen Hagan, Della Carlton, Carl and Lee Thorne, Michael Hammond and Rebecca Hendrickson, Ed and Sue Hendricks (and Chris and Lee), and Jon and Beverly Sensbach.

I have learned that doing the research is the easy part; formulating one's thesis and writing it in understandable form are the hard parts. Fortunately, many people have guided me along the way, and their opinions and advice have been most helpful. On my dissertation committee I would like to thank John Selby, Thad Tate, and Tom Sheppard at the College of William and Mary, and Michael Hammond, then of Old Salem. On getting from the dissertation to the book, I am indebted to the keen insight and suggestions of Jeff Crow, Dan Thorp, Warren Hofstra, Jean Russo, and Daniel Vickers. My colleagues at the University of Arkansas at Little Rock encouraged me (especially Stephen Recken, Michelle Fontaine, and Harri Baker), but having another colonial historian around was a true luxury and Charlie Bolton's comments and observations were instrumental to the final product.

I owe my largest debt to Jim Whittenburg; this book is as much his as it is mine. He suggested the topic to me, he supervised the dissertation, and he has read every draft of the book. Even more amazing, somewhere along the line we became fast friends in the face of adversity.

And finally, none of this would have happened without Michael. He knew, better than anyone, that having gone to Salem College and Wake Forest, I felt enveloped by Rowan County and the Wachovia Tract personally and historically. Not only has he read (and listened to) every draft; his love, support, encouragement, enthusiasm, and knowledge have made it all worthwhile.

Introduction

This book looks at artisans in Rowan County, North Carolina, during the third quarter of the eighteenth century. As a backcountry county, one west of the "fall line," colonial Rowan County contained some fairly populated areas to the east and the unsettled frontier to the west. In examining the craftsmen and their place in the social, economic, and political world of Rowan County, this study encompasses some of the most important and popular topics in the recent historiography of early America: artisans, the frontier, and the debate over self-sufficiency and capitalism in rural America.

For every direction this inquiry might have taken, the thesis is deceptively simple: far from being abandoned to their own survival skills in the great colonial wilderness, the inhabitants of the North Carolina backwoods patronized a small, but growing, population of artisan-farmers who supplied their clientele with basic necessities and even luxury goods that local merchants and their ties to the trans-Atlantic economy could not satisfactorily produce.

Perhaps the impact of this study lies not in its depth or attention to one issue, but in its portrayal of the role the artisan played in the everyday life of Rowan County. Such a portrayal allows the discussion of the presence of professional artisans in the rural South, the participation of backcountry businessmen in local, regional, and international trade networks, and the nature of the economy and the standard of living on the eighteenth-century frontier.

Although Rowan County artisans seem to lack many of the characteristics of other artisan groups that have been studied (they are not urban, they do not have an overwhelmingly cohesive political consciousness, and they are not faced with the economic consequences of changes in the organization of labor), these inadequacies may add up to the most distinguishing characteristic of all: they are "typical" artisans at work during the formative years of American history. Additionally, artisans working in a less economically developed area such as Rowan County probably played a more direct role in maintaining their customers' standard of living than did artisans working in large urban areas with fully developed market economies. In a more focused context, examining all of the artisans of Rowan County will explore how the Moravians, one of the only groups of artisans in the southern backcountry previously written about, fared against their competition.

The traditional interpretation of artisans in the colonial southern backcountry is brief and succinct: outside of those practicing the most basic crafts there were no artisans. This book seeks to revise that interpretation by exploring the role and experience of artisans in the settlement and early development of Rowan County, North Carolina, from 1753 to 1770. Research gathered from court records, deeds, wills, private records, and the voluminous records of the Moravians contradicts the earlier assumptions of historians; artisans were among the first settlers in Rowan County, and their development paralleled the growth of the county. In the early 1750s, a handful of artisans produced objects that the small groups of settlers needed to survive and create new lives in the backcountry. Blacksmiths, weavers, tailors, tanners, and saddlers made clothes, shoes, saddles, and ironware for backcountry inhabitants, and millwrights and carpenters built structures that helped Rowan county develop.

As more people poured into the county, so did more artisans. Hatters, joiners, masons, coopers, turners, wheelwrights, wagonmakers, potters, and gunsmiths joined the expanding community of craftspeople. Simultaneously, improvements and growth in the backcountry road and ferry system increased the range of local trade networks all the way to the coast and across the Atlantic Ocean. Where backcountry residents once had looked for their needs to Cross Creek, North Carolina, Charleston, South Carolina, or London, local silversmiths, cabinetmakers, gunstockers, and watchmakers came to fill the needs of Rowan County's conspicuous consumers. Public and private accounts record that artisans made raised paneled room interiors, silver shoe buckles, fancy beaver hats, walnut tables and chests of drawers, and fancy riding chairs for an exacting clientele. Anxious to take advantage of the economic opportunities the burgeoning backcountry offered, artisans expanded their operations to increase their profits.

Between 1753 and 1770, Rowan County covered approximately the northwest quadrant of North Carolina; for more than seventeen years it was the single largest county in the backcountry. The wide geographic area of Rowan meant that the county displayed all stages of settlement at any given time. Salisbury, the county seat, and Salem and Bethabara, two of the Moravian towns on the Wachovia Tract, provided a fairly refined lifestyle in the eastern half of the county, while the extreme western boundaries of the county featured the unsettled frontier. The artisans of Rowan County provided specialized skills and produced objects necessary for daily existence, as well as for decorative and ornamental purposes, that backcountry residents could not have easily obtained otherwise.

The study will answer such questions as: How did the artisans help settle Rowan County, and where did they come from? Were some crafts more necessary than others at different stages of settlement? Did any "nonessential" crafts ever appear? How did the non-Moravian artisans in Rowan County compare to their Moravian counterparts? And, finally, how successfully did artisans participate in backcountry politics?

To place the artisan's experience in Rowan County into context, chapter 1 presents the historiography of artisans and the economy of early America and the southern backcountry. Chapter 2 discusses how artisans participated in the early history and settlement of Rowan County and the Wachovia Tract, examining the motivation of the settlers to the region. Chapter 3 focuses on the growth and development of Rowan County and a series of events that caused the potential of the Wachovia Tract to remain undeveloped by 1759. The chapter explores the effect the early economic development of the county (east and west of the Yadkin River) had on both Moravian and non-Moravian artisans. The study of the economy's effect on the non-Moravian artisans of Rowan County from 1759 to 1770 continues in chapter 4. From the account books of three Rowan County merchants and the branch store of a Wilmington merchant in Cross Creek, the artisans' place in the expanding economy of the backcountry becomes increasingly evident. Not only do the account books show the importance of roads, merchants, and trading towns on the backcountry economy, they demonstrate the urban/rural dichotomy of economic specialization that artisans were quick to follow. In both chapters 3 and 4 a quantitative profile of artisans by craft and time period analyzes the changing artisan population.

Chapter 5 focuses on what happened to the Moravian artisans on the Wachovia Tract after 1759. The financial backing and organization of the Moravians make them an aberration when compared to the rest of the county. Their extensive records, especially regarding the planning of the first settlement and the subsequent development of the tract, make an interesting divergence to the less well-documented, "unsupervised" settlement and progress of the rest of Rowan County. The chapter begins with the belated construction of Salem, then discusses Moravian artisans' self-perceptions both within and without the church-run community.

Chapter 6 looks at the women artisans who formed a significant segment of the artisan population in Wachovia and Rowan County. Women contributed to the backcountry economy as professional artisans and as household practitioners. Records indicate that the ability to make and control an income afforded both married and single women a sense of freedom and self-worth that was most unusual for the colonial South.

Chapter 7 examines artisans in the public sphere of Rowan County. After a discussion of artisan participation (or lack thereof) in the War of the Regulators, the rural nature of Rowan County is shown to be a deciding factor in the lack of political organization among backcountry artisans. Artisans who were in the public eye as the result of political office, informal power through wealth, or criminal behavior got there because of individual motives and initiatives and not group action.

Rowan County artisans played a number of different roles in the colonial backcountry. As farmers, they helped settle and improve the land of the county with their houses, outbuildings, and fields. As professional artisans, they participated in the developing economy first by equipping county inhabitants with basic necessities, and later by producing some of the finer things in life. As providers of goods and services, along with local merchants, artisans helped to elevate the standard of living available to Rowan County residents. Finally, quite a few artisans, as individuals, exercised their best judgment by acting on behalf of the county's welfare. As such, Rowan County artisans are not the "typical" urban artisan group studied by historians. Instead, they provide us with a rare perspective of the rural society and economy found in the southern colonial backcountry.

ONE

Artisans and the Backcountry

From the time of its creation in 1753, artisans played an important role in the social and economic life of Rowan County, North Carolina. Whether they came individually with their families to obtain land and establish new lives, or they were chosen by the Moravian Church to settle the one hundred thousand-acre Wachovia Tract, all of these artisans were part of the huge wave of immigration to the western half or backcountry of North Carolina that occurred during the third quarter of the eighteenth century.

No other studies of Rowan County or the North Carolina backcountry have focused on the artisans of that diverse region. Research in Rowan County court records, apprentice bonds, deeds, and wills, as well as extant invoices and account books, indicates that artisans played a notable role in increasing the quality of life in backcountry North Carolina. The presence of artisans and the availability of their products in Rowan County show that inhabitants of the backcountry did not always live "in the most slovenly manner" that many historians have believed.[1]

While artisans in the North Carolina backcountry have not been written about previously, artisans in early America, especially in the colonial South, have generated a reasonable amount of interest over the years. Carl Bridenbaugh is the only historian to have given substantial notice of the importance of the craftsman in all of colonial society. His book *The Colonial Craftsman,* in which he delineates craft development in the colonies to meet the particular needs of an area and its inhabitants, remains the only general historical work on artisans in colonial America. Bridenbaugh has also included artisans and their place in economy and society in his books on colonial urban America and the South.[2]

More recently, the trend has been toward studying the craftsmen of a particular locale, or even artisans of specific crafts within a certain area. One characteristic of these works is that every author seems to investigate and interpret the artisan from a different perspective. With the onslaught of the new social history and interest in doing "history from the bottom up," as Jesse Lemisch called it, artisans became an easily identifiable segment of the "inarticulate" population, leading historians to scrutinize the craftsman as a typical example of the "working man." Consequently, quite a few historians have used the artisans of different locales to explore eighteenth-century labor history.[3]

In *The Social Structure of Revolutionary America,* Jackson Turner Main discussed the class structure of Revolutionary America and explained how an individual's occupation, income, and ownership of property influenced his status, prestige, and rank in the community.[4] While many of the more recent works in the new social history have superseded this book, the questions Main asked, his research methods, and his conclusions set the standard for all future studies of particular groups in society, including artisans. Following Main's lead, most historians have investigated artisans by analyzing the extant records involving artisans in certain localities to determine how they lived and how they fit into the society in which they lived.

To get a population of artisans large enough to study and recognize trends and patterns of behavior, historians have focused their studies on large urban areas, addressing those issues that tax, voting, court, land and other records can help answer. In these studies historians primarily emphasize the political and economic lives of the eighteenth-century artisan population and deal only tangentially with the more personal issues of standard of living and quality of life at home or work. As Howard B. Rock asserts in the preface of his book *Artisans of the New Republic,* politically-aware artisans often composed a decisive electoral block in the nation's major urban areas, playing a major role in the development of partisan politics. In the marketplace, too, artisans exerted influence as active entrepreneurs and, most critically, as adversaries in serious and sometimes protracted labor disputes, conflicts that have had a lasting effect on American working-class history.[5]

In fact, the majority of works written on artisans in early America deal with their participation in local and national politics, most notably the Revolution and the early Republic, to protect their economic interests. Sean Wilentz traces the political maturation of artisans from street mobs to well-organized political action groups in *Chants Democratic,* and Rock shows the impact that the economic realities of the new Republic had on artisans.[6] With artisans forming the largest segment of Philadelphia's population, Charles Olton's *Artisans for Independence* and Gary Nash's *Urban Crucible* show similar political activism among the city's mechanic classes.[7] In *The Mechanics of Baltimore,* Charles G. Steffen recounts artisans' efforts to liberate that city from the planter-dominated government at Annapolis by cooperating with the merchant class. Tina Sheller focuses on the effects the Revolution had on Baltimore artisans and their crafts in "Artisans, Manufacturing, and the Rise of a Manufacturing Interest in Revolutionary Baltimore Town."[8]

But political power was not everything to artisans, especially in the late eighteenth and early nineteenth century, when the economy and technology forced the reorganization of production to emphasize cost over quality and skill. The beginning of industrialization and the downsizing of the trained artisan labor force is the second most prominent topic among artisan studies. Some works, such as Sharon V. Salinger's "Artisans, Journeymen, and the Transformation of Labor in Late Eighteenth-Century Philadelphia," Steffen's "Changes in the Organization of Artisan Production in Baltimore, 1790-1820," and Susan E. Hirsch's *Roots of the American Working Class,* address the subject and its effect on particular communities directly.[9] Others, such as Nash's "Poverty and Poor Relief in Pre-Revolutionary Philadelphia," Billy Smith's "The Material Lives of Laboring Philadelphians, 1750-1800," and Bruce Laurie's *Artisans into Workers: Labor in Nineteenth-Century America,* discuss some of the consequences of the change of labor.[10]

The absence of large urban areas, the existence of a plantation economy based on staple crop agriculture, and the presence of a slave labor force in the prosperous areas of the South have led historians to a completely different approach with respect to artisans in southern society. Craftsmen in the colonial South have generated interest over the years because of the issue of bound versus free labor. In *Colonial Craftsman* Bridenbaugh reasons that outside of urban areas such as Annapolis, Williamsburg, and Charleston, the agricultural and rural nature of the South made it difficult for craftsmen to survive. Because they sold crops to England, the owners of large plantations frequently imported high quality consumer goods from there and used local craftsmen to supply only their most basic needs. However, as most southern plantations depended on slave labor, the owners gradually realized that making their operations self-sufficient by training their slaves as artisans would be cheaper than patronizing local free craftsmen. That investment also provided some economic protection against the crop market.[11] Thus Bridenbaugh argues that in the rural South the availability of goods from England, combined with the use of slave labor to produce "necessary" items, resulted in a serious shortage of free artisans throughout the region.

In an excellent historiographic review of the scholarship on free and slave artisans in the Chesapeake, Jean B. Russo points out that historians have reached an impasse in explaining the lack of free artisans amid the search for plantation self-sufficiency. Either the plantation owner's decision to make his plantation self-sufficient with slave labor caused him to rely less on free craftsmen, sending those artisans into other endeavors or locations, or the lack of free artisans forced the plantation owner to become self-sufficient with slave labor, causing artisans to abandon their trades for planting. Either way, Russo concludes, the debate has failed to address the role of local craftsmen who remained in their rural communities, as she does for Talbot County, Maryland, from 1690 to 1759.[12]

Russo answers a vital question in the historiographical debate over skilled slave versus skilled free labor in the Chesapeake with her research. Not surprisingly, she found that artisans who practiced basic crafts (carpenters, coopers, blacksmiths, shoemakers, weavers, and tailors) prevailed in the region; some artisans in secondary and allied crafts were also present at times. When the tobacco market prospered, free artisans' fortunes might decline, for planters who could afford to acquired skilled slaves who could expand the variety of plantation activity, thereby buffering the extremes of depression. Yet plantations (in Talbot County at least) were not self-sufficient, and the economy and society still depended on free artisans to provide them with the necessities of everyday life.[13]

Russo's work is important for another reason. Her dissertation does not merely scour the county records to construct another profile of how artisans, as a representative "inarticulate" group, fit into society, but also provides a portrait of artisanal life in Talbot County.[14] Rather than the highly trained, style-conscious craftsmen who competed for business from the wealthy inhabitants of Charleston or Annapolis, in Talbot County Russo found artisans in basic crafts who were willing to fit their skills into the framework of opportunity shaped by the tobacco economy of the region. Fortunately, other historians such as Christine Daniels have followed Russo's lead into the artisans of the Chesapeake region, filling in the details of her ground-breaking work.[15]

While Talbot County, Maryland, was a long way from Rowan County, North Carolina, Russo's conclusions about Chesapeake artisans parallel the situation in the backcountry South. Russo ascertained that a stable free artisan population did exist in an economy dominated by plantations, tobacco, and slaves. Similarly, this book will argue that artisans existed and improved the quality of life in a backcountry region once portrayed as lacking a market economy as well as most of the refinements of eighteenth-century life.

Although the backcountry in North Carolina was most decidedly rural, Russo's explanations for the lack of free artisans in the Chesapeake do not apply. In fact, the backcountry's reputation was quite the opposite of that of Chesapeake society. In the mid-eighteenth century the backcountry stood in stark contrast to the land of tobacco, slaves, and plantations: it was a frontier where newly arrived settlers began with nothing. This difference between the backcountry and the older, more established eastern areas of the South may explain why many authors, both historical and contemporary, have depicted the backcountry as a rural, *retardetaire* society.

Rowan County was a vital and active place to be during the third quarter of the eighteenth century. The westernmost county in the colony, Rowan was most decidedly backcountry, if not frontier. The settlers responsible for Rowan's growth and development were mainly farmers, who successfully produced enough corn, wheat, and other agricultural products to trade or export for profit.[16] Yet historians have been slow to correct the image of the backcountry resident as so isolated that everything he needed he had to make himself, or as only occasionally so fortunate that he could import some nicer items from more civilized places. The Reverend Charles Woodmason's 1766 description of "all new Settlers" near present-day Camden, South Carolina, as "extremely poor—Live in Logg Cabins like Hogs—and their Living and Behaviour as rude or more so than the Savages,"[17] leaves a vivid image in one's mind. Carl Bridenbaugh states that "back inhabitants lived by a mere subsistence farming [until] somewhat later [than 1750] in the Carolinas. This necessitated the fabrication in the home by the members of the family of all items needed except salt and iron—wooden furniture and utensils, homespun cloth, soap, and candles."[18]

Bridenbaugh was not the only proponent of the "make everything at home" theory of backcountry living. In *North Carolina: The History of a Southern State,* one of the most widely used reference books on the history of the state, Hugh T. Lefler and Albert Ray Newsome tell a similar story. "The small farmer and his family were engaged in self-sufficient or subsistence farming. They cleared the forest, tilled the soil, produced the bare necessities of life, and eked out a living—sometimes successfully and in an orderly way, but frequently, 'in the most slovenly manner.' . . . They had few conveniences and no luxuries; what they could not produce they simply did without."[19] In addition, similar statements appear in works by Julia Cherry Spruill and Rolla Milton Tryon.[20] With few exceptions, the interpretation of these older historians has remained the predominant view of the backcountry. As recently as 1991 Charles Sellers recounted this theory in *The Market Revolution,* noting that "people who settled at any distance from navigable water mainly produced use values for subsistence rather than the market's commodity values for sale."[21]

Studies concerning the exact economic nature of early rural America have dismissed much of the theory of total economic self-sufficiency or subsistence but have raised numerous other questions. As with artisan studies, the majority of the work historians have done on the economy of early America has focused on the interchange of mercantile and agricultural trade in urban areas.[22] In her article "How Self-Sufficient Was Early America?" Carole Shammas found not only that the costs of running a self-sufficient 125-acre farm in pre-Revolutionary Pennsylvania would have exceeded the financial resources available to many households, but that such households would require "a bewildering number of skills from their members." Shammas concluded in a later study that rural colonial homes never lived up to their potential as centers of household production for direct consumption because of the pressures exerted by the external economy in local communities.[23] Limiting her focus to self-sufficiency in food production, Bettye

Hobbs Pruitt proved that only the wealthiest farmers in Massachusetts could achieve self-sufficiency; for the vast majority "local exchanges of food were an essential and necessary part of subsistence."[24]

What these historians have left behind, however, is a raging debate over what type of exchange relations characterized the non-urban, agricultural areas of early America, what participants wanted from these relations, and how participants perceived such exchanges. Were the farmers of early America happy yeomen content to while away their lives on the family farm, taking care of their family with simple exchanges based on the reciprocal needs of their neighbors? Or were they, along with the merchants and artisans in the community, budding entrepreneurs, anxious to make a profit off their neighbors and anyone else, in order to climb the ladder of financial success?[25] Trying to characterize the actions, lives, and motivation of historical figures is a difficult business, and two historians can work with similar sets of facts and come up with the diametrically opposed views stated above—as did James A. Henretta and James T. Lemon.[26]

Why has the debate continued to rage? Allan Kulikoff states that the reason may be both confusion over the nature of economic development in America from the seventeenth century all the way through to industrialization, and a desire for a formal model to explain how the economy progressed and changed during that time. Kulikoff further suggests that the rural economy of early America be described as "transitional," i.e., as an intensification of capitalist production or from a noncommercial or at least a non-capitalist economy to a capitalist one.[27]

Unfortunately, the debate about and most of the models of the economy of early rural America mainly concentrate on farmers and agriculture, and Kulikoff's attempt to use the transition to capitalism to explain every incidence of social conflict in eighteenth- and nineteenth-century America falls short of the mark.[28] However, some other historians' theories can be applied to the larger economic picture in the southern backcountry. While Bridenbaugh would probably agree with the assessment of the backcountry as an economy in transition, his own work places him more in the Henretta "*Mentalité*," or what Kulikoff calls the social historian school of economic interpretation.

Bridenbaugh acknowledges the arrival of some artisans in the backcountry and their willingness to exchange their work for food and other necessities as "the time-honored European custom of rural artisans." While noting that the production of surplus crops stimulated the rise of crafts through local exchanges of goods and services, he maintains it also necessitated a search for markets and for a supply of much-needed manufactured goods.[29] Bridenbaugh concludes that "beyond the basic needs almost no crafts developed" in the rural South. Outside of a few exceptions such as the Moravians in North Carolina or Isaac Zane's Marlboro Iron

Works in the Valley of Virginia, "Quality goods for general sale were not produced." Furthermore, the few village crafts and rural artisans that did persist "were never able to satisfy the demands of the southern backcountry in the colonial period."[30]

For many of the same reasons that the urban areas of early America have attracted more attention from historians than the rural areas (bigger population, better records, more political and economic activity), the eastern region of the South has received much more discussion than the interior portion. In fact, the differences between the western and eastern portions of the South were what originally attracted historians to study the backcountry. However, the enormous surge of immigration to the backcountry, the ethnic and religious diversity of those immigrants, and those settlers' ability to adapt to their new environment have kept scholars' attention. Frederick Jackson Turner was one of the first historians to note the distinguishing features of backcountry life: a new and rapidly expanding, highly mobile, heterogeneous population, weaker local traditions and commitments to place than in older eastern settlements, less economic specialization and social differentiation, and inchoate or fragile institutions of authority. Turner argued that because frontier elites lacked personal prestige, affluence, and gentility, political hierarchies in the backcountries lacked clear definition. Therefore, politics was less deferential and more egalitarian, democratic, contentious, and disorderly.[31]

Scholars still credit Bridenbaugh in *Myths and Realities* with providing the first general sketch of life in the back settlements in terms of geography, immigration, ethnicity, economics, agriculture, labor, politics, society, religion, education and training, and culture.[32] Although Bridenbaugh generalized very broadly and his research was not thorough in some areas, he makes a crucial point about the history of the backcountry that most historians have overlooked: one of the most striking features of backcountry society was that in different areas various groups lived in several stages of development at the same time.[33] Furthermore, the different sections of the backcountry lived in several stages of development simultaneously.[34]

Most historians consider the geographic area of the southern backcountry to extend from Frederick County, Maryland, south through the Great Valley and that portion of the Virginia, North Carolina, and South Carolina Piedmont that lies west of the fall line and east of the Appalachians.[35] While the communities within this area shared such characteristics as an ethnically diverse population and a vast array of languages, religions, values, and customs, creating a multiform society, the ever-changing nature and the different levels of development present throughout backcountry society make comparing and contrasting colonies (or communities) a risky proposition.

As Albert Tillson notes in "The Southern Backcountry," the relationship between local backcountry governments and their respective provincial governments could determine the political atmosphere of the region, especially with regard to granting land titles and establishing local governments. In Virginia and Maryland, the colonial governments readily authorized local government in the newly settled western areas, and settlers experienced little sectional animosity. By contrast, in North and South Carolina the eastern provincial governments' refusal to grant the western regions local governments and equal representation in the colonial assembly resulted in disorders characterized by violence and corrupt and incompetent backcountry officials.[36]

Although more has been written about the Shenandoah Valley of Virginia, the back settlements of Virginia and North Carolina have been compared frequently, even though they differed on a number of crucial points. Virginia experienced political co-operation between the eastern and western counties; portions of the backcountry of Virginia were settled early, with a significantly greater immigration from the eastern part of the colony; finally, Virginia experienced a gradual extension of the slave-based, agricultural economy (and accompanying tobacco culture) into the backcountry by the close of the eighteenth century.[37] North Carolina had none of these characteristics until the nineteenth century. In fact, aside from a few early Indian problems, the Virginia backcountry never experienced the chaos and turmoil that the other southern colonial backcountries did.[38]

Specifically, in *The Evolution of the Southern Backcountry* Richard Beeman argues that most studies of the southern backcountry have ignored the obvious cultural and political connections between the traditional power centers in the eastern portion of those colonies and the western; a situation he tries to remedy for Lunenburg County, Virginia. Beeman believes that a variety of sources, including those commonly associated with the backcountry as well as those in the older, more established areas of the eastern colonies, affected the formation of the political institutions, economic systems, and cultural values of Lunenburg County.[39] Unfortunately, Lunenburg County's location on the Virginia Southside made it more susceptible to eastern influences than most southern backcountry counties. These influences include large-scale land speculation by Tidewater gentry prior to the formation of the county for personal gain during later expansion; an established Anglican Church; conscious imitation of Tidewater social, cultural, and political practices; a less-varied ethnic population; and (most strikingly) the adaptation of the most defining aspect of eastern Virginia, tobacco culture.[40]

For all the local variations in the southern backcountry, David Hackett Fischer makes a compelling case in *Albion's Seed: Four British Folkways in America* for the regional distinctiveness of the backcountry as determined by the cultural qualities (folkways) of the particular immigrants (and their descendants) who settled the area. Not only does Fischer's study complement Bridenbaugh's *Myths and Realities* by bringing a more up-to-date and synthesized approach to the backcountry; he seems to be the first historian to see conflict and confrontation as the essence of backcountry life and not an obstacle to progress. According to Fischer, backcountry society emerged not in spite of conflict, but because of it. Conflict and militancy were a part of the backcountry settlers' folkways when they were still in England, Germany, and Ireland; the question for historians is "how does that tradition of conflict and militancy manifest itself in the backcountry?"[41]

In North Carolina the tradition of conflict and militancy manifested itself in the Regulator movement, which left a legacy of political turmoil and confusion in the backcountry. Following John S. Bassett's lead, A. Roger Ekirch, Marvin L. Michael Kay, Lorin Lee Cary, and James P. Whittenburg have discussed and debated the origins and motivations behind the Regulators in great depth.[42] The Regulators' legacy in North Carolina was the chaos and bewilderment backcountry residents experienced deciding between loyalty to Great Britain and patriotism to the newly united American colonies during the War for Independence. Two books, *Uncivil War* and *The Southern Experience in the American Revolution*, have examined in great detail the issues of "which side are you fighting for," and the subsequent commotion for both British and American forces in the war.[43]

Certainly the Regulator movement and the American Revolution are in large part responsible for this historical interpretation of the backcountry as a region in which people were engaged in a constant struggle for power. In *The Moravian Community in Colonial North Carolina* Daniel B. Thorp writes that although conflict hardly was rare on the southern frontier, and the southern backcountry may well have been the most unstable region in Britain's North American empire during the mid-eighteenth century, a more complete picture of the social developments of the southern backcountry is desperately needed. He maintains that, outside of Beeman's *Evolution of Southern Backcountry* and Robert D. Mitchell's *Commercialism and Frontier*, both of which focus on Virginia, most historians are convinced that conflict was endemic to the backcountry. Such historians are more interested in finding the causes of conflict or debating its consequences than in exploring the society that emerged there in spite of the conflict.[44]

Thorp is correct. Only a few backcountry studies examine the economic makeup of the region and its effect on society. This gap is unfortunate because, as H.R. Merrens notes in *Colonial North Carolina in the Eighteenth Century*, even "if the administrative and judicial functions [of the backcountry] were sometimes disrupted by political partiality and civil disorders, at least trade and commerce seem to have been uninterrupted."[45]

As already noted, although it does discuss the political, economic, and social life of Lunenburg County without focusing on conflict, Beeman's study is a somewhat tenuous model for the North Carolina backcountry. He traces the development of the county's economy "out of the realm of subsistence agriculture toward the cultivation of tobacco for the world market" and the resulting increase in slavery, land prices, estate values, and the creation of a "gentry"—all attributes of the Tidewater's tobacco culture. His discussion of the quality of life in Lunenburg County singles out the "elites"—the objects they owned, the houses they lived in, and the merchants they patronized but *not* the participation of any artisans.[46]

Mitchell's *Commercialism and Frontier,* on the settlement and economic development of the Shenandoah Valley, is the most knowledgeable and useful model of the relationship of the southern backcountry to the larger colonial world. Noting that dissimilar areas of the valley evolved at different rates, Mitchell argues that the "pioneer economy" of mixed farming structures and multiple crops laid a broad base from which all of the region's specialties were derived, assuring farmers of a wide range of commercial options. While Mitchell agrees with Shammas, Pruitt, and Kulikoff when he writes that the "myths of frontier isolation and subsistence economy are inaccurate," he believes the growth of staple crop agriculture led to external commerce with the large eastern markets (where the variety of goods was greatest and extension of credit was most available). This, along with a decentralized trading structure based on individual artisans, peddlers, and farmer-merchants, delayed the appearance of small urban centers to provide local services.[47] Consequently, Mitchell maintains that crafts were mainly delegated to processing locally grown raw materials (such as hemp into linen, and wheat into flour) and fulfilling basic needs in iron, wood, and leather.

In their study of rural southern towns in the eighteenth century, Joseph Ernst and Merrens disagree with Mitchell's assessment of crafts and the appearance of small urban centers by postulating that, from the mid-eighteenth century forward, an urban system composed of towns of various sizes provided many functions to the rural population of the South, among them crafts, limited markets for neighboring produce, and administrative and judicial service centers. By emphasizing the functions, rather than the size of a town, they demonstrate that even the smallest towns acted as local service centers for the surrounding population.[48]

In an earlier work Merrens classified all the towns in North Carolina by the amount of their commercial activity—a feature of their geographic location. According to Merrens, the western towns traded agricultural commodities and deerskins to the midland towns, the midland towns traded them to the seaports, and the seaports traded them to other coastal cities or England. Therefore, the presence of Salisbury and Salem meant that the backcountry was anything but isolated and limited to local trade.[49] As Thorp notes in "Doing Business in the Backcountry," those same trade networks also provided backcountry artisans with an outlet for their overproduction, and a source for the tools and supplies of their craft.[50]

Not all the studies on the North Carolina backcountry center on the political upheaval of the Regulators or the Revolution, or on the economy of the region, and several of the best focus on Rowan County. Robert W. Ramsey's *Carolina Cradle: The Settlement of the Northwest Carolina Frontier, 1747-1762* investigates the people who settled the area of Rowan County between the Yadkin and Catawba Rivers. Ramsey delves into who the settlers were, where they came from, and how they settled the region. Local historian and journalist James Brawley's numerous works on Rowan County provide a more detailed chronological view of the county to complement the Rev. Jethro Rumple's nineteenth-century history of Rowan. Local histories of some of the counties formed from Rowan after 1770 also exist.[51]

Thorp's book is the most recent addition to a fairly large body of work dealing with the Moravians in North Carolina, of which the cornerstone is the multivolume *Records of the Moravians in North Carolina,* translated and edited by Adelaide Fries, et al. While Thorp focuses on the place of Moravians in backcountry society, most of the other histories deal solely with the society (or different aspects thereof) the Moravians created for themselves in the backcountry. Older works such as John Henry Clewell's *History of Wachovia in North Carolina* and Levin T. Reichel's *The Moravians in North Carolina* are traditional, chronological treatments of the Moravians' settlement and life in the backcountry.[52]

More recent scholarship by social historians and anthropologists has examined different facets of the Moravian experience in North Carolina. In some cases, the wealth of records kept by the Moravians has provided valuable insights into early America that otherwise would have been lost forever, such as the work on Moravian town planning and the water-powered mills of the Wachovia Tract.[53] Other historians have investigated from a variety of perspectives the Moravians' gradual acculturation into mainstream American society in the nineteenth century.[54] Archaeological excavations in Old Salem under the direction of Michael Hammond have provided a wealth of information about Moravian consumption habits and how the brethren lived, while digs outside of Wachovia have demonstrated the influence of the Moravians on the rest of the backcountry.[55]

Almost a half-century ago, the late Carl Bridenbaugh wrote *The Colonial Craftsman,* in which he combined the rural and agricultural nature of the South and the reputation of the backcountry as a crude, geographically isolated area to assume that no artisans, other than those in the most basic crafts, worked in the backcountry. The one exception to this situation was the Moravians, a group of German Protestants that settled the Wachovia

Tract in eastern Rowan County, North Carolina. Importing their artisans from Europe and their other settlements in Pennsylvania, the Moravians allowed the entire backcountry to benefit from their variety of craftsmen.

However, an examination of the artisan population of Rowan County from 1753 to 1770 through research gathered from court records, deeds, wills, and private papers contradicts historians' earlier assumptions about artisans in the southern backcountry. As the next chapter will show, all of the artisans working in Rowan County and in Wachovia during this time were part of the huge wave of immigration to the region from the middle colonies. While the Moravian and non-Moravian settlers had different reasons for relocating to Rowan, they all faced the same challenges and had similar needs in settling the frontier. Consequently, each group prepared to meet those needs by bringing along nearly identical complements of artisans.

TWO

The Early History and Settlement of Rowan County

The traditional portrait of the backcountry resident—as either barely scraping by in the wilderness, so isolated that everything he needed he had to make himself, or as fortunate enough to be able to import some refinements from more civilized places—needs to be re-evaluated. Artisans practicing basic crafts were among the earliest backcountry residents, and their presence along with merchants and tavernkeepers proves that more than a subsistence economy existed early in the history of Rowan County. Furthermore, the increase of identified artisans and trades and the growing number of merchants over the years this study covers point to the gradual development of a market economy and a continually rising standard of living, a standard dependent upon the manufacture of consumer goods and the trade those goods created within the backcountry.

Early settlement in Rowan County differed from other backcountry counties because of the Moravians, the German Protestant group that colonized Wachovia, a ninety-eight thousand-acre tract of land east of the Yadkin River in the northeast quadrant of the county. In essence, what the Moravians did on the east side of the river and what the various groups of English, Scotch-Irish, and Germans did on the west side of the river had no bearing on one another. Yet, despite the variances in the types of people who settled on either side of the Yadkin and their reasons for coming to the backcountry, the two areas share a striking similarity: the artisans each group included to provide basic necessities to the newly arrived backcountry residents.

This chapter will examine the early history and settlement of the area that became Rowan County in 1753. Beginning with some of the first descriptions of the backcountry and its inhabitants, the remainder of the chapter will look at how settlement proceeded on either side of the Yadkin River—with numerous ethnic and religious groups to the west and the highly organized church-sponsored Moravians to the east. The chapter concludes with a comparison of all the artisans present in Rowan County in 1753, proving that while the intentions and methods of settlement on each side of the river may not have had much in common, the artisans needed by the new settlers to maintain even a rudimentary standard of living did.

The earliest accounts of the North Carolina backcountry describe a lush country of fertile hills and valleys, criss-crossed by streams that emptied into larger rivers. In the journal of his "voyage" to Carolina in 1700, John Lawson commented that "were it [the backcountry on the Trading Path near the Trading Ford] cultivated, we might have good hopes of as pleasant and fertile a Valley, as any of our *English* in *America* can afford." The following day he recounted the travels of his party over twenty-five miles of "pleasant Savannah Ground, high, and dry," with few trees. Lawson described the land as "very good," but he was more impressed with the "curious bold Creeks" that traversed the region, flowing "into the main Rivers, that went themselves into the Ocean." Lawson erroneously assumed that the creeks would prove "very convenient for the Transportation of what Commodities this Place may produce."[1] In fact, a half century later, when surveying the same area to find a suitable place for the Moravians to settle, August Gottlieb Spangenberg came to the exact opposite conclusion. Spangenberg's description of the backcountry highlighted the lack of navigable rivers in the region and the effect on trade, concluding, "Trade and business are poor in North Carolina. With no navigable rivers there is little shipping; with no export trade of importance the towns are small and few."[2]

Yet the backcountry clearly captivated Lawson, who continued in his journal to describe the area near present day Rowan County as "delicious Country (none that I ever saw exceeds it)" and the east side of the Yadkin River (where the Moravians eventually settled) as having "as rich a Soil to the eye of a Knowing Person with us, as any this Western World can afford."[3]

During Lawson's trip through North Carolina in 1700, no white men were seen (save those of the traveling party) after they left the eastern counties. Eight years later, writing from New Bern to an English audience about the advantages of settling in the backcountry, Lawson noted that "the vast Part of this Country is not inhabited by the *English*."[4]

As more people came to eastern North Carolina from Virginia, some brave souls gradually moved westward into the wilderness. As a member of the survey party trying to settle the boundary dispute between Virginia and North Carolina in 1728, William Byrd II kept a journal of the trip. The backcountry fascinated Byrd as it had Lawson; he acquired 120,000 acres on the Dan River (in Virginia) and called it "Eden," and at least 20,000 acres more in what became Rowan County, North Carolina.[5] His observations of the western section of the colony on that journey provide some of the first descriptions of English settlement on the North Carolina frontier. When Byrd wrote his *History of the Dividing Line Betwixt Virginia and North*

Carolina, only a handful of people lived in the backcountry, and standards were no doubt rough. Byrd recalls how "I beheld the wretchedest Scene of Poverty I had ever met with in this happy Part of the World. The Man, his Wife and Six Small Children, liv'd in a Penn, like so many Cattle, without any roof over their Heads but that of Heaven. And this was their airy Residence in the Day time, but then there was a Fodder Stack not far from this Inclosure, in which the whole Family shelter'd themselves a night's and in bad weather."[6]

One theme that emerges from almost all descriptions of the early backcountry (which are primarily by male authors) is the idle and shiftless manner in which the settlers lived. About another family Byrd wrote, "We saw no Drones there, which are but too Common, alas, in that Part of the World. Tho', in truth, the Distemper of Laziness seizes the Men oftener much then the Women. These last Spin, weave and knit, all with their own Hands, while their Husbands, depending on the Bounty of the Climate, are Sloathfull in everything but getting of Children, and in that Instance make themselves useful Members of an Infant-Colony."[7]

Byrd's impression of the backcountry has influenced generations of historians about the settlement of the southern frontier in the colonial period. In *"Poor Carolina"* A. Roger Ekirch notes a difference between those settlers who moved to the eastern or central part of North Carolina early in the eighteenth century and those who went further west to the backcountry later in the century. Most of those settlers in the former category were probably industrious "small farmers and craftsmen" who had left areas of diminishing land and rising prices in Tidewater Virginia and "shared the hope of achieving success" in North Carolina. By contrast, the early small planters on the western frontier lived in "primitive, rude and perhaps semibarbaric" conditions as a direct result of their limited expectations, lack of industry, and lethargy.[8]

Who were these people who came to the backcountry of North Carolina, and why did they come? Southeastern Pennsylvania served as a major source of immigrants from Scotland, Ireland, Germany, and England who moved farther south and west in the colonies. Advancing land prices and the rapid diminution of unoccupied land in the hinterlands of Philadelphia led to the opening of new areas and the rapid spread of middle colony settlement patterns into the backcountry. Between 1730 and 1760, as southeastern Pennsylvania exploded in terms of population growth, rate of occupation, and the organization of new counties, towns, and trade, many new people moved west and then south into Maryland, Virginia, and North Carolina.[9]

Consequently, these settlers came mainly for land. Historical geographer Merrens states that early written accounts of North Carolina created a favorable image and influenced the consequent course of settlement. Most writers emphasized the opportunities available in North Carolina: the abundance of land and the temperate climate. Although early descriptions of the colony were limited to the Albemarle and eastern regions (where settlement had taken place), Lawson acknowledged the differences between east and west in *New Voyage* and, as the descriptions show, he gave an enthusiastic endorsement of the backcountry's features.[10]

In the eighteenth century North Carolina consisted of three geographic regions: the Coastal Plain, the Piedmont, and the Mountains, although the rugged mountainous area long restricted settlement to the first two regions. The outer coastal plain ranged in elevation from sea level to about one hundred feet above, and included the barrier islands and the amphibious landscape of the coast, consisting of flat, poorly drained surfaces punctuated by tidal estuaries. Further west, the inner coastal plains had higher elevation, with gently rolling hills and more pronounced river valleys for slightly better, although hardly adequate, drainage. The forest cover of the eastern portion of the colony consisted of loblolly, longleaf, and pond pines. In this section bottomland hardwood forests formed distinctive clusters among rivers, although the marshes, dunes, and beaches of the outer coastal plain had no forest cover.

After what Merrens calls a zone of transition from the sandy soil of the coastal plains, the undulating rhythms of the Piedmont begin at five hundred feet above sea level and gradually increase three to four feet per mile until this rolling upland surface reaches one thousand feet at the foot of the Blue Ridge in the west. Rounded hills and ridges aligned northeast to southwest occur above the general level of the surface in the western and eastern areas. A complex pattern of stream valleys weaves through the Piedmont, the channels of major rivers running between two and five hundred feet below interstream areas with valleys deeper than the Coastal Plain. The bottomlands of rivers and streams (which provide rich, fertile soil), varying from a few feet to approximately a mile in width, are the only type of recurring wetland within the region. The vegetation of the Piedmont stood in great contrast to the Coastal Plain: oak-pine forests were common to the section, with Virginia pine found close to the Blue Ridge in the west, short leaf pine in the central area, and loblolly pine to the east near the fall line. In addition to oak, hickory trees were also common to the entire Piedmont.[11]

When Rowan County was formed from Anson County in 1753, it encompassed almost the entire northwest quadrant of North Carolina. This area included the Piedmont region and ran west into the Blue Ridge Mountains. The original boundaries of Rowan County also comprised approximately the western half of the Granville District, a tract of land owned by and named for Sir George Carteret, Earl (and later Lord) Granville, one of the eight original Lord Proprietors of Carolina in 1663. In 1728 seven of the eight proprietors sold their interest in the colony back to the Crown, but Granville declined to sell his share. Finally, in 1744 George II granted Granville's great-grandson, John Carteret, all the territory lying between the Virginia line on the north and the parallel of 35°34' on the south to settle the matter. Surveyors ran the southern boundary from the coast to Bath Town in 1743, and then to the corner of present day Chatham County on Deep River. In 1746 they extended the line westward to Coldwater Creek at a point about fourteen miles southwest of the town of Salisbury, in Rowan County. This strip of land sixty miles wide included approximately two-thirds of the colony's population.[12]

The descriptions of Rowan County provided in early local histories draw heavily upon Lawson, as well as "the recollections of older citizens" of the county, and they generally agree with Merrens's geographical assessment of the Piedmont. These histories do offer a few more specific details about Rowan County. For instance, in 1881 Rumple noted that the county was not covered with forests in the colonial era, but was generally clear land covered with grass and peavines with occasional groves of trees, especially along streams.[13] Thirty-five years later Samuel Ervin mentioned the mineral wealth of Rowan (coal, iron, gold as well as other metals, ores, and minerals) and the wide variety of trees (white oak, white hickory, white ash, elm, maple, beech, poplar, persimmon, black walnut, yellow pine, and mulberry) in his colonial history of the county.[14]

Basing his analysis on twentieth-century conditions and what can be surmised of former environmental variations, Merrens theorizes that the early eighteenth-century legend about the superior resources of the interior section of North Carolina, as compared to the more maritime portion, was largely true.[15] Later eighteenth-century settlers much preferred sections of the backcountry to the coast. In *Carolina Cradle*, Ramsey states that the area between the Yadkin and Catawba Rivers lured colonists with its fertile, moist, virtually treeless meadowland and abundance of game.[16]

Lawson's favorable descriptions of the western portion of North Carolina and numerous other reports about the abundant resources of the interior began to attract settlers to the area in the 1730s. After receiving the royal grant for his land, the land office for the Granville proprietary opened in 1745 to accommodate the increasing rate of settlement. The land offered was not free, but the availability of freeholds enticed colonists to leave older established settlements in colonies to the north.

During this time two thoroughfares made the area that would become Rowan County accessible to incoming settlers. Indians created the older road, known as the Trading Path, which ran from Fort Henry in what is now Petersburg, Virginia, southwest into the North Carolina backcountry, crossing the Yadkin River at the Trading Ford, to connect the Catawbas and the Cherokees with the tribes along the James River in Virginia.[17]

The newer, more frequently traveled road was the Great Wagon Road from Pennsylvania. It began at Philadelphia on the western bank of the Schuylkill River. By the 1720s it reached to settlements in Lancaster County, where the Susquehanna River made an end of the trade. This section, gradually widened and improved, passed through the town of Lancaster. At the Susquehanna the main road went south through York and Gettysburg and across the Monocacy River in Maryland to Williamsport on the Potomac. The ferry crossed the Potomac into the Shenandoah Valley. By the mid-eighteenth century, towns such as Martinsburg, Winchester, Stephensburg, Strasburg, Woodstock, and Staunton had grown up along the road in the Valley. At Buchanan on the James River, Looney's Ferry took passengers to Roanoke at the end of the Valley. The road then went briefly eastward through the Staunton River gap of the Blue Ridge, crossed through hilly country over minor streams (Blackwater, Pigg, Irvine, and Dan) and entered North Carolina. It ran along a branch of the Yadkin River in eastern Rowan County and then followed open country between the Yadkin and Catawba Rivers. By 1760 it had reached Salisbury, the Rowan County seat.[18]

Although the Granville district land office opened in 1745, the first wave of settlement in the backcountry did not occur until two years later. A host of reasons existed to motivate people to move from the Delaware Valley and Chesapeake Bay region into the North Carolina backcountry, but Ramsey observes that Pennsylvania Gov. George Thomas's call to raise troops from New York, New Jersey, Pennsylvania, Maryland, and Virginia for King George's War in Canada in June 1746 may have provided some extra incentive. Within a year of this proclamation, the first settlers entered the Yadkin Valley from New Jersey, Pennsylvania, Maryland, and Virginia.[19]

Ramsey's analysis of the settlement of the land between the Yadkin and Catawba Rivers reveals that while many of the early settlers had known each other prior to their arrival in North Carolina, and many of them chose to live as neighbors in the backcountry, establishing planned communities (on the level of the Moravians) was not among their motives for migrating to North Carolina. Most settlers to Rowan County were not recent immigrants to the New World; they had already lived in Pennsylvania, New Jersey, Maryland, or Virginia, and they traveled south to procure greater landholdings at lower prices than in the northern colonies. The early backcountry settlements maintained the ethnic flavors of migrants to particular regions, be they English, Scotch-Irish, or German.[20]

Previous relationships and ethnicity notwithstanding, the abundance of land and lack of settlers in the backcountry attracted land speculators and farmers first. According to Merrens, those individuals who came to sell skills and services, rather than to live off the land, formed a numerically small but economically significant minority of the incoming population.[21] Despite climbing land prices in Pennsylvania, Maryland, and Virginia, most artisans were not overly anxious to leave an established area where they could easily sell their services to ply their trades on the frontier where they would have to live off the land. While the backcountry offered great opportunities to artisans, achieving success meant working as farmers and craftsmen until the economy and population developed to the point of supporting their skills.

In addition to farming as a primary occupation, the first artisan settlers had two criteria in common. They all practiced trades that answered basic human needs (food, clothing, shelter, transportation) and for which the raw materials were readily available on the frontier. The weavers, shoemakers, and tailors produced textiles and clothing from flax, wool, and leather; the tanner processed skins into leather; the blacksmith crafted and repaired tools and miscellaneous items necessary for farming and building; the millwright designed and built water-powered mills to process enough grain to feed a community of people; and the saddler made saddles, an indispensable link in the backcountry transportation system.

The early settlers to the northwest Carolina frontier had a seemingly unlimited amount of virgin land from which to choose. Having come from less than desirable circumstances in colonies suffering from overcrowding and soil depletion, these immigrant colonists selected their land wisely. Most settlement took place either west of the Yadkin River on the fertile land near the numerous creeks and rivers that traversed the region, or next to the established roadways.[22] Not surprisingly, settlers who had lived together previously and traveled down to North Carolina in groups congregated around one another again in the backcountry, virtually replicating the society they had left.

As early as 1747 people with similar ethnic and religious backgrounds formed loosely knit communities on the northwest Carolina frontier. The Bryan Settlement, the first located in what would become Rowan County, was formed that year. Named for Morgan Bryan, a prominent English Quaker from Chester County, Pennsylvania, the Bryan Settlement consisted mainly of English Quakers and Baptists from Pennsylvania and Delaware.[23] These non-Anglicans had migrated first to Pennsylvania because of its reputation for religious toleration. When they made the decision to seek cheaper land elsewhere, North Carolina offered the same promise of toleration.[24] Situated on both sides of the Yadkin River on the land between the River and Deep Creek, the Shallow Ford, Panther Creek, and Linville Creek, the settlement was located directly west of what eventually became the Wachovia Tract.[25]

Of the seven men and their families who founded the Bryan Settlement, at least two men and possibly a third were practicing artisans. Edward Hughes and James Carter were both millwrights; Squire Boone (father of Daniel, the hunter, and Jonathan, a joiner) had worked as a weaver in Pennsylvania, although no North Carolina records identify him as such.[26]

Immigrants to the region organized two other settlements on the land between the Yadkin and Catawba Rivers in the late 1740s. Southwest of the Bryan Settlement, some Scotch-Irish Presbyterians made up the Irish Settlement on the creeks that ran east into the Yadkin River. Further southwest of the Irish Settlement was Davidson's Settlement, created by Scotch-Irish and German immigrants in 1748 around Davidson's Creek, a tributary of the Catawba River, Rocky River, and Coddle Creek.[27]

Again, artisans constituted a small minority of the original settlers to those communities. (See Table 1.) Of the twenty-four grantees in the Irish settlement between 1747 and 1749, only five were artisans. George Cathey Jr. was a millwright, Andrew Cathey a shoemaker, Richard Graham a saddler, James Graham Jr. a blacksmith, and John Brandon Jr. a tailor.[28] At Davidson's Creek between 1748 and 1751, three grantees out of the original twenty-five were artisans. George Davidson Jr. was a tanner, John McConnell a weaver, and Thomas Cook a tailor.[29]

Although enough settlers streamed into the backcountry to organize three distinct settlements before 1750, the migration from Pennsylvania had only just begun. As the exodus continued, a new community just north of the Irish Settlement on the banks of Fourth Creek took shape about 1750. Of the sixty-two grantees who settled Fourth Creek over a twelve year period, merely four were artisans.[30] Andrew Allison was a tailor, Thomas Hall a weaver, Samuel Reed a shoemaker, and William Watt a clothier.[31]

In the years following 1751 a group of twenty-seven settlers, including mainly English but also a few Scotch-Irish and German families, chose to live on a parcel of land between the Irish Settlement and the Yadkin. The settlement's location southwest of the Trading Ford gave it the name of the Trading Camp Settlement. Three of the original settlers were artisans: Michael Miller, a cooper, and Richard Walton and James Carson, both tanners.[32] The Trading Camp Settlement and the Irish Settlement grew together by 1762. Artisans were a larger percentage of the later grantees. In fact, the artisan population in the Irish and Trading Camp settlements rose from eight (five in the original Irish settlement and three in the original Trading Camp) in the early 1750s to forty-four by 1762.[33]

The 1740s immigration into the North Carolina backcountry was only the beginning. Writing to the Board of Trade in June 1753, Governor Matthew Rowan commented, "In the year 1746 I was up in the country that is now Anson, Orange, and Rowan Countys, there was not above 100 fighting men there is now at least three thousand for the most part Irish Protes-

Table 1. Artisans in Early Rowan County Settlements

Settlement	No. of grantees	No. of artisans	% of total population
Bryan (1747)	7	2 men (3?)	28.5
Irish (1747-1749)	24	5 men	20.8
Davidson's (1748-1751)	25	3	12.0
Fourth Creek (1750-1762)	62	4	6.4
Trading Camp (1751)	27	3	11.1
Irish & Trading (1762)	177	44	24.8

SOURCE: Information on the number of grantees from Robert W. Ramsey, *Carolina Cradle: The Settlement of the Northwest Carolina Frontier, 1747-1762* (Chapel Hill: Univ. of North Carolina Press, 1964), 32, 35, 45, 95, 102, 108-9.

tants and Germans and dayley increasing."[34] By the late 1750s more than two thousand settlers passed through the Shenandoah Valley every year on their way to new lives in the backcountry. While the Valley of Virginia grew gradually from migration in the 1760s, with the population of southwestern Virginia doubling every eight years, western North Carolina witnessed a stampede. In a ten month period of 1755 one observer noted that five thousand migrants crossed the James River headed for North Carolina, and the number was increasing daily. By the early 1760s Benjamin Franklin estimated that ten thousand families had left Pennsylvania for North Carolina over a three year period.[35]

The influx of people into the region necessitated the formation of additional counties to handle the needs of the new inhabitants. On April 12, 1753, the section of Anson County north of the Granville line became Rowan County.[36] The justices of the County Court of Pleas and Quarters, the principal institution of local government, first met on June 15, 1753, to tend to the business of the new county's residents by recording livestock marks, registering deeds, designating public mills, issuing licenses to keep ordinaries, appointing men to various offices, resolving various legal cases, designating the location of new roads by the needs of the settlers, and deciding the size, specifications, and location of the future courthouse, jail, and stocks.[37] In later sessions (the court met quarterly), the justices would exercise the additional power of the court to settle estates, to appoint guardians for some orphans and apprentice others, and to fix the price schedules for ferries and ordinaries or taverns.

As settlements sprung up west of the Yadkin River and the county began to get organized, John Carteret, Lord Proprietor of the Granville tract, worried about still empty tracts on his land. He wanted more settlers on his North Carolina land in order to collect more quit-rents.[38] While living in London in 1749, Granville met a nobleman from Saxony, Count Nicholaus von Zinzendorf. More than a quarter of a century earlier, Zinzendorf had allowed a group of religious refugees, followers of the *Unitas Fratrum* (the United Brethren known today as the Moravian Church) to settle on his estates. After watching the brethren live their practical religion, which they understood to be vital in the everyday life of everyday men, women, and children, Zinzendorf threw himself unreservedly into their cause, becoming their generous patron and much-loved leader. The brethren often referred to Zinzendorf as *"der Junger,"* meaning the Disciple, a title suggested by his fervent love of the Savior.[39]

Coming from quiet, secluded communities in Bohemia, Moravia, and Poland, the brethren decided to establish settlements in the New World that centered around carefully arranged and regulated towns. After receiving a land grant in the colony of Georgia in 1734, the Moravians settled in Savannah with hopes of doing missionary work among the Creek Indians. Even with an unhealthy climate and bad soil conditions, the Moravians cleared all their debts in the colony by 1740, when war between England and Spain broke out. The Trustees of the colony of Georgia pressured the peace-loving Moravians to abandon their individual conscientious objections to bearing arms. Refusing to do so, the brethren turned their back on everything they had accomplished in Georgia and left the South for Pennsylvania. Following their arrival in Philadelphia, the brethren traveled forty-seven miles north along the Delaware River to two tracts of land they owned and founded what eventually became their largest town in America, Bethlehem.[40]

The Moravians' settlements in Pennsylvania were extremely successful. In the three largest towns they established—Bethlehem, Nazareth, and Lititz—the brethren continued the same pattern of life that had characterized the first European congregation town, Herrnhut.[41] The congregation was considered a family, with the governing bodies of the church acting as the patriarch. To advance Christian growth and activity, the church divided members into "choirs" according to age, sex, and marital status.

One of the major reasons for the Moravians' many accomplishments in Georgia and other early settlements was the integral and indispensable role work played in their Christian lifestyle. In the brethren's perpetual effort to pattern their lives after Christ, virtues of diligence, simplicity, frugality, punctuality, conscientiousness, and continence were not just highly desirable attributes; they were essential qualities. Work, though not causing or guaranteeing salvation, became imperative to maintaining a state of grace; labor thus provided a powerful ethical justification and impetus to the vast enterprises of the church. To Zinzendorf, each individual's work should become his goal in life. In 1738 the Count wrote, "One does not only work in order to live, but one lives for the sake of one's work, and if there is no more work to do one suffers or goes to sleep."[42]

Controlled by the church in Europe, all the early American Moravian settlements were *Gemein Orren* (congregation towns), and had to be run according to Unity principles. Only members of the congregation could live and work in the town, and the governing bodies of the church rigidly controlled all civic, material, religious, and personal affairs.[43] In addition to carefully planning all their activities through various church boards, the Moravians also wrote down their plans in exacting detail, and their community diaries, church board minutes, and land records still exist today.

The brethren earned the reputation as thrifty and industrious settlers, which made them much sought after as colonists.[44] In 1749, when Lord Granville met Zinzendorf in London and became familiar with the brethren, the church was actively pursuing new settlement locations. The brethren had just abandoned two church communities, Herrnhag and Marienborn, in the German principality of Wetteravia rather than join the state church. Granville suggested that the brethren buy land from him in North Carolina, where they could begin another settlement. This offer accommodated the Moravians' desire to establish a settlement in the southern colonies that would be free from the interferences that annoyed them in Pennsylvania, and they decided to accept Granville's offer.[45]

In the late summer of 1752, the Moravians sent Bishop August Gottlieb Spangenberg and a survey party of five to North Carolina to find a large tract of fertile land. To meet their settlement purposes, church leaders wanted a single tract of a hundred thousand acres that included little unusable land. Unfortunately, when the party reached the colony to begin the search, Spangenberg noted in his diary that "Land matters in North Carolina are . . . in unbelievable confusion." Francis Corbin, Lord Granville's land agent, did not know what land was vacant, and suggested that the Brethren "go to the 'Back of the Colony,' that is west to the Blue Mountains, taking a surveyor, and that perhaps there we can find a suitable tract of land that has not hitherto been surveyed."[46] The suitability of this area in terms of fertility and climate for the European-trained Moravian farmers made the survey party approve this geographic area.[47]

After scouring the backcountry at the foot of the Blue Ridge Mountains for more than two months, the survey party finally found one acceptable tract on January 8, 1753.[48] Spangenberg calculated that half the land on the tract was good, a quarter of it was poor, and another quarter was medium. The land was level except for a few rolling hills, the air was fresh, and the water was good and plentiful. The following spring Spangenberg went to England with his report of the trip to Carolina and maps of the various tracts. The German and English Moravian Church was under great financial stress at the time, and raising the money necessary to purchase and colonize the land appeared impossible. Considering all their options, the brethren decided to abandon the project and asked Lord Granville to release them from their contract with him. Not wanting to lose the enterprising settlers, Granville refused, but he then offered the brethren a new contract, with more favorable terms, that they accepted. On August 7, 1753, Lord Granville conveyed 98,985 acres (approximately 157 square miles) to the Unity of Brethren in nineteen separate deeds.[49] Wachovia lay in the southeastern corner of what had just become Rowan County, North Carolina's newest and largest county.[50]

The traditional version of the Moravians' settlement of Wachovia, as told in the "Foreword" to volume one of the *Records of the Moravians in North Carolina,* maintains that instructions to the first colonists in Wachovia included plans "to establish a settlement in the heart of the wilderness, and make it a center of service to neighbors," and "to preach the Gospel to the Indians."[51] Yet Thorp's research on the settlement of Wachovia revealed a "conspicuous absence . . . [of] the strong missionary spirit that had marked many of the Moravians' earlier colonizing ventures." Instead, Thorp maintains the brethren came to Wachovia for its location in the backcountry which would allow church members "to practice their religion and raise their families in relative security," and "provide the Brethren with good economic prospects." Apparently, "the principal motive underlying the Moravians' plans for Wachovia was the desire to establish an exclusive community in which the will of the Moravian Church would prevail," a perspective readily supported by the records of the brethren.[52] In other words, the brethren went to the backwoods of North Carolina to create not a sympathetic settlement of religion and service from which their neighbors would benefit, but rather an autonomous community that asked nothing from its neighbors.

According to Gillian Gollin in her book *Moravians in Two Worlds,*

Zinzendorf had expected Herrnhut and Bethlehem to strive for communal self-sufficiency. A desire to flee from the snares of the sinful world did not inspire Zinzendorf's model of an exclusive settlement. He wanted to establish a degree of independence from the outside world that would permit the Moravians to pursue their religious goals unhampered by the limitations imposed by a dependence upon non-Moravian resources.[53] As Spangenberg wrote to a church official in England, North Carolina interested the Moravians because they needed a place where they could "live together as Brethren, without interfering with others & without being disturbed by them."[54]

In all their Moravian settlements, the brethren looked for places in which they could build both the kind of society that they desired and the means to protect it from what they considered the corrosive influences of the outside world. The brethren did not want to withdraw completely from contact with the rest of the world. In fact, they envisioned a wide variety of social, political, and trade relations between themselves and their neighbors. They pledged, however, to create a society in which virtually every detail contributed to the maintenance of autonomy and the elimination of any means of non-Moravian control over the community of believers.[55] In other words, they welcomed relationships with their neighbors as long as the Moravians could dictate and control the terms.

With these guidelines in mind, the church began to develop somewhat more specific plans for Wachovia. The Unity intended for one central *Gemein Ort* to dominate the entire tract. Planners stressed that the town had to be built as near as possible to the geographic center of Wachovia so as to be equally accessible to all of the settlement's inhabitants, even those near the borders. Unity elders did not want the brethren looking to a non-Moravian town for any of the urban functions that the *Gemein Ort* could provide.[56]

The final plan for Wachovia called for Moravian craftsmen, merchants, administrators, and their families to populate the *Gemein Ort*. Around this town Moravian families would occupy thirty thousand acres of farms, and around that seventy thousand acres would be sold through the church to investors and occupied by them (many of whom would eventually join the church), their tenants, servants, and slaves.[57] Such detailed plans were decidedly dissimilar to the settlement that occurred west of the Yadkin.

Before any of these plans could take place, though, the Moravian leaders in Pennsylvania had to choose a group of men to begin the new settlement in North Carolina. Since the church acquired Wachovia to accommodate at least some of the brethren from Wetteravia, the Unity originally intended for most of the colonists to emigrate to North Carolina directly from Europe. However, his familiarity with backcountry North Carolina led Br. Spangenberg to argue against this plan because he felt it failed to respect the rigors the first colonists would encounter in North Carolina. Spangenberg believed that "the work of building a colony" demanded people who were "prepared for it already," i.e., brothers who had experience creating settlements.[58] In the end he won out, and most of the men selected to settle the tract came from Christianbrunn, Pennsylvania, a small town run by the Single Brothers one and a half miles from Nazareth.[59] In this aspect the Moravian settlers resembled the other North Carolina backcountry settlers: they all had previous wilderness settlement experience, whether in Pennsylvania, Maryland, or Virginia.

The Moravians did have one great advantage over the rest of the settlers in Rowan County: the financial backing of the Moravian Church. From 1753 to 1772, most of the Moravians in Wachovia belonged to the settlement's *Oeconomy*, a semi-communal institution formulated by the church that controlled the economies of each settlement to ensure its success. The *Oeconomy* did not abolish private property.[60] Members could retain whatever resources they brought with them to North Carolina (although ownership of land and cattle was restricted), but cash had to be deposited with the *Oeconomy*'s directors. In the *Oeconomy* the church expected all members to give their labor to the community in return for food, clothing, shelter, and education for their children. During these years the community also had the right to assign a man or woman to whatever task it desired. Various economic and trade supervisors controlled occupational assignments, not individual choice. The directors of the *Oeconomy* decided how to utilize all of the resources to Wachovia's greatest benefit.[61]

Unity leaders picked fifteen men to make the trip to North Carolina, twelve bachelors to settle in Wachovia and three to return to Pennsylvania after a brief stay to serve as advisors and guides between the two regions. In order to have a party that was truly capable of creating a successful settlement, each man specialized in one area, but was also able to do other necessary work.[62] Among the men and their skills were Frederick Jacob Pfeil, a shoemaker; Erich Ingebretsen, a millwright and carpenter; Henrich Feldhausen, a shoemaker, carpenter, millwright, cooper, sievemaker, turner, and farmer; and Hans Petersen, a tailor. Rev. Bernhard Adam Grube, a minister and leader of the group; Jacob Loesch, the business manager; Hans Martin Kalberlahn, a surgeon; Hermannus Loesch and Johannes Beroth, both farmers; Jacob Lung, a gardener; and Christopher Merkly, a baker, rounded out the group.

The creation of settlements in Rowan County west of the Yadkin River before 1753 meant that the Moravians were not the first settlers to the North Carolina backcountry, nor did they bring the first artisans to the region. In fact, the trades already represented by the early non-Moravian artisan settlers included six weavers, three millwrights, three blacksmiths, two tailors, a shoemaker, a tanner, a saddler, and a carpenter. Without any knowledge of who already lived in the backcountry, the Moravians practically duplicated these skills in the group they created to settle the Wachovia Tract. The brethren did not have a weaver, a blacksmith, a tanner, or a saddler at the beginning, but with Henrich Feldhausen, jack-of-all-trades, they counted a cooper, sievemaker, and turner in their midst.[63]

The existence of these trades among two distinct contingents of early backcountry settlers signifies their necessity in establishing a rudely sufficient quality of life in nascent communities. The eight trades established in the county prior to 1753 accounted for two-thirds of all the tradesmen found in Rowan County records prior to 1770. Obviously, the artisans in these trades fulfilled some basic human needs of food, clothing, shelter, and transportation with products created from readily available raw materials at a cost and quality that local residents could not equal by trading with the outside. The continued dominance of these trades in the county also confirms the demand for basic skills in developing communities with a growing populace.

The artisans in both groups knew that coming to the wilderness meant (in most cases) putting their crafts to the side until a rudimentary level of survival and comfort was achieved. As Mitchell notes in *Commercialism and Frontier,* pioneer settlers were the real risk takers, temporarily sacrificing their crafts and in some cases their lives to take advantage of the economic potential of an unsettled area.[64] Although the financial backing and long-range settlement plans the Moravian Church provided for the brethren are not typical of most backcountry settlement experiences, the similarity in the craftsmen the Moravian and non-Moravian groups brought to establish their communities strongly indicates that the way in which the two groups initially created their communities may have had much in common. Fortunately, the Moravians' penchant for recordkeeping and the survival of daily diaries, church board minutes, and correspondence with church leaders can describe the early settlement process on the eighteenth-century frontier.

After traveling for five and a half weeks on foot from Pennsylvania, the brethren arrived at the area designated by the Unity for the first settlement on the night of November 17, 1753. The brethren slept in a small log cabin abandoned by Hans Wagner, a frontiersman.[65] The brethren called the area Bethabara, Hebrew for "House of Passage." As the name indicates, the Unity did not intend Bethabara to be the large central *Gemein Ort* called for in the long-range plans. While Bethabara would have *Gemein Ort* status until the new, larger town was built and inhabited, Spangenberg only wanted a place where the brethren "can make a farm, meadows, orchard, and build a mill and a saw-mill." This place should be near the spot "suitable for the building of a Town, for then when the Town is built the farm and mill can still be used."[66]

The Wachovia diary reflects the plans and priorities the brethren had in establishing Bethabara; the daily work assignments placed men on the most urgent tasks, regardless of their training. Rule number one was to take care of the essentials for survival. The brothers cut down trees and cleared fields to grow crops and surveyed the land for other food sources and natural resources. The opportunity to practice their crafts or professions would come later; exactly how much later would depend on necessity and demand.

For instance, the ability to grind corn or other grain in a mill was paramount, as the main staples of the brothers' diet were bread and mush. Purchasing large amounts of processed grains from the nearest mill nineteen miles away was financially risky; flour and meal had a short shelf life and the likelihood of spoilage was great. Therefore, the inclusion of two trained millwrights in the settling party is not surprising. In fact, the brothers brought a small mill with them from Pennsylvania. Only ten days after arriving at Bethabara, a party of brothers began searching for mill sites, and the diary records that the day after Christmas the brethren's corn meal mill ran for the first time.[67] Although the records are not entirely clear on the power source, they suggest that the two brethren trained in mill work, Erich Ingebretsen and Heinrich Feldhausen, constructed a horizontal water wheel at one of the nearby mill sites to power the small mill. A number of facts support this hypothesis. Both millwrights had been trained in areas of Europe that used the horizontal water, or Norse, mill, extensively. The construction of this type of mill is relatively quick and easy, especially since the brethren had brought the gears and stones from Pennsylvania. And the brief construction time of an early corn meal mill at Bethabara, noted by William Murtaugh in his book on Moravian architecture and town planning, further supports this thesis.[68]

In an article on the urban process in the colonial South, Ernst and Merrens point out that certain key structures, such as mills, indicate the role of a settlement as a regional or local service center rather than merely a cluster of residences. Using water power to process grain into meal or flour signifies that settlers had neither the time or the energy to grind a sufficient amount of grain by hand and that the mill would be used enough to make it worth the investment of time and money needed to build it. The importance of mills to the settlement process explains the presence of three millwrights west of the Yadkin and the Moravians' desire to construct their own mill east of the river.[69]

The Bethabara Diary records the brethren's pride in having prepared so well to settle Wachovia. During the first year the Unity instructed the brethren to allot their time carefully: craft activity should be limited to producing items essential to the settlement or the brethren, after clearing fields, planting crops, and building houses had been completed. However, some crafts were so essential the brethren had to learn by doing. Even though three tanners worked west of the Yadkin in 1753, the Moravians would not patronize them so as not to become dependent on "strangers." Instead, the brethren tanned some cowhide by themselves in the spring, and in September Br. Pfeil made shoes for the company. After other brethren cut down trees and sawed planks from them, the multitalented Br. Feldhausen used his extra time to make barrels for storing food.[70]

The early history and settlement of Rowan County were dictated by people's desire to escape the increasing crowds and land prices of the older settlements of Pennsylvania, Maryland, and Virginia and to come via the Great Wagon Road to a new, unsettled area of fertile land where they could live cheaply and achieve financial success. As this chapter has shown, the initial settlement that took place west of the Yadkin River varied greatly from the later settlement of the Wachovia Tract by the Moravians on the east side of the river. Nonetheless, the complement of artisans on both sides of the river in 1753 was nearly identical, confirming that while an artisan may not be able to practice his trade full time on the burgeoning frontier, trades such as blacksmithing, weaving, saddle making, shoemaking, tanning, tailoring, carpentry, and building mills were a necessary part of settling the frontier.

THREE

The Development of Rowan County, 1753-1759

The development of, and artisans' participation in, the commercial economy of Rowan county is a story of both success and failure. The success occurred west of the Yadkin River, where population growth and a concentration of artisans helped Salisbury, the county seat, to become one of the earliest backcountry commercial centers. The failure occurred east of the Yadkin on the Wachovia Tract, where a singular lack of leadership and realistic vision on the part of the Moravian Church prevented a group of talented and dedicated church members from becoming as successful as their counterparts on the other side of the river. The church, in essence, wasted the potential of Wachovia and its inhabitants by delaying important decisions about the development of the main town on the tract, thus consigning them to secondary economic status within the county during this period. Consequently, a dichotomy occurred in the economic development of Rowan County in which the Moravian Church organized and controlled its members east of the river, while nascent capitalism and the desire to achieve financial success motivated the settlers west of the river.

A number of striking contrasts separate the Moravians from the rest of the settlers in Rowan County. The Moravian Church sent pre-selected members from its older settlements to Wachovia with specific instructions to create an autonomous community. The other settlers rumbled down the Great Wagon Road in hastily organized groups of relatives, friends, and neighbors without any plans except to start anew in the North Carolina backcountry. However, the Moravians and the other settlers in Rowan County did share one major goal: to make a profit from the developing backcountry economy. Here the similarity ends. Each group's expectations of the backcountry, their definitions of financial success, and their strategies for achieving it differed greatly. Consequently, even though the Moravians had advantages in creating their planned communities on the tract, church control from Europe and Pennsylvania stifled artisan development. Salisbury, a non-Moravian town and the county seat, therefore became the premier commercial town of Rowan County before the Moravians even began construction on their "center of trade and manufacture." This chapter will explore how the early economic development of the county affected artisans who worked on the Wachovia Tract and elsewhere in Rowan County.

The Moravians differ from all the other settlers of Rowan County because of their determination to create a specific type of settlement in the backcountry: namely, an exclusive, self-sufficient community in which the will of the Moravian Church would prevail. The highly-organized and well-financed Moravian Church (two other features uncharacteristic of most backcountry settlers) formulated plans in Europe and Pennsylvania for their utopian community in North Carolina that left absolutely nothing to chance. Short-range plans called for the creation of a temporary town with a skeletal crew of men to begin in the wilderness by planting some crops and establishing some trade networks with their fellow backcountry settlers. Then the settlers would embark upon the Unity's major project: the creation of a town of trade and manufacture filled with Moravian artisans destined to return large profits to the church.

Artisans had an important, even pivotal, role in the Moravian strategy for developing Wachovia. From the beginning their skills were crucial to the success of the principal motive for settling the tract: the artisans' abilities insured that the brethren would not have to look to outsiders to provide anything of great consequence, decreasing the chance of becoming dependent on non-Moravians. Once the main town was built, the artisans would make money for the church from those same non-Moravians.

The brethren did not expect to conduct business with outsiders during the initial phase of settlement. The leaders of the Moravian Church chose backcountry North Carolina for their newest colony because they believed that the region lacked a significant white population. Thus, as the first inhabitants to the region, the brethren could settle Wachovia and build the main town without interference from outsiders. Then, when the outsiders finally arrived in the backcountry, the Moravians would be ready to make a profit from them.

One can easily imagine the brethren's surprise when, one cold afternoon at the end of January 1754, two men appeared in Bethabara with work for Br. Petersen, the tailor.[1] The demand for their crafts should not have astonished the brethren. On the survey trip to North Carolina, Bishop August Gottlieb Spangenberg observed that "Almost nobody has a trade. In Edenton I saw one smith, one cobbler, and one tailor at work, and no more; whether there are others I do not know."[2]

The unexpected demand for the brethren's crafts outside of Wachovia, combined with what church officials in Bethlehem, Pennsylvania, considered remarkable progress for the first year of settlement, resulted in a series of short-range programs to develop the tract. These plans had contradictory and sometimes detrimental effects on the original long-range plans for Wachovia. The first plans called for maintaining only enough men at Bethabara to build the main town elsewhere on the tract, and then sending tradesmen, merchants, and their families to Wachovia when the central town was finished. Instead, officials tried to relocate as many settlers as possible to North Carolina to help enlarge the colony quickly. What Church leaders refused to recognize was that the additional people, as well as the new directives, would require the expansion of Bethabara beyond that of a staging area for the permanent town.

If the Unity did not realize the need to support the growing population with additional artisan services, Br. Jacob Loesch, the business manager in Bethabara, certainly did. In a letter dated April 27, 1754, to Peter Boehler, a bishop of the church in Bethlehem, Loesch said he would welcome "a larger company here," but did not think he could accommodate them without some more trades and "much provision."[3]

Loesch got his wish. Seven months later, after Boehler visited Bethabara to check out conditions, a party of eight brethren from Pennsylvania joined the settlement. Six of the eight men were artisans. Church officials sent Hans Christian Christensen and Jacobus van der Merk to build a permanent water-powered grist- and sawmill, with assistance from Jacob Kapp, a turner. The group also included George Schmidt, a blacksmith, Andreas Betz, a gunsmith, and George Holder, a carpenter.[4] While Loesch certainly had justification for asking for more artisans to meet the needs of a growing population, by sending those artisans the church contradicted its original position that the brethren should stress self-sufficient food production first and that artisan development would not occur until the completion of the main town.

The eight newcomers to Bethabara provided enough extra manpower to ease the load of everyday chores and to help build the settlement. As a result, the individual craftsmen had more time to work at their trades. The new craftsmen wasted no time getting to work: two days after they arrived, Christensen and van der Merk began measuring the fall of water in various creeks around Bethabara in their search for a good mill site; within three weeks Schmidt was shoeing horses for strangers.[5] Br. Pfeil made more shoes, Br. Peterson did some tailoring for the brethren, Br. Feldhausen produced a barrel for an outsider, Br. Christensen built a turning lathe, and Br. Schmidt created baskets, sieves, and a pair of bellows for his forge.[6]

In 1755 Bethabara also underwent major expansion in terms of both construction and population. Migrations of small groups from Pennsylvania in June, August, September, and October, and a large group in November brought a total of thirty-six new inhabitants to Bethabara, including seven women.[7] These women were not merely pawns in the church's demographic plans for Wachovia; they also fulfilled an economic role in the colony's ability to support itself. Even though the brethren had planted and raised flax, they continued to obtain linen clothing and yardage from Bethlehem.[8] Shortly after the sisters arrived, the brethren began to break and hackle flax and hemp, and they put together spinning wheels so the sisters could begin spinning.[9] The sisters spun flax into thread and wove it into linen. They then made linen into clothing and other accessories.[10]

Spangenberg realized that spinning and weaving would save the brethren at Bethabara a considerable sum of money. Anxious for the success of the new venture, he asked, "How would it be, if you, like many of our Brethren in Nazareth and Bethlehem, too, were to help spin in the evenings or when at other times the weather is bad so that they cannot do anything outdoors?"[11] Having survived in the backwoods of North Carolina for three years without spinning, the brothers apparently did not feel the need to participate in "women's work," especially once the sisters had come to Wachovia. They ignored Spangenberg's suggestion, preferring instead to encourage the women in their spinning with special lovefeasts.[12]

The influx of new residents to Wachovia and the progress of the brethren pleased the church, but the discrepancy between the colony's short-term success and the original long-term goals divided officials. The church hierarchy continually reminded the brethren not to progress too far, as Bethabara was not to become the central town of trade and manufacturing that Count Zinzendorf envisioned, but that church leaders still had not planned. In 1755 the Unity sent the brethren in Bethabara somewhat contradictory instructions, advising them to remain at Bethabara and to "spread out there to the degree your time and circumstances permit. . . . Only we would not like to have many craftsman located at the place you now live, for if the *town* should be removed elsewhere this would involve double construction and settling down for a second time."[13]

The phrase "if the town should be removed elsewhere" indicates that the leaders were reconsidering Bethabara's role as a "house of passage." Nonetheless, the instructions were more than just advice; the leaders in Pennsylvania and Europe had direct control over what really happened at Bethabara. Regardless what the brethren in Wachovia asked for, the church had final say over what artisans and supplies Bethabara would receive and what projects brethren would undertake. The Unity based decisions on their experience in establishing other settlements, the number of men currently available in either Pennsylvania or Europe, the amount of money the church had available to invest in Wachovia, and their understanding of the will of God.

An example of the role of religion in governance among the Moravians was the drawing of the lot. Every time the brethren did not feel qualified to make an important decision without knowing the will of God, they drew lots. After posing a question, they chose one of three reeds from a bowl. One reed was marked "yes," another "no," and the third was blank. The last, if drawn, indicated that the time was not appropriate to ask the question. The Wachovia brethren often drew lots to determine whether or not they should ask church leaders for certain artisans, and church leaders used lots to decide which artisans were appropriate for Wachovia. In October 1757 Br. Spangenberg explained to the brethren and sisters at Bethabara why the leadership could not send them "a mill-wright, wheel-wright, saddler, etc. We were indeed willing to do so but our Lord did not approve of it at this time."[14]

Original church ambivalence over policy for the Wachovia tract, coupled with financial troubles, prompted an official change of plans. During the initial phase of settlement, the church had financed all operations in Wachovia. Officials stressed that the skeletal crew of the brethren should become self-sufficient in food production as soon as possible and then begin building the central town on the tract. The brethren concentrated on clearing the fields and planting crops to prepare for future arrivals. They also received money from Pennsylvania to purchase the foodstuffs for present needs from neighbors. Establishing the "plantation," as the brethren called it, took top priority; the craftsmen devoted their time to constructing buildings or producing clothing articles for their brothers, accepting business from non-Moravian customers only when their schedules permitted it. Clearly, making a profit was not a responsibility of the early settlers at Bethabara; that task would be left to the merchants and artisans in the main town.[15] Church officials also wanted to avoid having to relocate any artisans (and their workshops) to the town and therefore tried to keep the number of skilled artisans in Bethabara to a minimum.

However, as the church failed to implement these first plans and sent more people (and artisans) to Bethabara, the cost of supporting Wachovia ballooned, and the church could not find any outside investors. By the winter of 1755-56 officials decided that the Wachovia settlers would have to bear their colony's cost sooner than expected. Consequently, they allowed additional artisans to go to North Carolina and take advantage of the unanticipated backcountry market that Br. Petersen, the tailor, had already served. Officials also sanctioned a reorganization of priorities in Wachovia until construction on the "center of trade and manufacture" had begun.[16] Namely, accepting business from outsiders became a high priority for artisans, who also received workshops in which to ply their trades. In addition, the brothers began to experiment with ways of fulfilling their obligations to the church in the most efficient manner possible, thus freeing up more of their valuable time to serve the "for profit" sector.[17]

Church officials and the inhabitants of Wachovia operated under these reorganized priorities for the next decade. The church's acknowledgment that Wachovia needed to support itself before the central town could be built meant that church officials never forgot Wachovia's primary mission was the creation of that town. Consequently, while the brethren did experience some craft development in terms of additional artisans and capital expenditures, during this time the brethren did not always get everything they requested. After 1755 the growth of trades in Wachovia actually declined.

Church officials sent ten artisans and three new crafts to Bethabara in 1755. Building trades—masonry and brickmaking—represented two of the three new crafts. The church also dispatched three tailors and two shoemakers to keep up with the clothing needs of all the new settlers. The 1755 Bethabara "Memorabilia," a year's end capsulation of events and accomplishments, reflected the Brethren's hard work and dedication to Wachovia. Construction projects for that year included the new Brothers' House, the kitchen, the smithy, the mill, a storage shed by the mill, the new *Gemein Haus*, and a little house for the miller. In addition the settlers built two bridges, opened two roads, cleared sixteen acres of land, and planted twenty-six acres of crops.[18]

The third new craft to appear in Bethabara in 1755 explicitly signaled the new economic priorities for Wachovia. Officials sent Gottfried Aust, a 33-year-old potter, to North Carolina to answer the Wachovia Brethren's repeated requests for a potter to provide both earthenware for their own use and a source of income for their community.[19] As late as June 29, 1755, Spangenberg told the brothers, "If you can make do with iron kettles, with some copper vessels, and such milk containers as you can fashion out of wood until such a time as the pottery can be built at the right place where it belongs, this will save you a lot of time in the first place and then lead to better results."[20] With church revenues down, however, Spangenberg decided not to wait for the new town. Since the Wachovia settlers had to bear more of their colony's cost sooner than expected, church officials sent Aust down to assist them by opening a pottery.[21]

The Unity's decision to send a potter to Wachovia paid off handsomely. Once his shop was finished in March 1756, Br. Aust fired his first batch of pottery in August and his second batch in September, leading the diarist to comment that "the great need [for pottery] is at last relieved. Each living room has the ware it needs, and the kitchen is furnished. There is also a set of mugs of uniform size for Lovefeast." Two and a half months later, "Br. Aust burned stove tiles, and when they were ready he set up stoves in the *Gemein Haus* and the Brothers' House, probably the first in Carolina."[22] Outsiders began to inquire about the availability of earthenware as soon as they heard of Aust's arrival, and the diarist recorded the first "great sale of earthenware" on July 19, 1757.[23] After Aust artisans arrived only sporadically; one or two a year came, such as Thomas Hofman, a tanner who arrived in 1756, or Johann Heinrich Herbst, who replaced Hofman in 1762.[24]

The mill complex designed and built by Brn. Christensen and van der Merk from Bethlehem constituted another successful Unity investment in Wachovia. Originally planned as a grist- and sawmill, the complex brought in so much business from outsiders that the brethren in Wachovia determined that the water power should be harnessed for some additional uses.[25] The intrepid Br. Loesch instructed Br. Jacob van der Merk to adapt the gearing at the mill to power a bark mill and an oil mill, but he did not tell church officials about the project until it was complete.[26] Fortunately, Loesch had made a wise decision. He knew that the bark mill would increase the production capability at the new tannery (where the recently-arrived Br. Hofman worked), and the oil mill would produce enough linseed oil to sell to backcountry residents, giving the church more profitable businesses in Wachovia.[27] Loesch was right. In December 1756, Br. Spangenberg sent a letter to the brethren at Bethabara expressing his happiness that "Your mill [is] of service to the whole countryside."[28]

In 1758 the two most successful crafts in Bethabara were the blacksmith shop and the pottery—together with the permanent water-powered mill that Loesch convinced the church he needed—the brethren in Wachovia began to partially support themselves. The church, however, retained rigid and total control over the colony, using its financial needs and settlement experience to determine which trades would become part of Bethabara.

Sometimes the Wachovia brethren's desire to make money for the church, even on a lesser scale than the central town would eventually provide, was not encouraged by the leadership. For instance, in early 1758, Br. Loesch wrote to Br. Spangenberg asking permission to set up a gunsmith's shop and requesting a carpenter and a miller for Bethabara, but Spangenberg rejected his appeal. Spangenberg explained that a severe shortage of Moravian carpenters in Pennsylvania had forced the church to hire outsiders to work on the Single Sisters' House in Bethlehem. No millers were available at present, either, but Spangenberg had asked for some to be sent from Europe. Bethabara's designation as a temporary village and plantation probably gave it low priority for assignment of skilled help. During the 1750s the growth and expansion of the Moravian Church in Pennsylvania made the construction of the town of Lititz imperative.

Not all the news the brethren received at Bethabara was bad. Spangenberg approved establishment of a gunsmith shop and arranged to send some high quality steel as an inducement to start work.[29] This gesture was a small concession on Spangenberg's part, as Andreas Betz, a trained gunsmith, had been living in Wachovia since 1754, working (at least some of the time) in the blacksmith's shop.[30]

Selling the handiwork of the Wachovia artisans to a willing backcountry market was not the only way the church could make a profit from Wachovia before the main town was operating. The brethren also traded or sold some of their products such as flax, thread, or skins to Moravian town stores in Pennsylvania or, occasionally, to merchants in Wilmington on the Cape Fear River and Pine Tree (now Camden), South Carolina, in exchange for items such as textiles that they needed but did not produce.[31] Not surprisingly, the leaders in Bethlehem tried to direct this aspect of the Moravians economic life as well. Spangenberg even worried about the practicality of what the Wachovia brethren might bring to Pennsylvania to trade for supplies. He finally instructed them to bring rattan, cotton, flax, hemp, furs, deerskins, heavy ox hides, sole leather, and other similar items to trade for basic goods they did not produce, such as blankets and saddles.[32]

Spangenberg's reference to saddles in his instructions to the brethren reveals the church's desire to curtail the brethren's trade with local artisans (which would have benefited the Wachovia brethren directly) in favor of cultivating trade networks which would profit the church as a whole. The Wachovia brethren could have procured saddles from Richard Graham, a saddler who had been working in Rowan County since 1749.[33] Instead, Spangenberg advised them to bring their raw materials to Pennsylvania to trade through the church store in Bethlehem. This plan not only benefited the church; it also insured that the Wachovia brethren would not become reliant on a non-Moravian for any necessities of colonial life.

A weaving operation was not established in Bethabara until 1758. A number of factors delayed the start of this trade in Wachovia. As Spangenberg's instructions suggest, Wachovia brethren could obtain virtually anything they needed from their trade networks in the backcountry and Pennsylvania. Although the brethren resisted trading for or purchasing supplies from local artisans, they did try to keep abreast of other "local" artisans and the services they offered. Periodically, the brethren would check the availability of the linen produced by weavers around Bethabara by sending a brother out to purchase some yardage. In the spring of 1758, Br. Petersen took a week's trip though the country in search of linen. He returned home on May 6 with eighty yards. After closely inspecting the material and evaluating their own labor situation, the brethren decided they could beat the competition and began weaving linen on a full-time basis May 23.[34]

If the church leaders were so determined to control the economic destiny of Wachovia until the original plans could be carried out, why did they wait until 1765, twelve years after the original settlers arrived on the tract, to select a town site on which to construct their center of trade and manufacture? In the twelve years prior to selecting the site for Salem, problems with the Indians in Pennsylvania and North Carolina during the Seven Years' War, the unanticipated establishment of the village of Bethania some three miles northwest of Bethabara,[35] and the death of Count Zinzendorf had distracted officials in Europe and America. The net effect of church leaders' neglecting to pay full attention to the first twelve years of settlement in Wachovia was simple: Salisbury, the Rowan County seat west of the Yadkin River, usurped Salem's intended role as the premier commercial town in the county, and artisan development on the Wachovia Tract remained at a rudimentary stage until the construction of Salem began in 1766.

The rapid, if chaotic, settlement of the rest of Rowan County stood in stark contrast to the Moravians' carefully planned selection, organization, and colonization of the Wachovia Tract in the northeast quadrant. The non-Moravian settlers of Rowan County were an ethnic mix of English, Scotch-Irish, and German. Even though many settlers came to Rowan County in groups,[36] no corporate body had a higher authority to do central planning for them and, consequently, they did not generate the sort of detailed plans and revisions the Moravians left. However, county records do reveal that even without the constant aid and interference from a higher authority, the non-Moravian inhabitants of Rowan County swiftly began the transition from an agrarian, subsistence-based economy to a market, capitalist economy complete with artisans, merchants, and innkeepers. Those settlers also created the county seat, Salisbury, more quickly and efficiently than the Moravians began Salem, and it became the center of commerce, administration, and justice (an advantage Salem would never enjoy) for the county.

This discussion of the non-Moravian artisans of Rowan County will begin by explaining the methodology used to identify these artisans; then it will examine the growth of this community of tradesmen as it paralleled the commercial development of Salisbury, the Rowan County seat from 1753 to 1759.

The task of identifying the non-Moravian artisans who worked in Rowan County is very different from the task of identifying their Moravian counterparts because the Moravians were devoted to record keeping and identified their members by skill or trade. The artisans living and working outside of the Wachovia Tract must be identified from public and private documents from Rowan County, in which noting a skill or trade was always incidental to the purpose of the record. These artisans have been identified from the Minutes of the Court of Pleas and Quarter, deeds, wills, apprentice bonds, and the civil and criminal action papers of Rowan County; and from the Salisbury District Superior Court civil and criminal action papers and the several dockets of that court.[37] With the exception of women artisans, the identification of whom will be discussed in a later chapter, this study includes only those artisans identified from a trade following their names, from documented responsibility for training an apprentice, or from invoices, ledgers, and account books. Consequently, the number of artisans working in Rowan County during this time frame almost certainly has been underestimated. James T. Lemon's study of early southeastern Pennsylvania, the area which many migrants left for Rowan County, described most of its inhabitants as skilled craftsmen and farmers.[38] Yet the number of identified artisans working in Rowan County appears low by comparison.

In 1767, George Marshall took William McCulloch, orphan of James McCulloch, as his apprentice "to Larn him the Art and Mistry of a House Joiner." Seventy-one of Rowan County's non-Moravian artisans were identified as masters from such undetailed apprenticeship agreements in the Orphan's Court sessions of the Court of Pleas and Quarter.[39] William was one of forty-eight children who were bound to adults in Rowan County between 1759 and 1770, all under provisions of statutes passed by the North Carolina legislature.[40]

North Carolina passed its first "Act Concerning Orphans" in 1715 to "educate and provide" for orphans "according to their Rank and degree." Orphans of both sexes whose parents did not leave estates were "bound Apprentice to some Handycraft Trade," and the masters would instruct the orphans in the trade as well as feed and clothe them in exchange for their labor.[41] Although the Assembly made minor changes in the laws concerning the care of orphans in 1755 and 1760, the 1762 "Act for the better care of Orphans, and Security and Management of their Estates" remained in effect through the Revolution. Section nineteen of the law provided that, should an orphan's inheritance be so small that no guardian could be found to care for the child for the estate profits, a male orphan could be bound apprentice to some "Tradesman, Merchant, Mariner" until he was twenty-one. A female orphan could be bound apprentice to "some suitable Employment" until she was age eighteen.[42]

Of the forty-eight children apprenticed in Rowan County between 1753 and 1770, thirty-five were male and thirteen were female. Thirty-nine agreements about those children mentioned an occupation or tools of the trade they would learn. Three girls, Mary Sawyers, Rachal Burch, and May Johnson, were identified as spinning apprentices by their receiving spinning wheels at the close of their terms. Thirty-four boys were placed in thirteen different trades (although thirty-six different apprenticeships were negotiated).[43] The trades to which boys apprenticed most often were blacksmithing (seven), weaving (five), and shoemaking (five).[44] Other trades, such as coopering (four), saddlery (three), carpentry (three), tailoring (two), hatmaking (two), tanning (one), saddletreemaking (one), silversmithing (one), farming (one), and vicaring (one), were found with less frequency. However, the twelve trades which appeared in the Orphan's Court records as apprenticeship opportunities did not reflect the same variety of trades present in the artisan population of Rowan County in 1770. While some craft categories, such as the clothing or leather trades, had a strong apprenticeship following, other categories, like the transportation and consumer item trades, had few, if any, apprentices. (See Table 2.)

Although the apprenticeship system met an important need in Rowan County—taking care of poor orphans—it did not supply the immediate area with an adequate number of artisans during the early years of settlement. First of all, only forty-eight children became apprentices prior to 1770, and the majority of them did not complete their terms until the mid- to late-1770s. Second, the former apprentices of Rowan County artisans hardly ever appeared in a survey of backcountry artisans through 1790, indicating that they rarely remained in the geographic area. Of the ninety-eight children apprenticed to non-Moravian artisans working in Rowan County prior to 1790, only one, Martin Basinger, a hatter who trained with Casper Kinder, worked as an artisan in Rowan County.[45] The reasons why these young people apparently left Rowan County after completing their apprenticeships are many and varied, but the most compelling reason appears to be that they moved west to the frontier to take advantage of the opportunities in unsettled territory, just as their masters had a generation earlier. Their move to the frontier might also be the consequence of improper instruction and low-quality workmanship, rendering their products unmarketable in all but the crudest of circumstances.[46]

Unfortunately, the primary sources for Rowan County only hint about the extent to which other types of bound laborers, such as slaves or indentured servants, helped to ease the shortage of skilled labor. The only mention of a bound servant working as an artisan in Rowan dates to 1770, when James Simison, a turner, paid an anonymous individual three pounds proc, "the price of one cow," through William Steele "for the use of Daniel Huffman," whom later court records identify as a shoemaker.[47] Indentured servitude was a popular method for immigrants to get to the colonies, and servants with artisan training were in demand in urban areas such as Philadelphia and Williamsburg.[48] However, the lack of records about indentured servants in Rowan County suggests that they were not a significant presence in the North Carolina backcountry.

Table 2. Apprentices in Rowan County, 1753-1770

Year	Name	Sex	Age	Trade
1758	Holland, John	M		shoemaker
	Roachment, Paul	M		blacksmith
1759	Holland, Hugh	M		shoemaker
1761	Smith, Ralph	M	17?	cordwainer
	Beard, Andrew (PB)	M	10	cooper
	Brandon, Mary (PB)	F	3	
	(Walter), Ann (PB)	F	5	
	Man, Else (O)	F	5?	
	Hicks, John (O)	M	15	blacksmith
	Welsh, Mary (O)	F	14?	
1763	Neide, John (O)	M	6	saddler
1764	Haddicks, William	M	18?	weaver
	Millsaps, William (O)	M	15?	saddler
	Kelly, Thomas (O)	M	7	cooper
	Anderson, James (O)	M	13	hatter
1765	Sawyers, John (O)	M	14	
	Sawyers, Mary (O)	F	12	
	Sawyers, Sarah (O)	F	7?	
1766	Sawyers, Mary (T)	F	13	spinster
	McCulloh, William (O)	M	10	tailor
	McCulloh, John (O)	M		carpenter
1767	McCulloh, James (O)	M	9	weaver
	Payne, Agness (O)	F	9	
	Asalvin, William (O)	M	13	saddler
	McCulloh, William (O,T)	M	11?	house joiner
	McCulloh, Jane (O)	F	7?	
	Sawyers, John (O,T)	M	16	farmer
	Burch, Rachal (O)	F	14	spinster
	Burch, Richard (O)	M	9	wicar
	Anderson, James (O)	M	15	shoemaker
1768	Allin, William (M)	M		
	Crunk, John Watts (O)	M	10	blacksmith
	Grup, Menery (O)	M	10	hatter
	Bartlett, John (O)	M	1	shoemaker
	Johnson, Nathaniel (O)	M	13	tailor
	Todd, Joseph	M		silversmith
1769	Jones, John (O)	M	14	saddletree maker

(Cont.)

Table 2, cont.

Year	Name	Sex	Age	Trade
	Cross, Phillip (O)	M	10	blacksmith
	Cook, William (O)	M	2	tanner
	Shaver, Sarah (B)	F		
1770	Crouse, Peter (O)	M	8	blacksmith
	Jones, John (T)	M	16	blacksmith
	Crosby, Paul (O)	M	19	joiner
	Grant, Rachel (O)	F	12	
	Grant, Michael (O)	M	3	weaver
	Adams, John (O)	M	19	blacksmith
	Johnson, Thomas (O)	M	11?	weaver
	Johnson, May (O)	F	8	spinster
	Baltrip, Hannah (M)	F	9	
	Baltrip, John (B)	M	7	cooper
	Mullens, William (PB)	M	2	weaver
	Donnolly, David (PB)	M	9	cooper

B: bastard; M: mulatto; O: orphan; PB: possible bastard; T: transfer

SOURCES: Lynne Howard Fraser, "'Nobody's Children': The Treatment of Illegitimate Children in Three North Carolina Counties, 1760-1790" (master's thesis, College of William and Mary, 1987), 80-95; Kathi R. Jones, "'That Also These children May Become Useful People': Apprenticeships in Rowan County, North Carolina from 1753 to 1795" (master's thesis, College of William and Mary, 1984), 70-94.

Lemon estimates that during the period 1725-1755 most of the European immigrants to southeastern Pennsylvania were poor and served as indentured servants of one type or another. The lack of indentured servants in Rowan County may be explained by the fact that many settlers to the area were former indentured servants themselves. After working off their period of service, they found Pennsylvania too expensive and headed down the Wagon Road to start their own lives over again in the Carolina backcountry.[49]

The presence of slaves in Rowan County is easier to document; they appear in county tax lists and individual wills as valuable property. However, one of the distinguishing features of Rowan County society was the relative scarcity of slavery, especially when compared to eastern North Carolina or even the backcountry counties east of the Yadkin River, such as Granville. The 1759 Rowan County Tax List includes approximately 38 slaves as taxable property. Out of 652 taxables, 24 owned slaves (3.8%). In 1767, out of an estimated population of 13,516 in Rowan County, only 719 (5.3%) were blacks. In contrast, with an estimated total population of 5,902, Granville County included 1,712 blacks (29%).[50]

Whether Rowan County slaves worked as skilled artisans is more difficult to document. Of the twenty-four slave owners on the 1759 Rowan County tax list, only six, or less than one percent of all taxables, were artisans. The only Rowan County slave known to have been trained and working as an artisan was "Ester" [*sic*], a mulatto girl bound to Joseph Hickman "to learn the art and Mistery of a weaver."[51]

In addition to bound labor such as apprentices, slaves, or indentured servants, the farmers and artisans of Rowan County may have hired free laborers to help them with their chores. In southeastern Pennsylvania, craftsmen and laborers who did not own land often hired out for food and board and sometimes a small fee. They could be distinguished from bound labor in their appearance as tax-paying citizens on county lists.[52] In Rowan County, the presence of such free labor is difficult to judge based on the extant records. The only specific reference to a laborer comes from March 1770 in the Civil Action Papers of the Salisbury District Superior Court, when "William Courtney Labourer otherwise called William Courtney Mason" was summoned to appear in front of the court.[53] Courtney did not own any land, and his name does not show up on any of the Rowan County tax lists. In both of his appearances before the Rowan Court of Pleas and Quarter, Courtney won sizeable sums of money, which indicates that he made his living traveling throughout the county selling his labor and his skills as a mason to those individuals who could afford it. Courtney's survival depended on his wages; therefore, he had to take people who owed him money to court.[54] Another likely laborer was the anonymous "free negroe" listed on the 1759 tax list as living in the household of Joseph Jackson.

The majority of artisans living in Rowan County migrated to the backcountry as adults, and many of them cannot be identified from apprenticeship agreements. Some of these artisans were experienced craftsmen prior to relocating in Rowan County. Because the same ethnic strains populated the entire southern backcountry, many common surnames existed with no method to distinguish between them. Consequently, craftsmen often identified themselves by their trade in legal documents. Michael Miller, a cooper who came to Rowan in 1751 from Cecil County, Maryland, or New Castle, Delaware,[55] was so well known by his craft that the sheriff summoned "Michal Miller, Cooper," to appear in Criminal Court for a case of indebtedness.[56] Fifteen artisans were identified from the Rowan County criminal and civil action papers.[57] When Stephen Elmore sold 495 acres of land on the east fork of Polecat Creek of Deep River on both sides of the Trading Path to John McGee, the deed identified Elmore as a blacksmith.[58] Approximately eighty-two artisans were identified from Rowan County deeds.

Occasionally, extant documentation concerning other matters helped to identify certain individuals as artisans. An account from Rowan County Sheriff Francis Lock to Samuel Smith for "making Two pair Large Bolts for the legs of Criminals" and "2 Pair of Strong Handcuffs" in *The Colonial Records of North Carolina* positively identified Smith as a blacksmith, even though he is not identified by trade in any other legal records.[59] The discovery of two other blacksmiths in Rowan with the same surname, David Smith and John Smith, confirmed Samuel's trade and a probable family connection.[60] The few account books and papers with this type of information for Rowan County have limited to nine the number of artisans identified this way.

Probate evidence proved less satisfactory as a means of identifying artisans. Unless the decedent stated his craft in describing certain tools or implements, men have not been identified as artisans through the contents of their wills or estates because the presence of tools does not necessarily indicate that the owner was a professional artisan. This is especially true in an agricultural community such as Rowan County, where carpentry tools were integral to the creation and maintenance of a farm. Quite a few artisans did mention their specialized tools or their craft in their wills, however. Robert Milagin, for example, was identified as a weaver by a loom and tackling willed to his landlord, as well as by his descriptions of the textiles he bequeathed to his friends.[61] Henry Wensel's trade as potter was discovered in his will from his specification that when his sons reached seventeen years of age "they shall go to trades and if one of my Sons will Learn the Potters trade the same shall have all my Tools & Necessaries for the Potters business & also all my Glassing."[62] Rowan County wills identified thirty-six artisans.[63]

Following their identification as artisans, recording the activities of these individuals as documented in the Minutes of the Court of Pleas and Quarter, deeds, and wills for Rowan County, and in some instances the counties later formed from Rowan, became the next task. The necessity for absolute identification of these individuals as artisans has surely resulted in an underestimation of Rowan County's artisan population.[64] Other secondary sources have identified certain individuals as artisans for whom no primary source evidence can be found. In addition, the available primary sources can be misleading. For instance, the Minutes of the Court of Pleas and Quarter often mentioned reimbursing individuals for artisan-produced objects. The court paid William Nassery £1 5s. for making a pillory outside of the jail and Francis Lock for repairing the "Gaol & Irons."[65] However, as Samuel Smith's account proves in the case of Francis Lock, the men named in these accounts (who were both sheriffs) did not make the objects for which they received money. Often they were only contractors, responsible for hiring and paying the artisan for his work. For the same reason, individuals who received contracts for erecting buildings and bridges in the county have not been counted as artisans. Consequently, William Hide's successful bid to build a bridge across Grant's Creek in August 1769 does not identify him as a builder.[66]

While artisans certainly participated in the organization of every settlement in the area which became Rowan County, not all artisans were overly anxious to come to the backcountry in the first wave of settlement. Who made the journey down the Wagon Road to Rowan County in the early years and why? All of the people who moved to Rowan County in the late 1740s and 1750s believed they had something to gain by relocating. Whether they were immigrants to the New World or first generation colonists, they shared a common vision of success. To a large extent they were entrepreneurs who sought to use their skills and their financial reserves to pursue an improved life in the material, social, and spiritual senses, and they believed the opportunity to create such a life could be found at the terminus of the Wagon Road in Rowan County, North Carolina.[67]

According to Mitchell in *Commercialism and Frontier*, commercialism was a key factor in how these people created new societies in America. They believed in private property, freedom of trade, and competition within an economy understood to be inclined toward some kind of internal, self-adjusting, market equilibrium. Consequently, they viewed exchanges between man and land, and between man and man, from a utilitarian, exploitive perspective, and surplus items from productive enterprise were potential sources of trade and profit within a money-based economic system.[68]

Research by Lemon and Mitchell indicates that as early as the 1720s recent immigrants to southeastern Pennsylvania had trouble finding suitable land at a price they could afford. This led to settlement further inland, to the Lebanon and Lehigh Valleys in northern Pennsylvania and the Susquehanna and Cumberland Valleys in western Pennsylvania. The Susquehanna and Cumberland Valleys were part of the Great Valley of the Appalachians, and they emptied into the Shenandoah Valley of Virginia, providing a natural escape route as the land in Pennsylvania continued to fill.[69]

This pattern—in which an area became settled, more settlers came, and land prices eventually escalated beyond the capabilities of the more recent arrivals—repeated itself throughout the backcountry. The people most likely to migrate because of overcrowding and expensive land prices were these newcomers or the children of the older settlers who found themselves unable to afford to live where they had been raised. A third type of pioneer migrant was the farsighted man who realized that he had everything to gain from being the first arrival to a region and (especially if he had settlement experience) nothing to lose.

The migration corridor down the valley provided a constant supply of potential buyers of land and farms, so that property owners who sold their land and moved on often were able to do so at a considerable profit. By moving to the new location they got first selection of land at low prices and the opportunity to be the first to practice their occupations while they helped develop the settlement. If they decided to move elsewhere, they profited from selling their land with its improvements at a hefty profit to the second wave of migrants, who were willing to pay more for the land in exchange for the security provided by the settlement. Settlers began to move out of the upper Shenandoah Valley of Virginia and into North Carolina by the mid-1740s.[70]

The first wave of migrants to backcountry North Carolina formed the settlements described in the previous chapter. Every settlement in the region that became Rowan County had artisans among its founders. While artisans settled throughout the county, professional artisans were clearly in the minority to farmers. Mitchell theorizes that permanent agriculture stood at the forefront of developing frontier economies; other activities, such as artisan production, were supplemental to commercial farming. Although early inhabitants of backcountry communities were primarily subsistent during the first years of settlement, they were not self-sufficient.[71] In fact, breaking out of local exchange networks and establishing contacts with outside markets were among the farmers' chief goals. To become connected to external markets meant that settlers could obtain a variety of goods, both necessities and luxuries, that were not available locally.[72]

Economic cooperation among all residents of Rowan County was necessary before the farmers could establish those ties with external markets. If an external market is absent, inhabitants have no alternative to subsistence or semi-subsistence production. Such limited (or non-existent) participation in a commercial market economy meant that most farm families had enough land, equipment, and labor to raise as much food as they could consume. During the earliest period of settlement, barter transactions took place in which established settlers exchanged surplus foodstuffs, seeds, and livestock for the scarce currency and manufactured items new arrivals brought. Then the local economy diversified somewhat more as the few artisans and traders created a small demand for farm produce. However, the migrants quickly planted their own crops, and most rural artisans had extensive gardens and possibly a few head of livestock, so the economy stabilized at a low level of specialization.

This rudimentary form of a market economy was really more of a system of direct exchange without a middleman. Farmers traded surplus crops to artisans for a specific product or service they needed: excess wheat for an ax, or a few dozen eggs for repairs to the porch roof. In these exchanges acquisition of a needed product on both sides was the motive, not profit. While both the farmers and the artisans played an important role in developing this early exchange network and low level of economic specialization in Rowan County, any further economic development (including trade with external markets) would be dependent on someone concerned with making profit, namely a merchant.[73]

The merchant could organize the economy of the county in an effective and efficient manner through the three functions he performed: first, as the only source of goods from the outside world; second, as a market for local farm surplus; and third, as a reliable source of long-term credit.[74] Stores would not be found during the earliest stages of settlement and economic exchange because Rowan County lacked what they needed to survive: a permanent, sizeable population to form a customer base and a centrally located town from which to operate.

With small settlements scattered throughout the North Carolina backcountry, developing economies frequently had to wait on politics, for the formation of counties and selection of county seats usually determined the central location most merchants desired. As in other county seats, the large number of people who would come to Salisbury to conduct their legal affairs were potential customers to storeowners, tavernkeepers, and craftsmen who, in turn, transformed the town into the economic center of the county.

In 1753 the population of the backcountry had increased to the point that the Assembly passed "An Act for erecting the upper Part of Anson County into a County and Parish by name of Rowan County, and St. Luke's Parish," so local inhabitants could attend Court for business and civic purposes more easily.[75] The creation of Rowan County brought local government to the northwest backcountry of North Carolina through a Court of Pleas and Quarter that filled the civic, administrative, and judicial needs of the area and its residents. It also formally acknowledged the growing backcountry population previously ignored by the eastern-dominated colonial government. The Court of Pleas and Quarter heard cases wherein the amount of litigation was between forty shillings and twenty pounds, a variety of minor civil and criminal offenses, and all cases involving legacy, intestate estates, and matters concerning orphans. In addition, the court administered the physical and financial needs of the county by deciding the construction of official structures and roads, supervising land deeds, setting and collecting the local taxes, and issuing licenses and fee structures for owners of taverns and ordinaries.[76]

Immediately following the formation of the county, the court met at the houses of private individuals such as James Alexander and John Brandon. After the first licenses were issued to establish public ordinaries, however, later sessions probably convened at those locations to be more accessible to the public.[77] Given the economic benefits the county seat could bring, the court was eager to have its own facility. The Moravians may have had a difficult time choosing a site for their main town, but the justices of the Rowan Court immediately selected the courthouse location at a crossroads between the Irish settlement and John Brandon's land. They next drew up construction specifications for the courthouse, the prison, and stocks during the first session, in June 1753.[78] When court sat for the second session, in September, the justices ordered a tax of four shillings and one penny half-penny proclamation money be levied on each taxable in the county to defray "the Publick Charges of this Province and Also debts Due from this County and Publick buildins &c."[79]

Having lived in the backcountry long enough to be recognized as prominent residents worthy of appointment to the court, the justices (who clearly had their own private economic interests) knew the importance of establishing a county seat and courthouse as soon as possible. Virtually every county resident would have to come to the courthouse at some time or another to register a cattle mark, record a deed, prove a will, obtain a license for an ordinary, ferry, or public mill, witness any of those documents, sit on a jury, participate in a case, or accompany someone with business at the court.

With a built-in, county-wide clientele, the town was the perfect location to start a business and the best way to promote the economic cooperation necessary to gain access to external markets. Edward Cusick realized the potential of the still unbuilt town and applied for a license to keep "public House at the Court House" on September 21, 1753.[80] Cusick had excellent instincts: he was the first of four innkeepers to establish taverns in Salisbury by 1755. Two years later there were eleven innkeepers.[81]

Although the justices may have claimed the 640 acres of land for the town as early as December 1753, the first mention of obtaining a warrant for the land for the sum of £1 6s. 8d. did not come from James Carter, Esq., Lord Granville's Deputy Surveyor (and a millwright) until the March 1754 court.[82] The formal creation of the town occurred on February 11, 1755, when William Churton and Richard Vigers, agents for Granville, granted 635 acres to Carter and Hugh Forster (a saddler), trustees for the town, to grant and convey lots in the town "by name of Salisbury." Similar to the Moravians, local authorities had a town plan for Salisbury, yet they only took two years to create and implement the plan, in contrast to the fourteen years the Moravians took before they selected a site for Salem, requiring a new plan to be drawn. Salisbury was laid out in a grid pattern: two main streets traversed the square plot of land, dividing it into four smaller squares that were subdivided into individual lots.[83] Carter and Forster issued the first deed to the Justices of the Peace in Rowan County for part of lot number four "adjacent Corbin & Water St. whereon the Prison is erected together with the Diamond where the Court House offices & stocks are erected."[84]

Innkeeper Cusick and at least two other individuals, James Alexander and Peter Arndt, lived on town lands before the formal survey of Salisbury in February, 1755. Shortly thereafter James Carter and John Dunn probably established residences in town.[85] In mid-June 1755, Governor Dobbs visited the western part of North Carolina and in his report to the Board of Trade noted that he "arrived at Salisbury, the County town of Rowan the Town is but just laid out, the Court House built and 7 or 8 log Houses erected."[86] In addition to the above mentioned individuals, Ramsey postulates that John Ryle and William Montgomery owned inns or ordinaries on town lots at this time, and that Johannes Adam, a potter, also lived in town. Before the end of the year Joseph Woods, William Cadogan, George Cathey Sr., John Newman Oglethorpe, Theodore Feltmatt, Nathaniel and Moses Alexander (a blacksmith), Alexander Dobbin (merchant and shoemaker), and James Carson (tanner) also had purchased lots in Salisbury.[87]

The sales of Salisbury town lots rose in 1756 and 1757 and they grew steadily more popular. However, the short periods of ownership and lack of building indicate a high level of speculation in town lots. Not everyone was afraid to take a chance on residing in a backwoods town, however, and artisans became increasingly aware of the financial opportunities afforded by the new urban center. A few astute businessmen ran taverns along with their craft shops. Henry Horah, a weaver from Cecil County, Maryland, obtained a license to operate an ordinary in Salisbury in 1756, and, according to Ramsey, he may have started a weaving shop the next year.[88] In the following years other artisans, such as hatter Casper Kinder and weaver Henry Zevily, to name but two, followed Horah's lead.[89]

In the first six years after the site for Salisbury was selected and settled, the population of the town may have remained small, but the functions of the town constantly expanded. Because of the agricultural nature of the colonial South, the population was located overwhelmingly in rural areas. Therefore, the functions or services provided by a town such as Salisbury are a more accurate indication of its size and importance to the region than its population.

According to Ernst and Merrens's model of functional elaboration in southern towns, the appearance of craft shops, inns, a courthouse, a jail, and mills in or around Salisbury by 1755 proves its role as a service center for the entire county. Salisbury was well on its way to becoming an urban center that would offer even more functions, such as retailing imported or manufactured goods, gathering, warehousing, grading, and distributing commodities from the local area, and administering justice and government both locally and regionally.[90] On the other side of the Yadkin River, the Moravians at Bethabara (and, later, Salem) were enjoying their own inn, mill, and craft shops, but their commercial enterprises would never attract or serve the audience who came to Salisbury for political and legal reasons and then stayed to eat and shop.

By 1759, the date of the earliest extant tax list for Rowan County, the artisan profile had changed dramatically from that of 1753. In all, 126 artisans in 21 professions were located for Rowan County; 62 craftsmen practicing 18 different trades appeared on the 1759 Tax List;[91] 86.5 percent, or 109, of the artisans were non-Moravians who made their living outside of the Wachovia Tract. Although the number of trades present had increased since the county's formation, the majority of the 109 Rowan County artisans still participated in trades necessary to daily life (i.e., not luxury): 29 percent of all artisans were in the clothing trades (clothiers, weavers, tailors, spinsters, or hatters); 20 percent of the craftsmen processed or made finished goods out of leather by tanning, shoemaking, or saddlemaking; 19 percent were involved in building trades as either carpenters, millwrights, joiners, bricklayers, brickmakers, or masons; 14 percent were blacksmiths; 9 percent participated in allied wood trades as coopers; and 5.5 percent of the craftsmen were wagonmakers or wheelwrights. Even at this early date more than 3 percent of the artisans participated in consumer item trades: one potter and two gunsmiths were successfully plying their crafts within the backcountry community. (See Table 3.)

The growth in the number of non-Moravian artisans in Rowan County, from 18 in 1753 to 109 in 1759, indicates the desire of an increasing number of backcountry inhabitants to own a wider selection of the objects made by artisans. Even though artisans in the necessary trades continued to compose the majority (70%) of the artisan population, they were not restricted in what they could produce. Surely some of those artisans (probably the majority of them) continued to fulfill the basic needs of the settlers continuing to migrate into the region. However, the growing number of artisans in the same craft also signifies further specialization within the trade. Weavers probably concentrated in certain fibers and special weaves, and some blacksmiths may have preferred to make tools, lighting devices, or decorative hardware rather than to shoe horses. For example, Paul Rodsmith's account with the Steele family shows that the smith steeled and sharpened various tools, made tools and hardware, and even repaired a wagon for the family, but he never shod a horse. In contrast, an account

Table 3. Rowan County Artisans in 1759

	Number	(Moravians)	% of total population
Clothing trades	**37**		**29.36**
weavers	22	(1)	17.46
tailors	10	(1)	7.93
hatters	3		2.38
clothiers	1		.79
spinsters	1		.79
Leather trades	**25**		**19.84**
shoemakers/ cordwainers	12	(2)	9.52
tanners	9	(1)	7.14
saddlers	4		3.17
Building trades	**24**		**19.04**
carpenters	12	(2)	9.52
millwrights	6	(2)	4.76
joiners	3		2.38
bricklayers	1	(1)	.79
brickmakers	1	(1)	.79
masons	1		.79
Metal trades	**18**		**14.28**
blacksmiths	18	(2)	14.28
Allied wood trades	**11**		**8.73**
coopers	9	(2)	7.14
turners	2	(1)	1.58
Transportation trades	**7**		**5.55**
wheelwrights	6		4.76
wagonmakers	1		.79
Luxury item trades	**4**		**3.1**
potters	2	(1)	1.58
gunsmiths	2		1.58

(Cont.)

Table 3, cont.

Total number of artisans in the county:	126
Total number of trades represented:	21
Number of Moravian artisans:	17
Number of artisans on tax list:	62
Number of trades on tax list:	18
Percent of artisans who were Moravian:	13.49

Sources: Artisans' figures generated from data base of artisans in Rowan County in dBase III+ sorted by trade and year of arrival. Information on artisans on Rowan County 1759 tax list provided by data base created by James P. Whittenburg.

of the costs to establish Oliver Townsley's blacksmith shop includes "1 Set of Shoeing Tools."[92]

This profile of Rowan County artisans in 1759 further supports that a local market economy did exist in backcountry North Carolina, and that specialization of crafts to meet consumer demands was on the rise. This increase in the artisan population and the trades being offered may not be the sole product of the developing backcountry economy, however. The growth of crafts also may be the result of the ever-growing sophistication of backcountry inhabitants and their desire to establish a more comfortable standard of living. According to anthropologist Henry M. Miller, settlement on the frontier required that colonists take care of their basic needs of food, clothing, and shelter before they could develop a stable, sustainable adaptation to the environment. Like most permanent frontiers, pastoral and agricultural people settled the backcountry and adapted to the physical environment by exploiting the land through crop production and grazing. Once they completed this process the settlers then began to incorporate learned behavior patterns and cultural models (especially memories of their homeland) to establish their social environment.[93]

Following learned behavior patterns and cultural models may be the ultimate explanation of the different ways in which backcountry society and economy developed east and west of the Yadkin River. The artisan population of Rowan County exploded from 22 individuals (4 in Bethabara and 18 in the county) working in necessary trades such as blacksmithing, weaving, and carpentry in 1753 to 126 artisans (17 in Wachovia and 109 in the county) practicing at least 21 different occupations, including potters, spinsters, gunsmiths, and wheelwrights, in 1759. The Moravians clearly intended to use their settlement experience, financial resources, supply of labor, and religious teachings, coupled with the will of God, to create a commercial town in the midst of the North Carolina backcountry from which the church would profit greatly. But in the case of the brethren, the best laid plans went astray. The tightening of financial reserves, Indian problems in Pennsylvania and North Carolina, and the death of their visionary patron kept the church from selecting a site for and beginning construction on the "center of trade and manufacture" for twelve years following the settlement of the Wachovia Tract. Instead of reaping great profits for the church from its vast supply of artisans and trades to the backcountry market, only a handful of Moravian craftsmen existed at Bethabara. These few worked diligently to fulfill the needs of their fellow brethren and sell their goods to outsiders.

This review of the settlement east and west of the river shows that the Moravians should and could have become the commercial center of Rowan County, but they did not. While the brethren waited for money, instructions, supplies, and permission to build their center of trade and manufacturing, the unorganized but enthusiastic politicians and future entrepreneurs of Rowan County created Salisbury, the county seat. Without any plans for development, the clientele drawn by the courthouse attracted numerous businessmen, including artisans, to the area. Although not all of the crafts people of Rowan County lived in Salisbury, the town began to evolve into an economic center populated by merchants, tavern keepers, blacksmiths, saddlers, tanners, shoemakers, hatters, potters, and gunsmiths. As early as 1759, Salisbury reigned supreme as the economic center of Rowan County.

FOUR

The Commercial Development of Rowan County, 1759-1770

Salisbury achieved prominence as Rowan County's center of economic and legal activity by 1759. Although most trading of agricultural and manufactured projects occurred within local networks, indications of Salisbury's and Rowan County's later participation in larger economic networks were already present. In the following eleven years, the economic activity of North Carolina's westernmost county exploded from a partially semi-subsistent, local market economy to a regional and international commercial market economy with strong local foundations.

A combination of three factors helped transform the economy of Rowan County: roads, merchants, and the Cumberland County trading town of Cross Creek (now Fayetteville) on the Cape Fear River. Two of these factors—roads and merchants—were present in the county prior to 1759, but they were not a force for substantial growth at that time. The emergence of Cross Creek in the 1760s as the connection between the backcountry economy and the coastal, trans-Atlantic economy of Wilmington and Charleston turned the road system and the merchants into crucial players in the expanding economic prominence of Rowan County.

The years from 1759 to 1770 were also important for the artisans of Rowan County. Not only did the number of artisans more than double, but the number of crafts represented in the county increased by one-third, with the greatest expansion occurring in the consumer item or luxury trades. Artisans were drawn to Rowan County in numbers greater than ever before.[1] Like merchants, Rowan County artisans became intimately involved with the developing backcountry market economy. New crafts came into the county as soon as the economy and the population could support them.

During the colonial period the commercialization of Rowan County was not instantaneous, nor was it ever complete. Although Salisbury and other areas of the county became increasingly involved in the retail trade and tied to external markets, in the more rural and recently settled areas of the county, local trade networks and semi-subsistence economies persisted. In cultivating external trade networks next to subsistent economies, county residents may only have been replicating a familiar pattern of economic systems. According to Lemon in *The Best Poor Man's Country,* southeastern Pennsylvania was involved in two economic systems: a semi-subsistence economy and a trans-Atlantic trading economy. During the eighteenth century the commercial network within Pennsylvania and with other provinces became increasingly elaborate. Despite the complex connections, however, internal and external markets remained limited, contributing to the lingering subsistence aspect of the economy, especially on the frontier. In southeastern Pennsylvania, as in colonial Rowan County, those more rural areas were characterized by limited specialization of agriculture and the existence of family farms as the chief unit of production.[2]

Along with court records and some private papers, the key to understanding Rowan County artisans' place in the market economy lies in four different sets of merchant's account books from the county and its surrounding area. The books originated from William Steele's store and tavern in Salisbury in the 1760s; Alexander and John Lowrance's combination tavern and store on Beaverdam Creek ten miles west of Salisbury from the 1750s to the 1790s; an anonymous merchant's (possibly John Nisbet) store northwest of Salisbury near Ft. Dobbs in the 1770s; and the Cross Creek agent for the Wilmington merchant firm of Hogg and Campbell.[3] Not only do the account books show the importance of roads, merchants, and trading towns on the backcountry economy, they demonstrate the active role some artisans played in that economy as well as an urban/rural dichotomy of economic specialization within the county. And finally, a careful analysis of the merchants' account books to determine the type of goods they imported into the county and sold to local consumers also suggests (by process of elimination) what products or services Rowan County artisans supplied within the same economy.

The commercial economy of Rowan County was the product not only of roads, midland towns, and merchants, but also of the motivation of backcountry inhabitants. In other areas of early America the settlers' desire to establish trade networks with other regions made these networks reality.[4] In Rowan County, farmers and artisans wanted to progress beyond the low level of economic specialization that characterized the early years of settlement. Direct exchange may have supplied them with the necessities of life, but it also meant a static existence. Only through the active change of producing surplus for sale and gaining access to larger markets would residents be satisfied. That surplus, along with roads and merchants, led some Rowan County residents directly to the external markets they desired.

The first step in making contact between Rowan County and external markets was roads. A well-developed road system was essential for trade within the backcountry and outside of the region. Unlike the eastern portion of

North Carolina, which is criss-crossed by navigable rivers and streams, in the west dependable, reliable, and effective west-to-east transportation came in the form of roads and ferries. Access to major thoroughfares was a requirement for any backcountry town to succeed, and Salisbury was located on one of the main overland arteries of colonial North America, the Great Wagon Road, and in close proximity to another, the Trading Path.[5]

Building and maintaining roads came under the jurisdiction of the Rowan Court of Pleas and Quarter Sessions, and the record of petitions to the court and court orders for roads reflects the priorities in the settlement and development of the county. From 1753 to 1759 the justices sanctioned only six official roads in the county. Three of the roads connected Rowan County with areas outside of the county: a road to Virginia and a road to the Cape Fear Road (which led to Wilmington) in 1753, and a road to Charleston in 1756.[6] Two of the roads connected areas of the county to Salisbury, and one road ran across the Dan River between two mills.[7]

The effect of roads that ran from Rowan County to locations outside the backcountry was important and immediate. In the earliest years of settlement, backcountry inhabitants procured the objects they needed from the county's artisans because it was easier and more economical to produce basic textiles, clothes, shoes, and metalware for everyday use locally than to obtain them from outside the region. For those who could afford the transportation fees, imported goods could be purchased in Pennsylvania (and brought back via the Wagon Road), Virginia, or Charleston. But at this early date, the trip was made more often to sell loads of deerskins to a waiting market than to buy consumer goods. Even so, established trade routes to Virginia and Wilmington (to connect with the road to Charleston) probably explain the early court orders for official roads to those locations.

By 1755 trade with Charleston had become common. Gov. Arthur Dobbs wrote to the Board of Trade that settlers on his backcountry lands "have gone into indigo with success, which they sell at Charles Town, having a waggon road to it, alto' 200 miles distant . . . and from the many merchants there, they afford them English goods cheaper."[8] The following year, the governor ordered "a Good and Proper Road laid out from Salisbury to Charles Town by the way of Cold Water." He added, "I will Take it as a favour that you would lay it out as conveniently as you can . . . and make it as straight and Convenient as you can for Waggons."[9] The road brought two Charleston merchants, William Glen and Charles Stevenson, to Salisbury to set up a satellite of their Charleston store.[10] With deerskins the most frequently traded product, two German tanners, John Lewis Beard and Conrad Michael, set up shops in town as well.[11] More roads signaled merchants that Rowan County was progressing past a local economy, and the opportunity to become a middleman between markets had arrived.

Access to other markets was also extremely important to artisans, especially those who depended on outside markets for their materials. The only new trades to come to Rowan County between 1753 and 1756 were, like the earliest artisans in the county, those who could make their products from readily available resources: a clothier, a cooper, and a potter. In 1756 and 1757, the two years after the Charleston road was built, a hatter, two joiners, a spinster, and a gunsmith arrived in Rowan County. The need to transport objects between burgeoning backcountry markets also attracted three wheelwrights and a wagonmaker to the area.

The increased access of Rowan County residents to external markets in the early years of the county demonstrates that their economic needs could not be fulfilled totally within the county. As in the rest of British Colonial America, Rowan County inhabitants bought and sold a variety of local and imported goods through an active community of retail traders. Like the artisans who worked in the basic trades in the early years of settlement, the first retailers operated stores and taverns dealing in necessary merchandise rather than running specialty shops that only addressed particular needs.[12]

As western retail trade developed, so did the artisans of the county. Merchants throughout the backcountry provided the link by which local products moved out of the county and imported goods moved in.[13] Local merchants collected the backcountry products for which there was a market in Pennsylvania, Virginia, Wilmington, or Charleston, arranged the transportation, and exchanged the local products for imported and manufactured goods that could not be produced in the backcountry.

The merchant's ability to import items from larger markets was more important for most artisans than the ability to export products from the local market. Artisans depended on local merchants and the retail trade to obtain raw materials, tools, and other objects that were extremely labor-intensive to produce. Access to external markets meant that artisans could produce higher quality goods and a wider variety of goods at a price that was not prohibitive. Account books provide some insight into how artisans utilized those outside markets.

External trade was most crucial to those artisans who procured their raw materials through merchants. While some bloomeries probably existed in Rowan County, blacksmiths could save time, money, and effort by getting "all the Iron & Steel" they needed "bought from Charles Town."[14] For blacksmiths and gunsmiths, especially, access to great quantities of iron meant that they could concentrate on making objects rather than on reducing iron ore to molten and then pig iron. Access to different grades of steel was equally important for blacksmiths and gunsmiths. Steel, a combination of iron and carbon, was extremely labor intensive and could not be produced in the backcountry, yet its ability to be tempered and the resulting tensile strength were necessary in tools and gun making. Cutting tools such as planes and chisels may not have been essential for life on the frontier, but axes, mattocks, shears, and coulters were. And a longarm was only as good as the steel parts of its lock—the tumbler, sear, frizzen, and associated springs—that fired the gun. Blacksmiths John Dobbins, Adam Simonton, and Joseph Foster procured part of their supply of iron and steel from the general merchandise store located northwest of Salisbury.[15]

Saddlers and shoemakers were in a similar situation to blacksmiths. While they possibly could have supplied their own raw material, in this case leather, it was not the most efficient use of their time, especially when tanners existed throughout the county. However, shoemakers do not appear in any of the store account books as leather buyers, and only one saddler—Nathaniel Ewing—does.[16] A more likely scenario is that the saddlers and shoemakers procured their leather directly from local tanners or that their customers supplied it to them.

Artisans who worked the clothing trades such as tailors, seamstresses, and clothiers were as dependent on outside markets for their raw materials as blacksmiths were. Not only did they need a wide variety of fabric in different weights, weaves, fibers, qualities, and price to fulfill their customers' fashion needs and pocketbooks; they also needed notions such as buttons, back buckles, ribbons, and lace to hold the clothes together and decorate them. Clothier William Watt and tailors David Hill, Andrew Boyd, William Bones, and John Miller all patronized the store northwest of Salisbury, while John Miller also went to William Steele's store in Salisbury.[17]

The majority of artisans in Rowan County did not depend on external resources for their raw materials. However, many artisans in Rowan did trust outside suppliers to elevate the practice of their craft in terms of quality and efficiency with specialized tools and general hardware. Shoemakers frequently patronized the general merchandise store northwest of Salisbury because of their constant need for tacks, awls, and needles. Archibald Wasson, Samuel Wason, Joseph Wason Sr., Adam Campbell, Hance Hamilton, and Hugh McWhorter bought awls and needles by the dozens and tacks by the hundreds. Less frequent purchases were scissors, shoebuckles, gimlets, thimbles, and shoe knives.[18]

Tool production in early America was limited to agricultural implements such as mattocks, axes, and hoes; therefore, artisans and farmers had to get more refined devices from England.[19] The general merchandise store sold carpenters James Davis and George Marshall chisels, whipsaws and steel handsaws (and the files to sharpen them), hinges, augers, and files. The same tailors and clothiers who purchased textiles and notions also bought needles, thimbles, scissors, thread, and pins.[20]

On occasion artisans also bought ready-made objects from local stores.

Blacksmiths who doubled as gunsmiths often purchased gunlocks to either repair or assemble longarms for their customers. Not only was the lock the most labor-intensive part of the gun to produce; it also required great skill and experience, something a trained gunsmith was apt to have, but not a blacksmith. At least two stores in Rowan County sold gunlocks to blacksmiths: Joseph Foster bought a gunlock for eleven shillings from the store northwest of Salisbury and James Graham bought four gunlocks at eight shillings six pence at a store and tavern run by John Dickey.[21]

A second, and more frequent, reason artisans purchased ready-made objects from stores may have been to resell them to their own clientele. The artisans usually sold accessories to their own trade and in this way acted as middlemen between merchants and customers, capitalizing on the customers' buying moods. In these situations, saddlers sold horse fleems and saddle boxes, blacksmiths sold stirrups and penknives, and tailors sold handkerchiefs and hats.[22]

In addition to demonstrating the artisans' ties to the trans-Atlantic economy, these backcountry store account books refute the theory that the geographic isolation of the backcountry made it impossible to import objects into the region, which forced inhabitants to live on a subsistence or self-sufficient level. Most purchases reflect the needs of everyday life: patterns, fabric, thread, thimbles, needles, and pins for sewing; shoes, boots, shirts, and hats to wear; ovens, frying pans, sifters, funnels, knives, forks, and spoons for cooking and eating; nails, saws, and hammers for building; brushes, sheers, and combs for grooming animals; scythes, axes, mattocks, hoes, and plows for farming; flints, powder, and shot for hunting; and bridles, bits, stirrups, whips, saddle bags, saddle cloths and other equestrian accessories for riding horses.[23]

Other entries show that the nicer things in life were available in the backcountry: jewelry (rings, necklaces, watches), books (hymnals, bibles, spellers, songbooks, almanacs), bells, pepper boxes, snuff boxes, delft plates, teaware, pewter porringers, silks and lace, and wine glasses.[24] More specifically, a 1760 invoice from merchant William Glen[?] to fellow merchant and tavern keeper William Steele lists (among other items) a tea kettle for £6 10s.; a punch ladle 7s. 6d.; looking glass 45s.; 6 wine glasses [plain] 15s.; 6 flow[er]d Wine Glasses 22s.; 2 soup spoons 20s.; and pewter bowls, sugar dishes, mugs, and plates.[25]

Artisans purchased the same types of items from the backcountry stores as the rest of the population did. Aside from periodically buying the tools and materials of their livelihoods, they too bought fabric and notions, household accessories, and agricultural implements from the local merchants. Not all artisans could afford the luxury items that William Steele acquired, however. Of the artisans who appear in the account books, only a handful of them obtained luxury items. Three artisans purchased sets of teaware: tailor David Hill, shoemaker Archibald Wasson, and shoemaker Samuel Wason. Carpenter James Davis got a delft plate and some butter dishes, carpenter William Cowan bought some pewter plates, and tanner Moses Purvines bought a necklace.[26]

The purchases of numerous luxury items by some artisans suggests a knowledge of high standards of living, whether it be from experience or merely pursuit. For instance, at the same time he purchased the teaware Archibald Wasson also bought a wine glass, a tod[d]y bowl, spoons, knives and forks, and four pewter porringers. Likewise, David Hill procured some knives and forks as well as a glass tumbler along with his teaware; and Samuel Wason acquired some spoons.[27]

Local merchants were the important link between Rowan County artisans and external markets. Retailers and artisans frequently made reciprocal exchanges based on need. These exchanges fall into three categories: merchants who obtained goods from local artisans and resold them to a larger market; merchants who accepted goods and services from artisans in lieu of, or in addition to, cash; and merchants who acted as middlemen between artisans and the merchants' customers.

In the first type of exchange, the merchant used the artisan as a supplier of goods sold in his store. For bringing his product to the merchant, the artisan could select what he or she wanted from the store or establish credit to draw on later. These type of exchanges can be distinguished by the amount of product the artisan brought to the retailer. For instance, Salisbury textile merchant William Steele accepted large quantities of fabric from George Pattey, Cattrin [*sic*] Gibson, Widow Donaldson, and Sarah Moran.[28] The anonymous merchant who ran the general store northwest of Salisbury used local artisans to supply him with lots of blankets (James Herman), saddles (Nathaniel Ewing), shoes (Adam Campbell, Joseph Wason Sr., Hance Hamilton, and Hugh McWhorter), stockings (Marey [*sic*] Gayley) and yarn (Jonathan Barret).[29]

In the second type of exchange, artisans paid for the store goods they needed with their services or excess wares. These are by far the predominant type of exchanges between artisan and merchant in Rowan County and appear in all the account books but one. While the merchants may have resold these goods and services to their customers, they probably used these exchanges to fulfill their personal needs. For example, in 1756 blacksmith John Dobbins paid Alexander Lowrance for his liquor purchases by making him a mattock and an ax, and sharpening his grubbing hoe. A little more than a decade later Samuel Carson paid his bar tab to Lowrance by making him eight pairs of shoes and half soling an old pair.[30] The proprietor of the backcountry general store frequently exchanged goods with artisans. In fact, he took care of many of his necessities, including clothing, shoes, tools, the foundation for his house, a chimney, and a porch via his transactions with artisans. Clothier William Watt paid him "by 2 gowns making @ 3/6"; bricklayer James McCullough built him a chimney (£3 5s.) and underpinned his house (5d.); carpenter Valentine Callahan did £5 of "joiner work for the store"; blacksmith Adam Simonton made him two bells, fixed his ax, and sharpened some plow irons for him; and tailor Andrew Boyd's credit came from "making a jacket and Britches 10/" and "making a sertout 10/, a coat and jacket 15/."[31] William Steele accepted artisans' services in exchange for goods less frequently (possibly because his wife was quite particular about which artisans worked for them), but he let William Davenport and Samuel Coulter mend saddles. Coulter also gave him two pair of saddlebags, a saddle cloth, and a girth, and John Penell did some tailoring for him.[32]

Occasionally merchants acted as middlemen in their transactions, sometimes for themselves, and sometimes for their customers. For instance, deerskins were the most frequently traded product in the southern backcountry, and merchants took in skins constantly. The proprietor of the general merchandise store would exchange goods with tanners Moses Purvines and John Clemmens for tanning and dressing skins, and then he would resell the skins to customers like saddler Nathaniel Ewing.[33] The Lowrance account book indicates that merchants acted as go-between with artisans and customers, too. In 1768 gunsmith John Dickey incurred a debt with the Lowrance store for having thirty-two yards of cloth woven, which the storekeeper must have arranged with one of his customers who was a weaver.[34]

In addition to exchanges, merchants and tavernkeepers also granted credit to artisans to help them obtain supplies when their income decreased.[35] Usually artisans paid off their debts within months, but occasionally it took them longer. Weaver Samuel Woods took six years from the date of his last purchase at the general merchandise store to pay off his account with tallow, skins, butter, and cash.[36]

Not all transactions involving artisans were carried out as exchanges. As noted above, artisans frequently paid their bills, wholly or partially, in cash. Ledgers from the Lowrances' store and tavern and the general merchandise store show that artisans paid their debts with food (butter, oats, rice, wheat), cash, skins, leather, beeswax, tallow, and occasionally livestock. However, William Steele's customers almost always paid in cash, with only a rare exchange of goods for the artisan's handiwork.

Although there was a lack of specie in the colonies, sometimes artisans received cash from their customers, too. Invoices and receipts from the Steele family prove they paid their bills in cash. Absolam Taylor waited for two years before he finally received £5 6s. from William Steele's estate to compensate him for years of blacksmithing chores. Over a period of three years Taylor sharpened and mended tools for the family, made them small implements such as hoops for barrels, pails, churns, and hooks, and shoed their horses.[37] Carpenter Joseph Atkins' account with the Steele family ran for six years, beginning with building William Steele's coffin in 1769 and ending with payment of £5 18s. 3d. and items from the store run by his wife, Elizabeth. In between Atkins made her a walnut table, constructed a porch on her house, and did various repairs on the house and the back shed.[38]

With proper analysis, the account books of Rowan County merchants can reveal more than who sold items, who bought them, and how they paid their bills. A comparison of the objects imported into the county and sold at the stores and the artisans and their crafts may yield some important clues to the buying habits of Rowan County consumers.

From an examination of the contents of the account books, certain categories of objects become noticeable for both their presence and their absence.[39] For instance, the largest categories of objects purchased at the county stores were fabric and notions. Likewise, the majority of objects in the much smaller clothing category were hats, hose and stockings, garters, and shoes and boots. Actual pieces of clothing such as shirts, breeches, gowns, and capes appeared sporadically. Consequently, with artisans in the clothing trades comprising the largest group in the county, those Rowan County residents who did not make their own clothes probably patronized local artisans regularly rather than depend on their merchants' stock and taste. Furthermore, with weavers as the single largest artisan group in the county, their products did not compete with but rather complemented the trade in imported fabrics. Most fabric spun and woven in Rowan County was for everyday use. In fact, most backcountry residents probably wore shirts and shifts made from "homespun" (locally-made) fabric on a daily basis.

By contrast, other categories, such as furniture, silver, wrought metal work, common ceramics, or lighting devices, never showed up in the account books; these products were a rather unusual combination of everyday and luxury items. Again, a look at the artisan profile for the county may provide the missing pieces to the consumer puzzle. Many of the artisans working in Rowan County produced objects either impossible or impractical to import.

Furniture was too big and fragile (legs and feet snap off easily) to import into the backcountry, so those people who wanted to buy furniture had to go to one of the many carpenters or joiners in the county. Ceramics for everyday use were rarely imported because their cost would not cover the hassle and expense of breakage; only the more expensive ceramics (which could not be produced in the colonies) such as porcelain teaware were worth the gamble. With only eight potters in the county, housewives frequented the twenty-two coopers in the county for buckets, tubs, and barrels; they purchased the occasional piece of cast-iron cookware from a merchant; and they waited for the potters to have sales after firing the kilns.

Lighting devices, wrought iron, and silver may seem like a strange combination of categories, except that they speak to the specific needs of backcountry residents. Lighting devices and silver never appear in the account books, and while the absence of silver may point to the rougher-than-usual standard of living on the frontier, having a light in the dark was necessary at all economic levels. Possible replacements for lighting devices include candles without holders (placing the base of the candle in some melted wax), homemade holders, ceramic holders or oil lamps, or wrought-iron stands or hooks for candles. Along with candleholders and lamps they already owned, Rowan County residents probably attended to their lighting needs by themselves or through local potters and blacksmiths, depending on their exact needs.

The absence of silver from merchants' account books is fairly surprising, given the penchant of some county residents for luxury items, whereas the presence of silversmiths in the county by 1770 is equally surprising. Surely silversmiths in England or even Charleston and Philadelphia easily could have satisfied the demand for silver in the backcountry and not have worried about a lack of market. What advantage did the Rowan County silversmiths have with their clientele, and how did they stay in business? First and foremost, local silversmiths could make customized objects for their clients, in a style and form they liked, personalized with engraved names or initials. Second, the smith stayed in business by knowing and exploiting the backcountry market. Salvers and pierced tea strainers were too expensive for most people's incomes, but a pair of silver knee buckles or shoe buckles was an affordable investment for a man with aspirations.

The largest category of metal objects found in the account books are tools, followed by hardware. While the supply and demand for tools in the backcountry already has been addressed, the availability of hardware such as nails, tacks, brads, and occasionally hinges and locks raises some important questions about competition with local blacksmiths. Why did the Lowrance brothers and the general merchandise store sell objects that were the bread-and-butter of local artisans? A comparison of the account books and the invoices of blacksmiths Absolom Taylor and Paul Rodsmith reveals that a handful of county residents may have realized that purchasing nails and tacks from merchants was more efficient and economical than ordering them from the local smith. It was far more important for the blacksmith to apply his skills where they were absolutely necessary: in sharpening and repairing equipment and making new implements.[40] In addition, this meant that items such as locks for furniture, which were too time consuming or complicated for blacksmiths to make, also were purchased from a merchant.

This analysis of account books and the artisan population lends itself to a deceptively simple conclusion: the busiest and most numerous artisans in Rowan County were those who made items that could not be purchased at a store. Consequently, the majority of artisans in Rowan County made inexpensive, durable textiles and clothing; built and repaired houses and mills; created, fixed, and sharpened household and farm implements; or fabricated wooden vessels for home and farm use. Besides showing a preference for artisans who could provide services, this comparison of goods and artisans also reveals that (consciously or unconsciously) the merchants and artisans of the county accommodated each other: neither side tried to impinge on the other's economic viability.

The roads that connected Rowan County to southside Virginia, Philadelphia, Charleston, and consequently to London, made any product of Great Britain available in the North Carolina backcountry. According to Merrens, roads were important to large and small urban centers alike (Charleston as well as Salisbury) because they provided the means for trade—the most important function of towns—to take place. The amount of trade in a colonial town and the number of markets with which it did business were often the dominant factors in a town's growth or decline.

The opening of the North Carolina backcountry in the mid-eighteenth century led to an increasing importance of road transportation in the middle and western sections of the colony. In spite of outsiders' frequent complaints, the backcountry road system grew quickly and efficiently. This development, along with growing trade networks to the north, south, and east, made possible the emergence of inland trading towns. Inland or midland trading towns linked the coast to the backcountry. Located in the middle of the colony, these towns' primary function was to facilitate internal trade between the east and the west.[41]

With the evolution of the backcountry and midland towns in the third quarter of the eighteenth century came an interrelated system of urban economies. The coastal or seaport towns of Edenton, New Bern, and Wilmington acted as an exchange area for raw materials destined for export overseas and manufactured items imported for sale and distribution within the colony.[42] The western towns of Hillsboro, Salisbury, Salem, and Charlotte, all the results of the tremendous post-war influx of settlers into the backcountry, had local economies grounded in agriculture with trading ties to Virginia, Pennsylvania, and South Carolina.[43] The midland towns of Halifax, Tarboro, Cross Creek, and Campbelltown utilized the inland waterways of the eastern portion of the colony and the road system of the backcountry to bring the imported goods from the coast to the backcountry in exchange for deerskins (and later agricultural products) wanted in England.[44]

Salisbury and Cross Creek were both founded in the 1750s and grew into prominent regional towns during the 1760s. Located approximately half way between Rowan County and Wilmington on the Cape Fear River, Cross Creek became Salisbury's principal inland trading partner. The importance of Cross Creek as a trading center for Rowan County inhabitants becomes apparent from the number of roads built from various locations throughout the county to the Cape Fear Road during the 1760s. In the 1750s the court records only show one road to link the "Upper Inhabitants of the County . . . to the Cape fare Road."[45] However, in the 1760s the court recorded the building of eight roads to access the Cape Fear Road.[46] Another indication of Cross Creek's prominence as an urban center is the specific mention of the town in road petitions in 1767 and 1769.[47]

Merchants in Cross Creek were frequently the agents by which local products, such as skins, flour, and wheat, left the backcountry and imported goods came into the backcountry. As such, these traders quickly assumed an important post as middlemen in the southern colonial economy. Rowan County residents no longer sent their products via wagon to Wilmington, Philadelphia, or Charleston to exchange for imported goods; instead, inhabitants could fulfill their needs by traveling down the Cape Fear Road to Cross Creek. This decline in direct trade between the backcountry and seaport cities also forced seaboard merchants to come to Cross Creek to buy or trade for agricultural products. As the midland trade grew, most of the large merchants in Wilmington established agents in Cross Creek, promoting the flow of goods between seaports and trading towns and trying to replace the Charleston trade with trade (via Cross Creek) to Wilmington.[48]

Trading with midland towns had important benefits for Rowan County consumers: they could acquire imported goods more quickly, and they could go to Cross Creek and shop in person. The ability to go to a large, well-stocked store and get exactly what one needed instead of relying on someone else to fill an order was a luxury for some but a necessity for others. Shopping in Cross Creek was especially significant for artisans who depended on merchants to supply them with raw materials, specialized tools, and even small parts (such as gun locks) of their final products.

At least two, and possibly four, Rowan County artisans conducted business with Robert Hogg, a partner in the Wilmington firm of Hogg and Campbell, who had an agent in Cross Creek.[49] Robert Johnston and William Williams, both hatters, William King, a tailor, and John Dobbins, a blacksmith, all had accounts with the Cross Creek agent between 1767 and 1771.[50] Hogg's ledgers and day books for the Cross Creek enterprise reflect the midland town's connection to local, regional, and international trade networks. What could not be obtained in Cross Creek could be procured from Wilmington, Charleston, or England.

Rowan County artisans shopped with Hogg's agent in Cross Creek in much the same manner as they shopped locally, buying textiles, fashion accessories, tools, food, and "sundries," and taking months, if not years, to pay their debts. The major differences were that the selection of goods was greater, special orders were easier and faster to get, and debts were always paid in cash, goods, or skins, never in services.

The books list only a few tools purchased by the artisans. Robert Johnston bought nails, mill files, penknives, and "scizzors," and William King purchased nails, a plane iron, and a draw knife. Not surprisingly, textiles, notions, and clothing accessories comprised the largest category of objects acquired by artisans from the Hogg store. King and Johnston obtained callamanco, osnabrug, checks, plains, shalloon, "sup^{r} fine cloth," cotton Holland, linen, and "persian callico" in varying quantities, as well as worsted hose, "boys hatt," "mans hatt," breeches, garters, handkerchiefs, shoes, mitts, ribbons, buttons, thread, and pins. As artisans in the clothing trades, King and Johnston probably did not use all these materials but rather resold the accessories and clothing (with a markup) to their customers.[51]

Hogg's agent procured his merchandise through the main store in Wilmington, and he could make special orders to English suppliers when necessary. Prior to 1770 the agent sold mainly provisions; everyday items such as spices, clothing and household accessories, paper, and ink made up the majority of Hogg's business. He even filled special orders occasionally. For example, in June 1764 six "fine fowling pieces," all with different prices, were sent to Robert Hogg from England via Charleston on the schooner *Mary Ann Betty* for Wilmington and Cross Creek.[52] In all likelihood, the English longarms were destined for gunsmiths or blacksmiths, who could buy the guns for less than it would cost to make them, then resell them and make a profit. At 18d., the lowest price weapon was a functional, steel mounted, flintlock smoothbore, all that was necessary for life in the backcountry. At £2 10s., a top of the line fowler probably featured a higher quality barrel, bridled frizzen and tumbler on the lock (for smoother operation and longevity), brass or silver mountings, and brass bands adorning the breech area of the barrel.[53] Style and luxury could be brought to the backcountry for those who could afford it.

Salisbury played a vital part in the economic and demographic growth throughout the North Carolina backcountry during the 1760s. The reasons for Salisbury's success were many: its role as county seat and commercial center, its location on the Wagon Road and within the backcountry road system, and its reasonably close proximity to the Davidson's Creek, Fourth Creek, and Irish and Trading Camp settlements of Rowan County. Salisbury continued to appeal to numerous innkeepers, merchants, artisans, and professional men despite the rise of midland towns such as Cross Creek. As the county continued to grow between 1759 and 1770, Salisbury attracted more residents and fewer speculators. By 1762, 74 of the original 256 lots in the township had been purchased, as had 8 lots adjacent to the town land. More than 150 people lived in Salisbury in 1762, and 24 more had purchased lots in the town. Rather than the "7 or 8 log houses" Gov. Dobbs had seen in 1755, the townscape now included 35 homes, inns, and shops.[54] In fact, Salisbury became such a popular place to live that some wealthier individuals such as George Cathey (millwright and planter) and James Carson (tanner) may have had residences both in town and out of town.[55]

Salisbury profited greatly from its advantageous location and designation as the county seat. While there may have been at least 20 stores operating in Rowan County before 1776,[56] at least a quarter of the merchants were located in Salisbury. The 1756 arrivals from Charleston, Glen and Stevenson, were not the first or only merchants in town. Hugh Montgomery, a merchant from Philadelphia, moved to Salisbury earlier in the year, John Mitchell arrived in 1760, and William McConnell came in 1762.[57] In addition, there were 125 licensed taverns in Rowan County prior to 1775; their owners frequently entered into the retail business, as well.

The number of roads to Salisbury echoed the town's importance as the retail center of the county. More than one-fourth of the thirty-six official roads built in Rowan County from 1753 to 1770 tied various locations to Salisbury, and seven of those roads were laid after 1759. Most of the major roads to markets outside of the county ran through Salisbury, too. The account books of William Steele, a merchant and tavern keeper in Salisbury during the 1760s, clearly show the other areas in contact with the county seat. Steele did business with men from Carlisle and Derytownship [*sic*] in Pennsylvania; Winchester, Virginia; Maryland; and Charleston.[58]

Although Salisbury, like Bethabara and later Salem, eventually provided a wide range of goods and services to a far-reaching population, the urban areas did not contain all the business in the county. Like the majority of the population, more artisans and merchant/tavernkeepers lived in the rural areas of Rowan than in the towns. From an examination of the account books of Alexander and John Lowrance, a father and son who ran a rural tavern/store in Rowan county from 1755 to 1796, it is clear that rural retailers served mainly local customers on a regular basis. By contrast, the records of the church-run general store at Bethabara show a similar local customer base augmented by a few long-distance occasional customers and some one-time customers traveling through the region.[59]

A comparison of the range and types of objects purchased from merchants in rural Rowan County and Salisbury demonstrates that rural customers usually took their business to local businessmen, saving trips into town to purchase items unavailable in the immediate neighborhood. For instance, the general merchandise store southwest of Salisbury sold textiles (duffel, oznabrug, callico, linen, damask), notions (thread, pins, needles), fashion accessories (shoes, handkerchiefs, hats), hardware and tools (nails, hinges, locks, scythes, files, augers, awls), food (sugar, spices), household accessories (irons, skillets, plates, dishes, knives and forks), equestrian supplies (saddle boxes, saddle tacks, horse fleems, stirrups), and miscellaneous items (paper, tobacco, books). The Dickey and Lowrance account books show a somewhat similar, albeit more limited, range of items such as tools, food, liquor, fashion accessories, and household accessories. By contrast, William Steele's store in Salisbury sold almost exclusively a vast array of textiles, notions, clothes and fashion accessories. Occasionally, other items such as books or knives and forks appeared. Therefore, to procure fabric to make a dress for everyday wear, holland or calimanco could be purchased from the local merchant, but if attire for a special occasion were required, a trip into Salisbury was necessary to see the velvets and silks carried by Mr. Steele.[60]

Craftsmen in a number of basic trades such as blacksmiths, saddlers, tanners, tailors, and shoemakers lived in Salisbury between 1753 and 1770. Even so, a higher concentration of artisans producing consumer-oriented goods owned land or lived in Salisbury than anywhere else in the county, and most of them arrived in the county after 1759. For instance, all the non-Moravian potters (Johannes Adams, Henry Beroth, Michael and Susanna Morr) resided within the town limits, as did both silversmiths (German Baxter and David Woodson) and the tinsmith (James Townsley).[61] Andreas Betz, an ex-Moravian gunsmith, moved to Salisbury near his father-in-law who was also a gunsmith when he left Bethabara.[62] Two-thirds of the hatters in the county (James Bowers, Robert Johnston, Casper Kinder, and William Williams) lived in Salisbury, as well.[63] Customers probably purchased items from rural and urban artisans the same way they shopped in the stores: commonplace items were procured locally, while unusual needs were taken to town.

Even artisans who did not live in Salisbury came to town to do business. Clothier William Watt and blacksmith Tobias Forror traveled in from the Trading Settlement to do business with Elizabeth Steele.[64] More out-of-town artisans who worked for the Steele family included blacksmiths Absolam Taylor and Paul Rodsmith, carpenter Joseph Atkins, and tailor

Arthur Erwin. Other artisans, such as blacksmith John Keylaygler, came into Salisbury to do business for the court; Keylaygler made some iron bolts for the jail.[65]

With new artisans continually appearing in the county, the number of trades available in the county blossomed. In the same way luxury goods such as tea sets and wine glasses became more evident at the backcountry stores, non-essential trades grew in importance to the backcountry economy. Although by 1770 the number of artisans in Rowan County had more than doubled since 1759, the most significant change in the artisan profile is the increase in the number of trades represented, particularly in the consumer items category. In 1759, 126 artisans represented 22 trades in Rowan County; in 1770, 328 artisans represented 34 trades. However, even with the addition of 12 trades, the artisan profile did not change substantially. Clothing trades (weavers, tailors, spinsters, hatters, seamstresses, and clothiers) still accounted for a third of the artisans. The leather trades (shoemakers/cordwainers, tanners, and saddlers) dropped to 18 percent, as did the building trades (carpenters, millwrights, joiners, bricklayers, brickmakers, and masons), to 17.5 percent. Metal trades (blacksmiths, tinsmiths), allied wood trades (coopers and turners), and transportation trades (wheelwrights and wagonmakers) all remained basically unchanged. The largest area of growth, both in the number of trades represented and the percentage of total artisans, came in consumer item trades. (See Table 4.)

The number of artisans practicing consumer item trades increased from four (3.17%) in 1759, when the only trades were pottery and gunsmithing, to twenty-six individuals (8.23%) practicing twelve trades in 1770. New trades included cabinetmakers, silversmiths, gunstocker, clock/watchmaker, gravestone cutter, and a saddletree maker. Moravians were the sole practitioners of six of the new consumer trades (cabinetmaker, gunstocker, artist, clock/watchmaker, glovemaker, and gravestone cutter), monopolies probably attributable to the establishment and growth of Salem. However, four consumer item trades (silversmith, chairmaker, saddletree maker, and wicar) and at least six of the more common trades (hatter, seamstress, clothier, tinsmith, wheelwright, wagonmaker) could not be found as primary trades in Wachovia. Salisbury still reigned supreme as the consumer center of Rowan County.

A lack of primary documentation makes it impossible to tell whether the Rowan County artisans consciously fought the Moravians for a share of the backcountry market. However, the replication of trades on and off the Wachovia Tract and the known trading patterns of backcountry settlers suggests otherwise. The only Rowan County settlement that appears to have done business with the Moravians on a regular basis was the Bryan

Table 4. Rowan County Artisans in 1770

	Number	(Moravians)	% of total population
Clothing trades	**103**		**31.40**
weavers	46	(7)	14.02
tailors	25	(3)	7.62
spinsters	21	(?)	6.40
hatters	7		2.13
seamstresses	3		.91
clothiers	1		.30
Leather trades	**59**		**17.98**
shoemakers/ cordwainers	26	(2)	7.92
tanners	20	(4)	6.09
saddlers	13	(3)	3.96
Building trades	**58**		**17.68**
carpenters	30	(7)	9.14
millwrights	10	(2)	3.04
joiners	10	(2)	3.04
bricklayers	3	(3)	.91
masons	3	(1)	.91
brickmakers	2	(2)	.60
Metal trades	**46**		**14.02**
blacksmiths	45	(7)	13.71
tinsmiths	1		.30
Allied wood trades	**23**		**7.01**
coopers	20	(3)	6.09
turners	3	(1)	.91
Transportation trades	**13**		**3.96**
wheelwrights	11		3.35
wagonmakers	2		.60
Luxury item trades	**26**		**8.23**
potters	8	(4)	2.43
gunsmiths	6	(1)	1.82
cabinetmakers	2	(2)	.60
silversmiths	2		.60
artists	1	(1)	.30
gunstockers	1	(1)	.30

(*Cont.*)

Table 4, cont.

	Number	(Moravians)	% of total population
Luxury item trades, cont.			
chairmakers	1		.30
clock/watchmakers	1	(1)	.30
glovemakers	1	(1)	.30
gravestone cutters	1	(1)	.30
saddletreemakers	1		.30
wicars	1		.30

Total number of artisans in the county: 328*
Total number of trades represented: 34
Number of Moravians: 59
Percent of artisans who were Moravian: 17.98
Secondary trades not mentioned as primary trades include: pewterer, jeweler, butcher, and dyer.
*This includes artisans who have dates that end prior to 1770.

SOURCE: Artisans' figures generated from data base of artisans in Rowan County in dBase III+ sorted by trade and year of arrival.

Settlement, located on the west boundary of the Wachovia Tract and east of the Yadkin. Very few transactions took place between the Moravians and Rowan County residents west of the Yadkin River.[66] In the few documented exchanges between Moravians and Salisbury residents, for instance, the latter all tended to be ex-Moravians such as Andreas Betz.[67] Furthermore, the backcountry "strangers" that showed up at the Rowan County stores all tended to come from the extreme western portion of the colony: William Bay from near Tuits (*sic*) Gap, Samuel Gibson from Big Spring, and Leonard the smith at Stovertown.[68]

As individuals, Rowan artisans probably did compete with the Moravians in terms of quality and workmanship; otherwise they stood the possibility of losing their business to the artisans in Salem. In contrast, the Moravian records indicate that the church kept abreast of the products and prices offered by other artisans in the county in order to remain competitive. If the church leaders discovered their artisans were not producing competitive goods, they remedied the situation as soon as possible. For instance, even though Andreas Betz had worked as a gunsmith since 1758, gunstocker John Valentine Beck's arrival six years later signals that the Moravians required a more specialized artisan to help create a higher quality product to compete with the firearms being produced by the Bruner family and others in Salisbury.[69]

By the year 1770 at least 328 artisans practicing 34 different occupations came to live in Rowan County, North Carolina. The 269 non-Moravian artisans in Rowan County during these years practiced a variety of crafts that served, along with imported and manufactured objects available in local stores, to enhance the quality of life on the southern frontier. Artisans also played an integral role in the care and education of future artisans through the apprenticeship system, which bound out children bereft of funds to masters who would train them in their trade.

Land grants and deeds show that artisans in eight necessary trades were among the backcountry's first residents. A little more than a decade after the first settlers arrived, the artisan population of Rowan County had increased almost seven-fold, and the trades they represented almost tripled in number to include hatters, spinsters, coopers, potters, and gunsmiths. Salisbury, the county seat, also served as the center of commerce, with a thriving import/export trade and a contingent of artisans offering even more skills than the Moravians. Business was so good in the backcountry that the artisans continued to come to the county as other residents fled because of the Indian War. By 1770, the number of artisans in the county had more than doubled again to 328, and the continued expansion of trades to thirty-four reflected the specialization of labor and a growing consumer demand for luxury items such as silver, furniture, and even clocks.

The next chapter will show how the Moravian inhabitants of the Wachovia Tract progressed past the difficulties they experienced in the early years of settlement as a result of the church's indecision, ushering in a new era which featured the building of Salem and the commencement of the Moravians' strong economic presence in western North Carolina.

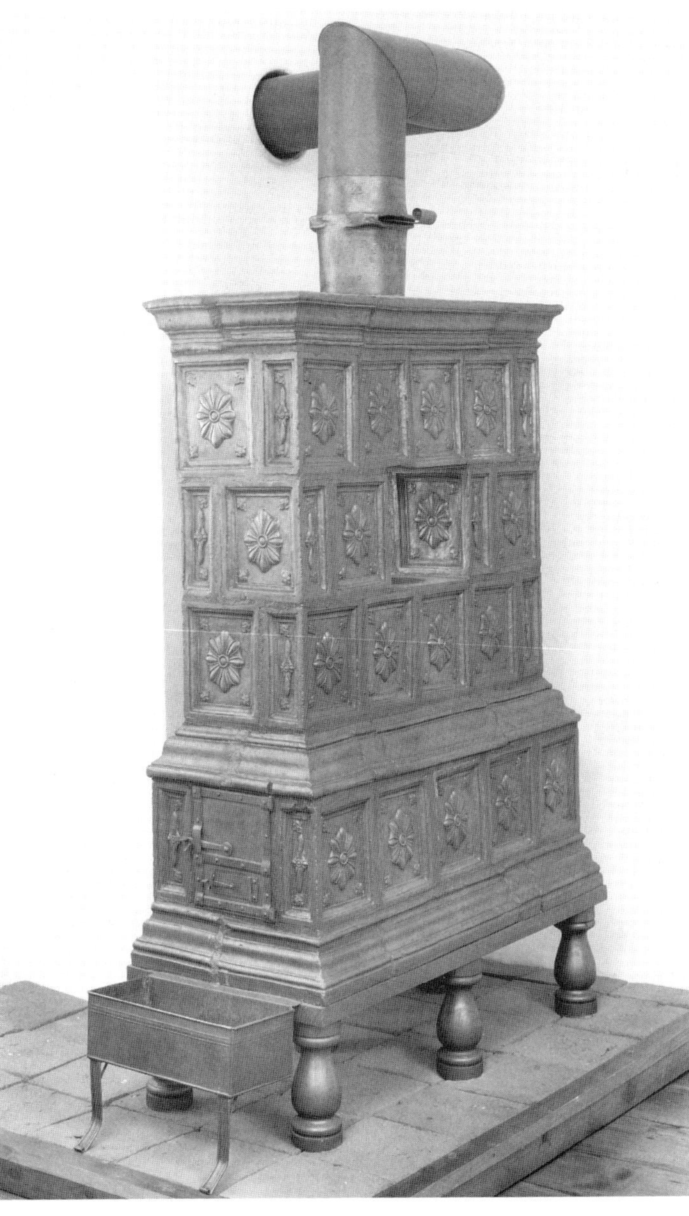

Tile Stove, "patera shell" pattern, Aust, 1755-1780, Salem; in the biscuit state; finished with black stove polish. Courtesy of Old Salem, Inc., accession number 435.

The work of Gottfried Aust, master potter for the Moravians, stands today as the largest extant group of artifacts made in Rowan County in the colonial period. Ceramic tiles for stoves were among Aust's first products in Wachovia. In November 1756 he fired tiles to build stoves for the *Gemein haus* and the Single Brothers at Bethabara. Aust also sold tile stoves to those "strangers" who could afford them; he even traveled to Salisbury to set one up for former Moravian gunsmith Andreas Betz.

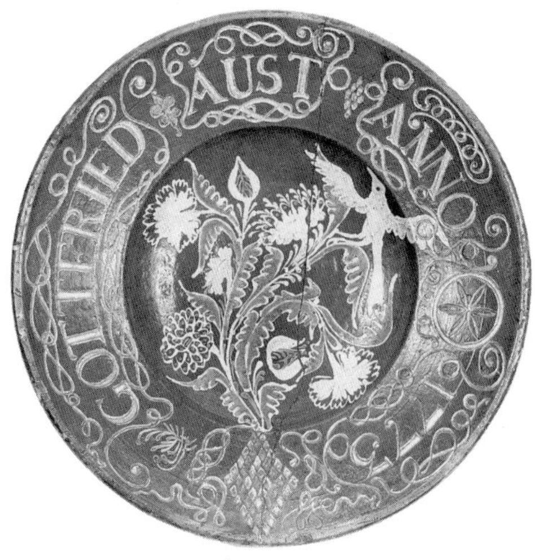

Trade sign, Gottfried Aust, 1773, Salem; decorated with white and green slip over red body; incised scrollwork filled with white slip. Courtesy of the Wachovia Historical Society, accession number B-180.

Below, plates, attributed to Aust, 1771-1780, Salem. *Left,* decorated with red and green slip over a white slip base. Courtesy of Old Salem, Inc., accession number 2934.
Right, leaves have a gray-tinted slip. Courtesy of the Wachovia Historical Society, accession number P-87.

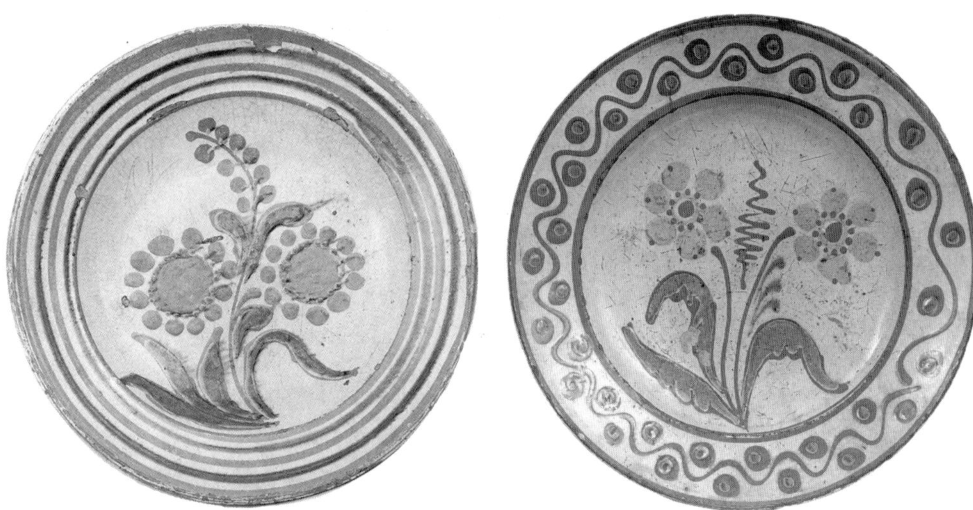

The most important stylistic group of surviving North Carolina Moravian pottery is the slip-decorated wares, which range from simple pans with annular banding to large plates with all manner of foliage. As these plates demonstrate, Aust's best production reflects his fondness for floral forms. Although such highly decorated wares as Aust's own trade sign, a 22" plate with lugs for hanging in front of his pottery at Salem, were not the bulk of his production, this plate still serves as a veritable "book" of slip decoration techniques in Wachovia. The heavily-fronded, fernlike leaves are characteristic of Aust's work, although the calligraphic-like flourishes, or *schnörkelwerk,* is a rare instance of sgraffito (incised work) on Moravian pottery. Here the cuts are highlighted with white slip painted into them—a reversal of usual sgraffito. Aust's floral decoration and use of polychrome slips link him more closely to contemporary European design than similar designs in this country, which tended to be more stiffly stylized.

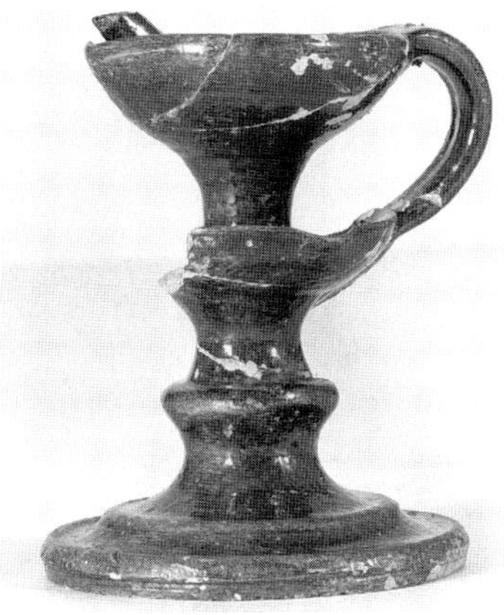

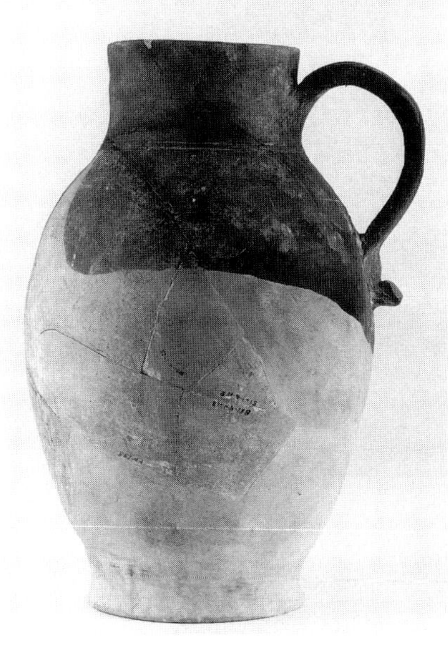

Above, oil or fat lamp, 1755-1771, Aust pottery site, Bethabara; brown manganese glaze. *Left,* water jug, 1755-1771, Aust pottery site, Bethabara; black glaze, probably iron, on interior and on shoulder and handle of exterior. Both photographs courtesy of Old Salem, Inc., archaeological collection

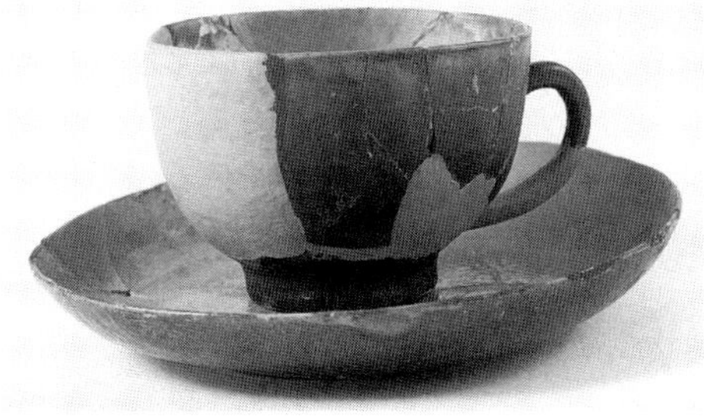

Cup and saucer, 1755-1771, Aust pottery site, Bethabara; cup has white slip and clear glaze inside with manganese brown outside; the saucer is glazed with manganese brown. Courtesy of Old Salem, Inc., archaeological collection.

The need for common, usable objects such as these was the reason the Moravian Church sent Aust to Wachovia. While these everyday objects comprised the majority of his work, Aust did not eliminate decorative touches. Although the exterior of the water jug is unglazed, the handle features a scrolled terminal. This fat lamp (which burned both animal and plant oils) derives a formal quality from its unusually fine baluster shape and protruding wick support. The very thinly potted cup and saucer exemplify not only Aust's recognition of prevailing Chinese ceramic forms but his ability to make earthenware emulate porcelain.

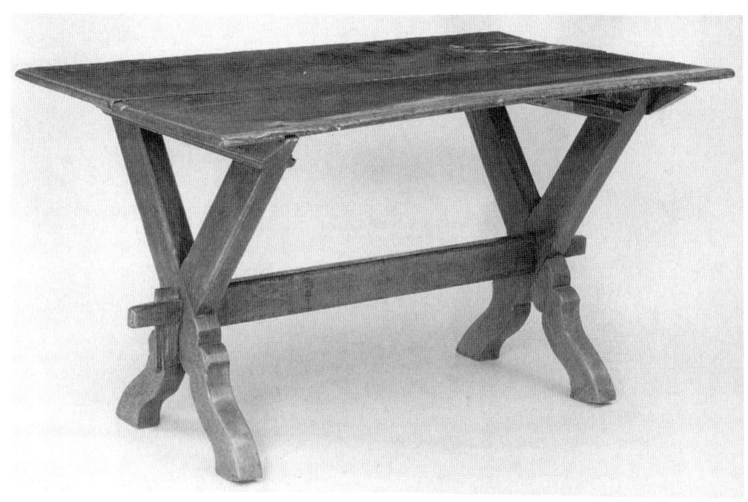

Table, 1753-1760, Bethabara; walnut. Courtesy of Old Salem, Inc., accession number 766.

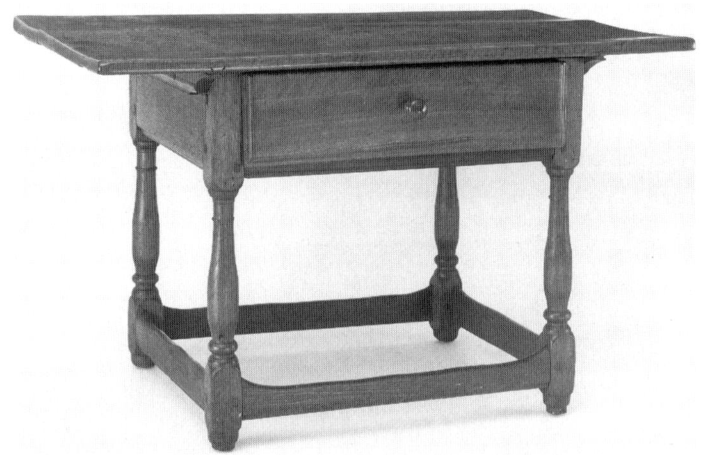

Stretcher table, 1760-1770, Bethabara or Salem; walnut with poplar and yellow pine secondary. Courtesy of Old Salem, Inc., accession number 2268.

Tables from the early Wachovia period largely follow central and northern European precedents in design. The rare "sawbuck" table (top) probably survives from the earliest settlement at Bethabara, as indicated by its simple construction, which well could have been carried out by a house joiner. Nonetheless, the table features decorative elements, such as the ogee curve in the lower portion of the legs. By the later period, stretcher tables with heavy vasiform-turned legs and attached tops were encountered more frequently in the backcountry. The example below, from Bethabara or Salem, is more functional than the sawbuck table because of the large storage drawer in the center of the skirt.

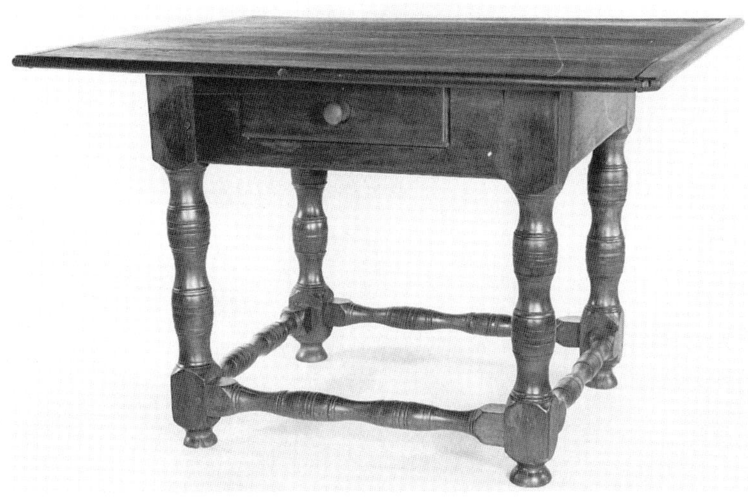

Stretcher Table, 1755-1785, central Piedmont North Carolina; cherry. Collection of the Museum of Early Southern Decorative Arts, gift of Mr. and Mrs. Ralph P. Hanes, accession number 1072.

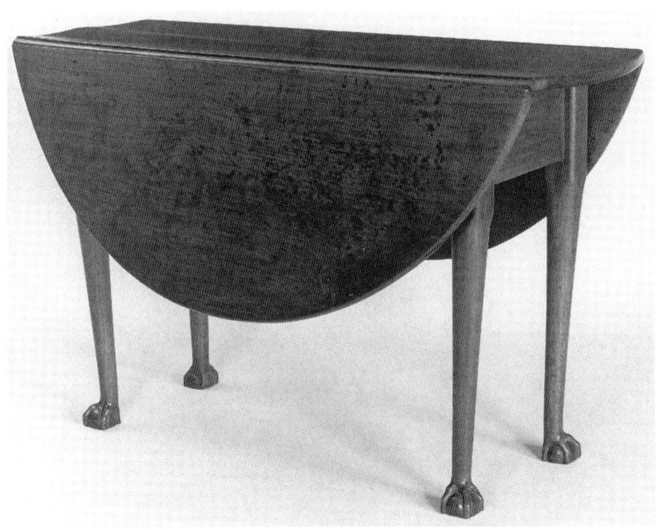

Drop leaf table, 1765-1780, Bethabara or Salem; walnut with yellow pine and oak secondary. Courtesy of the Wachovia Historical Society, accession number T-86.

These tables, one from Rowan County, the other from Wachovia, share a common Germanic heaviness. The stretcher table form was especially popular with German-American colonials, although this example, with its massive turned legs, is not as well articulated as its Moravian counterpart (opposite, lower). The drop leaf table below, English in form but Germanic in its heaviness and construction, has straight turned legs ending in claw-and-ball feet. Although built in the 1760s or 1770s, it brings to mind the 1754 diary entry by Jacob Friis of Bethabara: "I made the top of a table for myself, and cut wood for feet on the Table. They shall be Lyons Claws; is not that too much? One day I am a Joiner, the next a Carver; what could I not learn if I was not too old?" [*RM* 2:529]

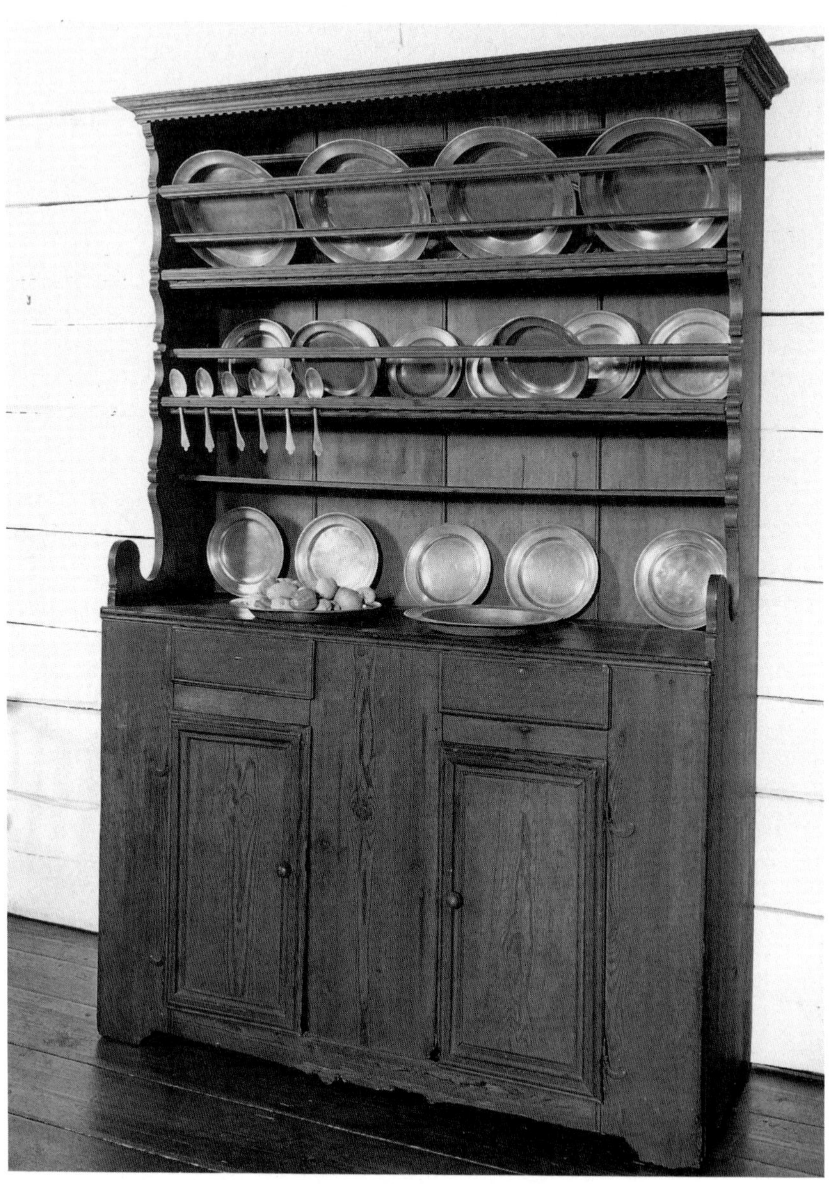

Kitchen cupboard, 1760-1780, Piedmont North Carolina; yellow pine. Collection of the Museum of Early Southern Decorative Arts, gift of the estate of Katherine Hanes, accession number 2073.21.

German-Americans adapted the popular kitchen cupboard (*küche schrank* in German inventories), from the rural British form. These pieces served dual purposes—storage and display of cooking and eating wares. Originally painted red, this piece would have graced a kitchen proudly showing colorful earthenware pieces like the ones made by Moravian potter Gottfried Aust.

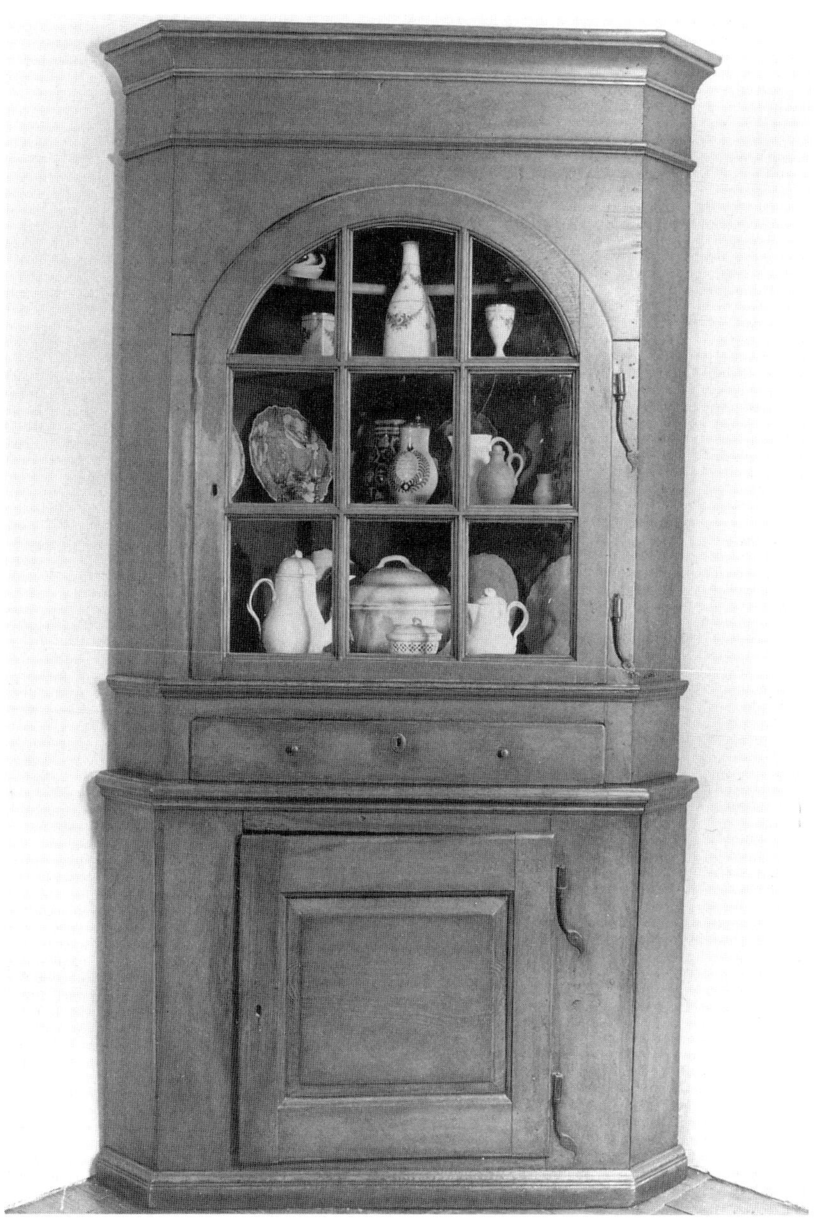

Corner cupboard, 1760-1775, Bethabara or Salem; all yellow pine with restored blue and orange paint. Courtesy of the Wachovia Historical Society, accession number C-432.

Although corner cupboards were not made in great numbers by early joiners in Wachovia, this example features a raised panel door on the bottom and a glazed door on top. Such a piece would have been more conspicuous than other units intended for storage and display because of the glass in the door.

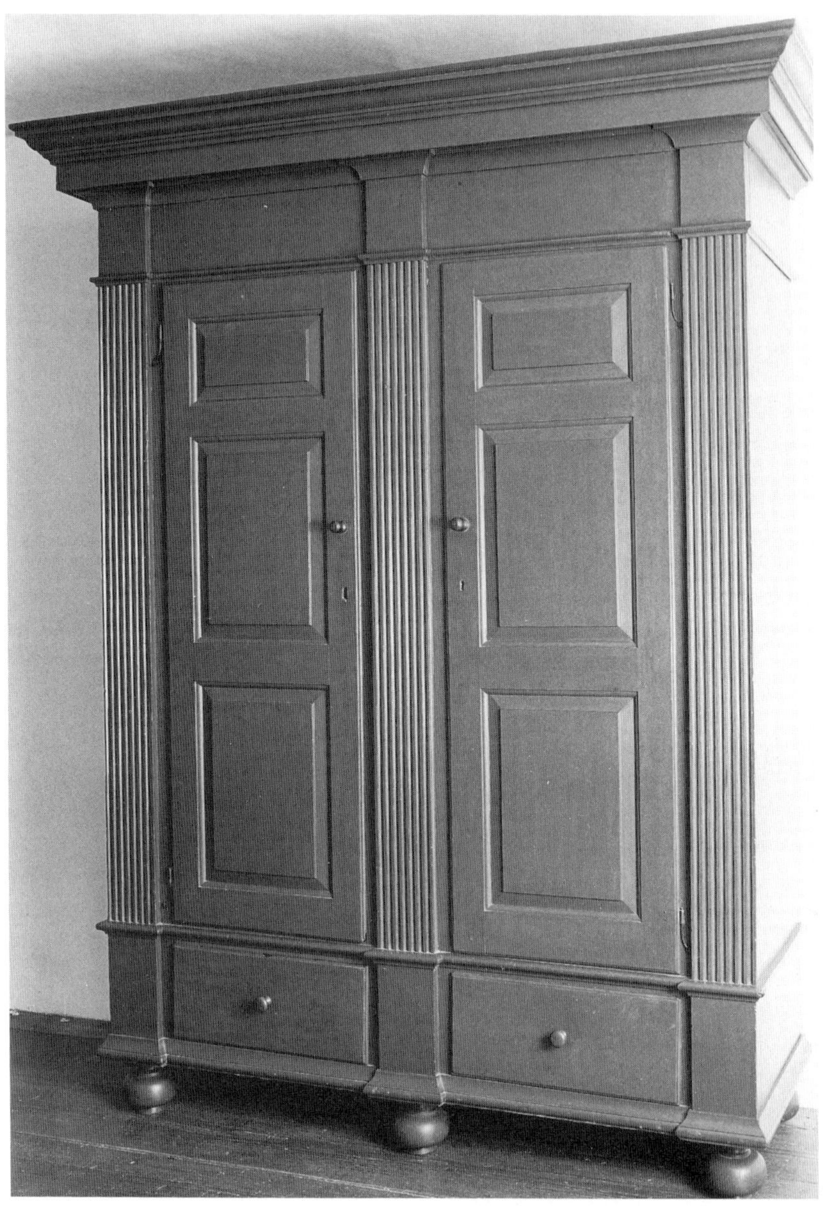

Schrank, 1760-1780, Bethabara or Bethania; all yellow pine with restored "Spanish brown" paint. Courtesy of Old Salem Inc., accession number 2360.1.

In Europe and the colonies, large storage pieces like this *schrank*, or wardrobe, were among the most characteristic Germanic pieces of furniture. Used to house clothing and fabrics, the *schrank* was fitted with hooks and shelves instead of drawers. This heavily architectural piece is uncommon for furniture made in Wachovia in its strong stylistic links to Pennsylvania-German *schranken* of the same period.

FIVE

Moravian Artisans on the Wachovia Tract, 1759-1770

As the portion of Rowan County which lay west of the Yadkin River and the county seat of Salisbury experienced unregulated growth and success during the first decade of settlement, in Wachovia church officials continually reminded the brethren that Bethabara was literally a "house of passage" until the main town became reality. The frustration these reminders caused the Wachovia brethren and sisters, and the lack of progress and instructions on the future town, overshadowed the exchanges between Bethabara and Bethlehem about what constituted necessary crafts and trades. Following the first survey of the Wachovia Tract to select a site for the *Gemein Ort* in 1759, and the founding of Bethania to relieve overcrowding at Bethabara, tensions eased, and the Bethabara residents and leaders began to believe that the new central town would finally be built.

With the prospect that the main town was only a few years away, Wachovia residents became instilled with a new purpose: preparing for it. After 1760 the squabbling with Bethlehem over which crafts were needed at Bethabara virtually ceased; instead, requests focused on filling any vacant craft positions and obtaining the crafts and labor necessary to build and operate the town as a center of trade and manufacture. At Bethabara administrators concentrated on keeping key personnel happy, discharging undisciplined craftsmen, creating an apprenticeship program, and organizing the artisans and their shops for the move to Salem. A Unity directive to end Wachovia's successful *Oeconomy* before inhabiting Salem also preoccupied administrators. Unlike most residents of Wachovia, artisans anxiously awaited the *Oeconomy*'s demise so they could share in profits. However, the church's financial and social restrictions proved too oppressive, particularly for artisans, some of whom chose to leave the tract prior to the completion of Salem.

This time, all of the efforts and energy the brethren put into creating the new town, along with their penchant for planning, would finally pay off. Even though Salem was not officially inhabited until 1772 (people began living there in 1766), the conglomeration of artisans in a well-planned town complete with signs advertising their shops helped make it a late-eighteenth and nineteenth-century success, surpassing Salisbury along the way.

Wachovia brethren may have welcomed the creation of Bethania, but Count Zinzendorf disapproved of allowing Society members to live with regular brethren in the town. In the Moravian Church "society," members were associates of the local congregation but not communicant members. Joining a society was frequently, though not always, a step toward becoming a church member.[1] In Bethania the brethren remained members of the Bethabara congregation until the Bethania congregation was organized in 1766, most of the Society members joining as communicants and becoming full members. Zinzendorf did not want any missionary activity in Wachovia, and he interpreted the founding of Bethania as a direct violation of his wishes. His death in May 1760[2] ended any Church opposition to Bethania but further delayed the creation of the *Gemein Ort*. As had been the case for Herrnhut and Bethlehem, Zinzendorf's ideas for the central town on the tract, including a town plan he drew in 1750, were more of a hindrance than a help. His plan called for a circular arrangement of the town with streets radiating in spoke-like fashion from an octagonally shaped central area.[3]

Even though Zinzendorf could envision the new town, other church leaders, whether in Europe, Pennsylvania, or Wachovia, apparently could not find the time to implement his concepts. The brethren took a full six years after arriving in Bethabara before they made their first inspection of a possible site for a new town.[4] Following Zinzendorf's death, the absence of his somewhat dictatorial and monopolistic leadership style left the Unity a host of leadership responsibilities to sort out. Finally, in 1763, the Herrnhut Board named an administrator, or *Oeconomous*, for Wachovia, Frederick William Marshall, and instructed him to find a site for the town and organize construction.[5]

Marshall was a man with a vision, and his leadership of Wachovia, beginning with a four month visit to North Carolina in late 1764 and early 1765, resulted in decisive action. On February 14, 1765, Marshall approved the selection of a site for the town located on a ridge. However, the ridge tops and lack of flat spaces led him to reject Zinzendorf's circular town plan and draw one himself.[6] Instead, the brethren used a grid system of streets around a centrally located square.[7] Construction of the town, named Salem by the Unity *Vorsteher Collegium*, commenced on January 6, 1766.[8]

Between 1760 and 1770 only three new crafts were added to Wachovia, and all three artisans arrived during the planning stages for Salem. Two of the trades they represented, cabinetmaking and gunstocking, were nonessential consumer-oriented crafts new to the county. The third, saddlery, had been practiced west of the Yadkin since 1751. The addition of these crafts clearly shows the Moravians' aspirations to maintain and enlarge their share of the backcountry market. In 1764 Enert Enerson, a cabinetmaker, and John Valentine Beck, a gunstocker, came, and two years later Charles Holder, a saddler (and brother to carpenter George Holder), arrived and became one of the first artisans to practice his trade in Salem.[9] Br. Johann August Schubart, an account clerk and "clockmaker of sorts" came to Bethabara in 1760, mainly for administrative duties. Unfortunately the records do not indicate if he ever acted on Spangenberg's suggestion to make a "large clock that strikes."[10]

For the most part, the leaders in Wachovia focused on running the businesses they already had at Bethabara and adding manpower to the construction trades that would be necessary to build Salem. By 1758 the two most successful crafts in Bethabara were the blacksmith shop and the pottery. As such, they appear in the records frequently, although for entirely different reasons. The economic success of the various crafts and businesses at Bethabara was extremely important to the church.

After telling Wachovia to take responsibility for its own finances in 1757,[11] Bishop August Spangenberg wanted to make sure the settlement survived and succeeded on its own. Consequently, church leaders at Bethabara had to accommodate their income-producing artisans. Blacksmith George Schmidt provides an example. Thirty-three-year-old Schmidt arrived in Wachovia in 1754 and, as one of the early settlers, helped to build Bethabara. In his enthusiasm he fell off the roof of the Single Brothers' House while shingling it in the winter of 1755, dislocating his leg; he then stayed busy by making baskets and sieves while he recovered.[12] He married Johanna Heckedorn in 1757, and they eventually had six children. Three years later Schmidt created enough trouble with his financial demands upon Wachovia leaders that three elders complained to Bethlehem that he "makes us little joy and honor with his profession."[13]

The elders neglected to mention that Schmidt *was* making them a substantial profit. Aware of his economic success and financial status within the *Oeconomy*, Schmidt probably asked for a share of the profits or for additional help, an attitude unheard of in that economic system. Not surprisingly, less than a year later Schmidt asked permission to leave the *Oeconomy* and move to Bethania, where he could operate with a little more latitude. This request left the Conference in Bethabara with a multitude of questions concerning whether Schmidt owned the smith's tools (they decided he did not), and whether the church should extend some financial assistance so he could start his own smithy (they approved a loan for him).[14]

Schmidt apparently did not move to Bethania,[15] but the records remain unusually silent about him until 1765. Even more puzzling is a 1763 letter from the minister in Bethabara to Nathaniel Seidel in Bethlehem: "The smithy is practically still, and if something must be done to wagon or horses at once, the other wagon is out of commission and no one can help the smith."[16] Schmidt may have held a work slowdown or stoppage to get what he wanted from the church, and it eventually worked: in February 1765 the Bethabara diarist recorded him working at the smithy with a new assistant, Dan Hauser, from Bethania.[17] The additional help evidently did not appease Schmidt, and the church finally let him out of the *Oeconomy* (simultaneously barring him from communion) in 1766. He continued to live at Bethabara and was readmitted to Communion in October.[18]

George Schmidt was looking forward to moving to Salem, which would not be run as an *Oeconomy*, but he continued to make demands on the church. Over the next six years he asked for specific apprentices, a certain location and size of lot in Salem, and a different type of house construction. As long as he made a profit (of which a portion would go to the church in Salem), the Conference usually fulfilled his request one way or another. Once he moved to Salem his complaints ended, and he became an active member of the congregation.[19]

Gottfried Aust, unlike George Schmidt, did not cause problems, yet he frequently appears in the Moravian records because of the immense popularity of his earthenware pottery on the backcountry market as well as his ability to produce almost enough pottery to satisfy the demand. After arriving in Wachovia in 1755, Aust filled the ceramic needs of the brethren before selling to outsiders.[20] The brethren soon held "great sales of earthenware" that drew large crowds of neighbors vying for Aust's product. On June 15, 1761, the Bethabara diarist recorded that "people gathered from fifty and sixty miles away to buy pottery, but many came in vain, as the supply was exhausted by noon. We greatly regretted not being able to supply their needs."[21] Church leaders did regret not being able to supply all of their neighbors' needs at these sales because every lost sale represented lost profits. However, the more pottery Aust made, the more his customers wanted. The demands of an ever-increasing market always outstripped supply. A few years later more people came even further (sixty to eighty miles) "to buy crocks and pans at our pottery. They bought the entire stock, not one piece was left; many could only get half of what they wanted, and others, who came too late, could find none. They were promised more next week."[22]

To get wider distribution and more profit from the sale of pottery, the brethren began to sell or trade it to backcountry merchants in exchange for goods they needed in Wachovia, as the Bethabara diary shows:[23]

February 14, 1763: A wagon load of pottery was sent to Salisbury.
January 31, 1766: The Irishman, whose wagon brought some of the goods of the

European company from Pinetree [South Carolina] Store, left this afternoon with a load of pottery.[24]

Church elders reciprocated Aust's industriousness and productivity, as well as his piety, by giving him first choice of apprentices, naming him to important church boards and committees, and allowing him to use outside potters to learn how to make Queensware and other English-style pottery.[25] Although Aust had a reputation as a harsh taskmaster, which frequently resulted in bad relations with his employees, his business success kept him a favored brother in the eyes of the church until he died of cancer in 1788.[26]

The church did not try to mollify all its artisans. Only talented craftsmen like George Schmidt and Gottfried Aust were deemed worth the extra effort. In some cases the craft was more important than the artisan. Bethlehem sent Thomas Hofman to Wachovia in October 1756, and he assumed responsibility for the tannery (from cooper Heinrich Feldhausen and shoemaker Frederick Pfeil) in February of the following year. In June a new tannery building was raised.[27] In 1760 church elders used the same letter to Bethlehem to complain about George Schmidt and Hofman: "[Hofman has given us] no end of trouble. . . . Therefore, if you could or would also think how better to provide for both these branches, it would be very agreeable to us, because they have many connections with the world and can contribute a great deal to our good or bad name in the region."[28] Hofman's problems with the Unity extended far beyond business or finance; he failed to fulfill his spiritual duties as a Single Brother. An inventory of Wachovia residents lists Hofman in Bethabara as having "for some time stayed away from Communion."[29] Church officials did not take laxity in religious responsibilities lightly, and the following year Spangenberg agreed to replace Hofman as soon as someone suitable could be found.[30] Br. Johann Heinrich Herbst arrived in Bethabara on June 8, 1762, and was appointed Master of the Tannery shortly thereafter. Hofman was still in Bethabara when Herbst took over the tannery from him, but the next mention of him in the published records is that of his death in Bethlehem eight years later.[31] Praised by the minister at Bethabara as "a sincere Christian," Herbst, like Schmidt and Aust, went on to have a long and illustrious career as an artisan, first in Bethabara and later in Salem.[32]

With a population totalling 147 in 1762—including 32 artisans[33]—the brethren needed help building the new town. In addition to moving all the artisans (and their families) who currently resided at Bethabara (the blacksmith, the potter, the tanner, the gunsmith, the tailor, the shoemaker, the weaver, the carpenter, and the mason) to new facilities in Salem, plans called for the construction of a gristmill, hemp mill, tawing mill, sawmill, oil mill, fulling mill, a slaughterhouse, a dyer's workshop, and a hattery.[34] All, of course, were in addition to other town necessities: the *Gemein Haus*, the Single Brothers' House, and eventually a church, a store, a Single Sisters' House, a tavern, and other shops.

To alleviate the labor shortage and organize the artisans into guild-style shop and personnel arrangements before moving to Salem, in 1760 the Conference at Bethabara began an apprentice program to train young boys in crafts. Unlike non-Moravian Rowan County, where apprentice programs were primarily a way of taking care of orphan children and providing them with skills, the church viewed apprenticeships as an opportunity to train young boys in their work for God and tried to control such training as a way of regulating the supply of labor. Not surprisingly, the same concerns the church had about overdeveloping Bethabara, as well as a shortage of space in the town, kept apprenticeship to a bare minimum. Only boys who resided in Wachovia could become apprentices. However, in much the same way that the brethren's backcountry neighbors heard about Br. Petersen, the tailor, shortly after their arrival in 1753, the neighbors heard about the apprenticeship program and wanted to enroll their sons.

The first correspondence from Bethlehem concerning the matter of apprentices came in 1761 when Spangenberg evidently responded to a question from the Conference about "outside" apprentices: "It is not at all our policy to accept non-Moravian boys as apprentices. But if Acum and Jos. Muller learn a craft, good. The latter would perhaps like to be a gunsmith, and would, I think, be well adapted to this. But I am unable to give any positive direction regarding this. Circumstances must have a say, also."[35] Five months later Spangenberg wrote that "Joseph Muller should probably be apprenticed. For he is of age."[36] Unfortunately, the records list three people with this name, and sorting them can be confusing. However, the 1762 inventory only lists one Joseph Muller, who must be the young boy who arrived in Wachovia on August 3, 1755.[37] Four years later an inventory listing of him as a gunsmith probably means that Muller reached journeyman status, although reports on his training (or lack thereof) under Andreas Betz, the gunsmith, still refer to him as an apprentice.[38]

Somewhat more mysterious is the reference to the other boy, Acum, and the remark about not accepting non-Moravian boys as apprentices. The name does not appear in the records, but in 1767 the minutes of the *Aeltesten Conferenz* at Bethabara record that "The *fremde* boy Even leaves his apprentice [*sic*] with Br. Fockel (the tailor) next Monday."[39] The term *fremde*, or stranger, indicates that the elders permitted an outsider to apprentice to the tailor; in all likelihood, he is the boy referred to in Spangenberg's 1761 letter.

The brethren in Bethabara began to formulate plans for a formal apprenticeship program in Wachovia to help supply labor. However, in February 1763 they decided against sending "a wagon to Pennsylvania this spring in order to get for our professions some boys which they had promised us," because too much work needed to be done at Bethabara before they would be ready for the boys.[40] Leaders in Bethabara may have wanted the boys partially to help stimulate the senior artisans who had become somewhat stagnant in their duties. Br. Gammern believed that many of the artisans were shirking their duties, and in March he complained to Nathanael Seidel in Bethlehem about the situation.

We cannot speak encouragingly about our tannery. If we had only half of a shoemaking establishment we would lack leather to keep it going.

It is so with the other trades. The pottery is best and bringing in something. The tailor makes hardly enough for our own use. Br. Fockel is master, but he has the misfortune to have Br. Nielson as apprentice. The gunsmith trade makes great talk but has turned out only two guns since I am here. The smithy is practically still, and if something must be done to wagon or horses at once, the other wagon is out of commission and no one can help the smith. Hardly anything has come out of the cabinetmaking trade: Br. Dav. Bischoff had been here eight weeks and has turned out nothing for the economy.[41]

Evidently, by the fall of 1764 the brethren at Bethabara were ready for the boys, and twelve arrived from Bethlehem to learn trades from the master-workmen. Most of the boys already had been training in Pennsylvania, and the rest were ready to begin. Shortly thereafter the masters held a conference to decide where the twelve boys should be placed.[42] Three months later Br. Johannes Ettwein, the minister at Bethabara, wrote to Nathanael Seidel that the boys had "all been allotted to trades," and he included a list of where all the boys were working: "We have put Matth. Reitz into the tannery (we do not know whether this will please his father); Lanius is also with Herbst. Stotz is with the gardener; Strehle with the carpenter. Mueche is with the brewer; Christ and Ludwig Moeller with the potter; Bibighausen in the store; Sehnert and Kaske with the shoemaker; Nielson and Joh. Mueller are to go to the tailor as soon as the shop is completed."[43]

By early 1765, however, construction on Salem had begun, which often diverted masters and apprentices from their usual responsibilities.[44] Obviously, the fifty-three men and boys at Bethabara would not be able to build the town overnight, even hiring outsiders to help. Because the brethren only completed three houses during the first year of construction,[45] throughout 1766 Bethlehem sent down forty-two individuals (twenty-four men out of whom six were artisans and nine apprentices) to hasten the building process. The first men to arrive in January, Gottfried Praezel (linen weaver), Bernhard Schille (farmer and linen weaver), James Hurst (weaver and mason), and John Birkhead (cloth weaver), were all seasoned brethren with prior settlement experience, enthusiastic about serving the Lord in Wachovia.[46] Although the extra help was appreciated, the *Aeltesten Conferenz* really wanted trained construction labor. Nonetheless, the brethren carried on with the task of building the new town. On October 5, 1766, Bethabara business manager Matthew Schropp reported to Bethlehem that four days earlier they "laid the corner-stone of the two-story house in Salem. How embarrassed I am at times for a couple of reliable masons and helpers, and carpenters, so that Salem can be advanced! With strangers nothing can be accomplished here. They come for a week, fill their belly and are gone."[47]

Five days after Schropp wrote the letter, a group of eight boys accompanied by four brothers reached Wachovia. One of the boys was apprenticed to Melchoir Rasp, the mason, and another went to live in Salem as apprentice to Gottfried Praezel, the linen weaver. The six others received assignments to work on "the plantation" at Bethabara. Schropp was persistent, however, he even wrote to Br. Marshall, who was visiting Charleston, to ask him "if he would bring some masons and carpenters in order to advance the building of Salem."[48]

Construction at Salem remained at a slow pace, and the town was not officially inhabited until 1772. Although they may have been frustrated by the lack of progress, church officials certainly needed the extra time to solve administrative problems before the move to Salem. Up until this point, apprenticeships within Wachovia were fairly informal arrangements between masters and boys, monitored by the *Aeltesten Conferenz* at Bethabara. If either side had a complaint, church officials investigated and made a ruling. In January 1769 two apprentices at Bethabara ran away, forcing the brethren to take legal action and whip the boys as punishment. "This incident led to a realization of the importance of legally binding apprentices to their Masters. Hitherto the Masters had stood *an Elternstatt*, which was just as binding, but less easily understood by the boys."[49]

To make the apprenticeships legally binding, the Master had to post a bond with the congregation business manager to assure, among other stipulations, that he would not keep the boy in any way contrary to the rules and regulations of the congregation, that he would not remove the boy from the community in case he, the master, moved away, and that he would not bind the apprentice out to any other masters without permission of community officials. The apprentice and the master had to sign identical indentures that laid out the obligations of both parties and stated when the apprenticeship would end. (See Appendix A.)

Eager to keep their matters private, the brethren always had their own justice of the peace witness the indentures rather than take them to Salisbury and the Court of Pleas and Quarter. In contrast to most of the other apprentice indentures executed in Rowan County, none of the Moravian apprenticeship agreements show up in the legal records.[50] The legal indentures benefitted church officials in many ways: not only did they have legal recourse in the event that an apprentice misbehaved or ran away, signing an indenture and posting a bond also made a master think twice about accepting just any boy as his apprentice. The relationship had to last.

The biggest problem facing church officials in Wachovia was Bethlehem's insistence on ending the *Oeconomy*. In the early years of settlement at Bethabara, the semi-communal economic system was a benefit for the brethren, but as Wachovia grew, officials in Europe and Pennsylvania believed the *Oeconomy* would become the same impractical administrative nightmare that it had in Bethlehem and Herrnhut. Church officials in Pennsylvania brought the *Oeconomy* in Bethlehem to a close in 1761 after complaints from residents and a significant drop in the population. The problems in Pennsylvania may well explain why Spangenberg created Bethania outside of the Bethabara *Oeconomy* in 1759.

According to Gillian Gollin in *Moravians in Two Worlds*, the *Oeconomy* in Bethlehem was doomed almost from the beginning. The main problem was the church's view of private property. In theory, the norms of private property were held inviolate, but in practice the Unity of Brethren had sole control, if not ownership, of all the land and property in Bethlehem. The individual immigrant to Bethlehem in the 1740s and 1750s had no opportunity to buy land or to start up his own business, since all land and property belonged by definition to the community as a whole.

Church officials spent so much money to buy the land in Pennsylvania that little or no capital was left to invest or to help pay for food, shelter, or clothing. This lack of capital in the early years kept the brothers and sisters busy trying to meet their own needs, and as time progressed they began to focus on making a profit by trading and doing business with the outside. As a result, the original plan, to create a place for skilled craftsmen in Bethlehem while agricultural pursuits were left to the brethren in nearby Nazareth and the Upper Places, failed.[51]

Instead of a balance of agriculture and trade, support personnel began to outnumber both groups. The number of individuals in administration, trade (bookkeepers, storekeepers, and secretaries), and commerce (innkeepers, guides for visitors, and food production including farming) increased while the number of practicing craftsmen decreased. Gollin attributes some of the elimination of the craft occupations to the gradual absorption of the immigrants into the economy of Bethlehem, a process which forced many persons to abandon their former occupations in favor of skills more immediately required in the new community.[52] However, with artisans in short supply throughout the colonies, Moravian craftsmen may have chosen to leave the community and go into business for themselves, opting to keep their profits rather than share them with the church. Bethlehem was in a particularly vulnerable location: with Philadelphia only forty-seven miles down the Delaware River, the brethren no doubt lost more than their share of artisans before ending the *Oeconomy*.

Because the church had not attempted to enforce a complete separation of crafts and agricultural pursuits in Wachovia, and because most of the brethren in Wachovia were ignorant of the problems with the *Oeconomy* in Bethlehem, brethren appeared to be content with the system. Occasionally, someone such as blacksmith George Schmidt complained, but, for the most part, everyone seemed satisfied. To most church members the *Oeconomy* was not an obstacle to making large profits and owning property; it was an economic safety net that insured their basic needs would always be met.

In fact, one of the most difficult tasks Frederick Marshall encountered as the administrator for Wachovia was convincing the brethren that the *Oeconomy* had to end. Even though the economy of Salem would not be divorced from agriculture, leaders planned to emphasize trades, with agriculture practiced mainly elsewhere. Church officials wanted to avoid repeating the Bethlehem debacle. In Wachovia's successful community, where contented church members were not leaving, ending the *Oeconomy* also meant less of a financial drain on the church. No longer would residents be totally supported by the church; now they would be responsible for their own financial well-being.

Shortly after being appointed administrator (but before the appointment had been announced to the residents), Marshall wrote to Ettwein, the minister at Bethabara, and explained his plans for Wachovia's economic future. The communal economy would end for everyone except the ministers, the choir houses, and "those who are absolutely essential in the domestic economy." Married people would become self-dependent either by their trades or by a salary from the Church. For artisans, Marshall proposed, "To the master of a trade I would first of all give a journeyman's wages and in addition he would receive 20 per cent or the fifth part of the clear profit, after the interest on his stock in trade had been deducted and his rent, and the wages of his journeymen; this would spur him on to be diligent and concerned about the success of his affairs to the benefit also of the economy."[53]

After announcing Marshall's appointment as administrator, the Administrator's Conference in Bethlehem gently broke the news about the end of the *Oeconomy*. The statement reiterated the "Savior's wish that Salem should really be the place for trade and professions in Wachovia," and, as such, moving the trades, professions, and administrators, as well as the *Aeltesten Conferenz* there as soon as the houses were ready, "will be the beginning of fulfilling the Savior's intention to make Salem the principle town." The end of the report stated that moving all the businesses and administration to Salem made it necessary for Salem to have congregation credit from the beginning, with new and accurate books to be kept so that each place would have its own account.[54]

Arranging the separate accounts for the construction of Salem was the extent of the church's progress in ending the *Oeconomy* for quite a few years. Clearly, officials in Bethlehem did not understand the delay. In Pennsylvania the brethren clamored for the end of the *Oeconomy;* in North Carolina they made it thrive. Occasionally Marshall and other church officials, both in Pennsylvania and Europe, would re-examine the situation in Wachovia and encourage the *Aeltesten Conferenz* to finish building Salem and stop communal living. Instructions from the Directing Board of the Unity in Herrnhut and Zeist to a company of brethren leaving for Wachovia in 1765 were sympathetic in tone, telling the North Carolina brethren that the *Oeconomy* had been intended only for the beginning of Wachovia, but the church had allowed it to continue because of the Indian War and Zinzendorf's death. However, with the building of Salem, communal living had to be brought to an end "in such a Manner as is suitable to our Congregation-Course."[55]

Two years later, when the *Oeconomy* was still going on in Wachovia, the Unity's *Vorsteher Collegium* in Herrnhut appointed a special committee to investigate and make plans for Wachovia. They discovered that "gifts, diligence, industry, and faithfulness, in the way of buildings, stocks, inventories, and improvements" had made the Bethabara *Oeconomy* profitable and even helped pay for the construction of Salem.[56] Nonetheless, seven weeks later the supervising board agreed that Salem should be separated from Bethabara as soon as possible and the *Oeconomy* in Bethabara abandoned. Fortunately, they realized that a deadline could not be set for this occurrence (too much of it depended on the construction of Salem), and as a precaution they instructed church leaders to explain the situation in Wachovia to any brothers or sisters going there from Europe or Pennsylvania (where communal housekeeping had ended) with the warning "that when they reached Wachovia they would have nothing of which to complain."[57]

In his 1768 Report to the Unity, Marshall discussed Wachovia's success, noting that in the past fifteen years "we have established, at least in a small way, all the really necessary businesses and handicrafts, which are greatly missed in other localities here. In addition to our farm of about 200 acres" brethren had

> a grist and saw mill, which can also be used for breaking tanbark and pressing oil; a brewery and distillery, a store, apothecary shop, tan-yard, pottery, gunsmith, black-smith, gunstock-maker, tailor shop, shoe-maker, linen-weaver, saddlery, bak-

ery, and the carpenters, joiners, and mason's, who do our building, and there is also our tavern. Even if these businesses are not particularly profitable they are indispensable, and with them we can provide ourselves with most of the necessaries of life.

Yet as soon as enough construction in Salem was finished, Marshall stated, "the handicrafts will move thither from Bethabara. From the beginning Bethabara was not intended to be a center of commerce . . . and there is still common housekeeping."[58]

Fear of the unknown may have been the main reason Bethabara residents resisted discontinuing the *Oeconomy*. From the beginning of the settlement of Wachovia, the brethren, and later the sisters, took comfort that the church would satisfy all their needs if they worked hard enough. In his 1769 Report to the Unity, Marshall explained that inhabitants of Bethabara could requisition items from the *Oeconomy*'s supplies that private persons "could hardly get" in the backcountry.[59] Having to obtain and pay for objects on one's own, even when receiving a salary from the church, was a daunting prospect for Bethabara residents.

The prospect of doing business on one's own may have seemed less daunting for certain members of the Moravian Church. For more than a century after settling in North Carolina, the Moravian leadership went to great lengths to protect their members from becoming dependent on, and unduly influenced by, the outside world. In establishing a settlement in the backcountry of North Carolina during the mid-eighteenth century, artisans were a vital link in the brethren's chain of self-sufficiency. The church's dealings with George Schmidt and Gottfried Aust suggest that the artisans were well aware of their importance within the Moravian community, but how did those Moravian craftsmen perceive the world outside of Wachovia? And how did the outside world perceive the Moravian artisans? Ironically, these two questions are more intertwined than they may first appear.

The records of the Moravians reveal that a demand for artisan services such as tailoring, blacksmithing, coopering, and turning greeted them upon their arrival on the Wachovia Tract in Rowan County. From analyzing the *Oeconomy*'s business records during the early years of settlement, Thorp found a steady stream of outsiders (three to four hundred a year), most of whom lived within a twenty mile radius of Bethabara, coming to do business with the Moravian craftsmen and the storehouse.[60] Obviously, a need for crafts existed in the backcountry, and the scarcer the craft, the farther people would come to buy the product. The pottery, for instance, sold wagonloads of pots, pans, jugs, etc., as far away as South Carolina. Not surprisingly, the presence of so many crafts in one location attracted the attention of many backcountry visitors. As early as 1765, the Rev. Charles

Woodmason, an Anglican cleric posted in the backcountry of South Carolina, described the Moravians as having "Mills, Furnaces, Forges, Potteries, Founderies, All Trades, and all things in and among themselves," and selling off their surplus in exchange for any items they might need.[61]

After the establishment of Salem, a planned town of streets lined with artisans' shops, each advertised by a unique trade sign, even more travelers recorded their impressions of the brethren and their "laudable example of industry, unfortunately too little observed and followed in this part of the country."[62] Another description of "the present state of the Moravian settlements, and the progress of manufactures and agriculture," written in 1789 and published on the front page of the Halifax *North Carolina Journal* in February 1793, waxed poetic about the plethora of artisans to be found in Salem, Bethabara, and Bethania.[63]

Clearly, these written depictions portray the Moravians and the crafts they practiced as an extraordinary occurrence for the backcountry, a generalization that research on artisans west of the river has proven false. The Moravians only practiced fourteen of the twenty three professions present in Rowan County in 1759; and only four of these—clothier, bricklayer, brickmaker, and turner—were found solely on the Wachovia Tract. The artisans not present among the Moravians in 1759 include a hatter, a joiner, a saddler, a wagonmaker, and a wheelwright.

Why were these "outside" artisans ignored? The artisans west of the Yadkin River were not so much ignored as the Moravian artisans, as part of a German settlement in the wilderness, attracted a lot of attention. First, according to the Moravians and their customers, until the county seat of Salisbury developed into what the Moravians characterized as a "rival" in 1767,[64] no other urban place existed, outside of Bethabara and then Salem, where a person could transact business with such a diverse group of artisans in one location. Second, the financial backing of the Moravian Church made it possible, after the initial settlement at Bethabara, for the Moravian artisans to work full time at their crafts. The opportunity to practice a craft as one's only occupation was highly unusual in early Rowan County, where deeds from sales of "improved land" reflect that virtually every artisan also worked his land to make ends meet. However, to find artisans exclusively pursuing their crafts on the North Carolina frontier, a phenomenon in the colonial era otherwise found only in urban areas such as Philadelphia, Boston, or New York City in the North and Annapolis, Williamsburg, or Charleston in the South, must have impressed both residents and visitors to the backcountry. The opportunity to work all day, every day at their trades like their urban counterparts may have resulted in the Moravian artisans' appearing more talented, more dedicated, or at least more experienced than other Rowan County craftsmen, as well.

As much praise as was lavished on the Moravian artisans, most observers did not fully understand the financial restrictions (both with the *Oeconomy* and the lease system in Salem) under which they worked. The brethren, on the other hand, understood perfectly the reputation they enjoyed throughout the backcountry as talented craftsmen as well as the market (and, they hoped, profits) that awaited them if they ever chose to leave the security of the *Oeconomy*. For some brothers, the lure of the outside world where they could have their own money and property proved stronger than their devotion to the church. Another attraction of living outside Wachovia was the absence of the church's direction of one's personal life; the restraints on Moravian social life and behavior seemed to affect artisans, in particular. Quite possibly the artisans' realization that they could leave Wachovia at any time, and conceivably be better off for it (at least financially), led a few individuals to dismiss their responsibilities as brethren. In *Moravian Community*, Thorp recorded at least ten men who were expelled or encouraged to leave Wachovia for their behavior between 1753 and 1772.[65] The records indicate that six of those men may have been artisans.[66]

Who were these men, and what happened to them? The records do not always disclose the story behind the man. Since the Moravians did consider the possibility that future generations might read their records, they took pains not to commit to paper and thus, to eternity, the sins of those unfortunate individuals. Today titillating phrases remain, enough to catch one's interest but devoid of the details to explain exactly what happened. A prime example of this type of treatment by the Moravians is Heinrich Feldhausen, the multi-talented cooper, shoemaker, carpenter, millwright, sievemaker, turner, farmer, and sometime tanner of the original settlement at Bethabara. Without any prior indication of a problem in the records, on June 17, 1762, the Bethabara diary recorded that "H. Feldhausen left today with many tears. He had put our brewery and distillery into the best of order, but yielded to carnal desires and fell into all kinds of sin and shame, so that we could no longer keep him here. The refugees have done us much harm."[67] Moravians forbid social relations and marriage outside of the church, which may have been Feldhausen's sin, but the records remain silent as to what really happened.

Gunsmith Andreas Betz experienced a similar fate at the hands of the brethren. Twenty-seven years old when he arrived in Wachovia in 1754, life seemed to be one disappointment after another until 1765, when he accompanied another brother to Salisbury on a routine trip to court. For the next two years a flurry of letters flew back and forth between the elders at Bethabara and church leaders in Bethlehem concerning Betz's "dangerous course," the heartaches he gave the brethren, and the possibility that Satan was working through him. They even asked the lot if Betz should be given the opportunity to leave in a friendly manner, and received the negative.[68] Finally, in January 1767, the mystery was resolved. The brethren discovered that Betz had become secretly engaged to Barbara Bruner, daughter of gunsmith George Bruner, who lived in Salisbury. Evidently, Betz saw more than the court on that visit to Salisbury in 1765, and the consequences of meeting Barbara tortured him: should he leave the church to marry her, or should he forget her and remain faithful to the brethren? Love won out, and within days of telling the brethren of his plans to marry Barbara, Betz was excommunicated from the church and expelled from Bethabara.[69]

A rather strange footnote to this story involves Betz's apprentice, Joseph Mueller. Although Lorenz Bagge wrote to Bethlehem that Mueller did not seem to learn much from Betz, he did pick up one thing: seven years after Betz left the Church to marry an outsider, Joseph Mueller did the same. In January 1774, he married Sara Hauser and moved to some land near Bethania.[70] Both Betz and Mueller remained on excellent terms with the brethren in Wachovia, however. Betz continued to do business with some of the craftsmen at Bethabara. In 1768 he purchased a tile stove made by Gottfried Aust, and in 1773 the Single Brothers accepted a loan of £1100 at 5 percent interest from him.[71]

Close ties existed between the craftsmen who had left the confines of Wachovia but remained in the backcountry. Michael Morr, a journeyman potter who came to work in Bethabara in 1762, probably disliked the restrictions of the brethren's lifestyle and left shortly thereafter for Salisbury. In the spring of 1765, Morr bought land in the east square of Salisbury from tanner John Lewis Beard and his wife Christian for his house and shop. Only two months after Betz came to Salisbury in 1767 and married Barbara Bruner, Morr witnessed the deed for Betz's purchase of two lots in the north square of Salisbury.[72]

The *Oeconomy* obviously did not offer enough to every segment of Moravian society, and the artisans seemed the most vulnerable to its rules and restrictions. Finally, in 1769 the General Synod of the Moravian Church issued an ultimatum to Wachovia to end the *Oeconomy*. In March 1770, the *Aeltesten Conferenz* began to discuss the transition of the administration of professions and trades from church control to private control.[73] A month later Marshall audited the accounts of all the master workmen in preparation for their going into business for themselves, and gradually, one at a time, the trades moved to Salem.[74]

Even though the semi-communal lifestyle had ended, the church did not relinquish social control over its members. No trade or business could be started or expanded without consent of the Moravian authorities. Apprentices could not be hired or fired without the consent of the church.

Restrictions applied to an individual's borrowing or lending of capital. Under this new regime, individual brethren operated most of the economic activities in Wachovia, doing business with anyone they chose, paying their own expenses, and keeping their profits. The church enforced its economic regulations through leases.[75]

The *Aeltesten Conferenz* took over governing trade and economic issues in Salem at first. However, as the town grew and the number of trades and business expanded, the elders formed a special board to oversee the financial welfare of the congregation and manage the trades. Beginning in 1772, the *Aufseher Collegium* regulated the number of people allowed to practice a particular craft (usually just one shop per town), set craftsmen's wages, and determined the price to be paid for items in the craft shops and the community stores. For the privilege of practicing their crafts in a protected economic environment, the artisans allowed the *Collegium* to audit and inventory them annually to evaluate their financial well-being and the quality of the items they produced. If a shopmaster was found negligent in his management duties or his workmanship, he could be demoted to journeyman or asked to train in a different craft.[76] Eventually, the effort to regulate the trades failed because of the elders' reluctance to cancel the leases of those who violated their commands. In 1856 the Church ended the lease system; afterwards Moravian businessmen operated in the same manner as their neighbors.[77]

Moravian leaders took advantage of the time lapse between selecting the area for Salem in 1759 and the end of the *Oeconomy* in 1770 to adapt their economy to a larger, permanent town. Social and economic dissent marked this transition period from life in Bethabara, the "house of passage," to Salem, the new center of trade and manufacturing. While the dissent was limited mainly to individuals, some Wachovia brethren's unwillingness to obey the Unity's order to end the successful *Oeconomy* characterized the discord which plagued the community. The *Oeconomy* may have benefited the overall community, but it restricted the financial futures of artisans. For example, blacksmith George Schmidt chafed under the communal system because he knew that in the unregulated economy of Rowan County his skills could make him wealthy. Well aware that Schmidt's skills could be a financial windfall for the church once the *Oeconomy* ended, the church willingly placated Schmidt until he could move to Salem and keep a share of his profits.

The need for skilled craftsmen in the backcountry, combined with the perception that Moravian artisans were more talented than their Rowan County counterparts, put Moravian craftsmen in constant demand on the east side of the Yadkin. Life outside the social and financial restrictions of the Wachovia Tract tempted many Moravian artisans. Not surprisingly, some artisans, such as Andreas Betz, Heinrich Feldhausen, Thomas Hofman, and Joseph Mueller, allowed the demand for their craft skills and their desire for a freer life to overshadow their devotion to the church.

Stress and anxiety often mark times of transition, and the Moravians were no different. Out of these chaotic times, however, the Moravians brought order. They began an apprentice program to train boys in the trades and to augment their labor supply, they succeeded in abandoning the *Oeconomy* for a market economy and the lease system, and they built a planned town in the wilderness that continues to stand today as a monument to their industry and devotion.

SIX

Women Artisans in Rowan County

In a spare minute from running her busy household and tavern in Salisbury, Elizabeth Steele walked over to see the seamstress Ann Crosby to pick up a dress she had ordered from Ann some weeks before. Although the dress was for everyday wear, Mrs. Steele could afford to have Ann make it from specially-ordered fabric that cost four shillings six pence a yard.[1]

Just how uncommon was Elizabeth Steele's order, and subsequent purchase, of a dress from Ann Crosby? Historians used to consider it nearly impossible. Spruill, in her 1938 book *Women's Life and Work*, described the backcountry woman this way:

> It was the housewife of the back settlements who had to depend most upon her own labor and ingenuity. The frontiersman's remoteness from the waterways and highways and his lack of a marketable staple crop prevented his trading much with the outside world and made it necessary for him and his wife to produce almost everything consumed in their household. With broadaxe and jackknife, he made his cabin, furniture, and many of the farming implements and kitchen utensils; and with spinning wheel, loom, and dyepots, she made all the clothing of the family, the household linen, blankets, quilts, coverlets, curtains, rugs, and other such furnishings.[2]

The previous chapters, which have shown the presence of artisans working in a wide variety of crafts and the extension of their trade networks far beyond Rowan County, have discredited this traditional historical interpretation of backcountry life. Thus, Elizabeth Steele's purchase of a dress from a seamstress was no more uncommon than a purchase from any other Rowan County artisan at this time. More importantly, Ann Crosby's work illustrates that women were professional artisans in Rowan County. Employed mainly in the textile arts, women held a monopoly on the craft of spinning, a crucial step in the production of cloth, in the backcountry.

Female artisans serve as just one example of the role women played in the economy of backcountry North Carolina. As working women, these artisans, whether married or single, possessed varying levels of economic autonomy, a circumstance that was quite unusual for the rural colonial

South. Their income and skills made them good credit risks, and merchants granted accounts to both married and single women. However, the legal tradition of *feme covert* prevented married women from having as much economic freedom as single women did. Single women artisans may have had more control over their finances than married women did, but court records indicate they paid a high price for that autonomy.

Because it has been difficult to identify female artisans in the rural colonial South, historians have not been able to study them in the same manner as male artisans. The first half of this chapter will focus on the identification of female artisans and on the training women received to become artisans. Special attention will be given to the largest group of female artisans in Rowan County, spinsters. The second half of the chapter will examine the place of female artisans in Rowan County's economy and society.

Women who practiced traditionally female skills such as spinning, sewing, weaving, or knitting for profit commonly have not been classified as artisans by historians. This situation seems to be the result of a combination of factors: women did not always receive the same craft training nor did they have the same economic opportunities as men; women usually worked at home and not in a shop; and the pervasiveness of women's skills led to the fallacy that they were a normal part of the housewife's duties and not a distinct trade. While these qualifications have some basis, they do not change the fact that these women, like male artisans, generated income by using special skills to manufacture a finished product from raw materials.

Mary Boone was the first woman artisan to appear in Rowan County records. In a deed dated April 31, 1756, Mary, wife of Jonathan Boone, a joiner, and daughter of millwright James Carter, one of the richest men in the county, is identified as a spinster.[3] Spinsters often have been overlooked as artisans because of the erroneous assumption that the label applies only to marital status. In fact, the *Oxford English Dictionary* primarily defines a spinster as "A woman (or, rarely a man) who spins, especially one who practises spinning as a regular occupation," and only secondarily as a term "Appended to names of women, originally in order to denote their occupation, but subsequently (from the 17th Century) as the proper legal designation of one still unmarried." Historians of colonial America have asserted that free women did not define themselves as artisans; they were either spinsters, widows, or wives."[4] Yet seventeenth- and eighteenth-century English county records used "spinster" as a reference to marital status and occupation.[5] The records of Rowan County (and its subsequent counties) show that in backcountry North Carolina women *were* defined as artisans, and at least a few free married women *were not* totally subsumed by their husbands' identity. Furthermore, research to delineate the differences between housewifery apprenticeships and spinning apprenticeships reveals that spinning probably was not a common skill of all housewives.

The assumption that the term spinster always referred to single marital status is not supported by the historical record. For example, court records identified Mary Carter Boone, a married woman, as a spinster, and Alexander Newberry's will called three women spinsters, when two of them were married. A fourth woman mentioned in the will received no such designation.[6] Clearly, the first three women worked as professional spinsters.

The Rowan County public records recognized only a few women as professional spinsters, and yet tradition holds that "the skills of housewifery [included] primarily sewing and spinning."[7] However, a comparison of the apprenticeships to learn housewifery and the apprenticeships to learn spinning reveals that spinning may not have been a commonly practiced skill of backcountry housewives.

Between 1753 and 1795, approximately seventy-five girls were apprenticed in Rowan County.[8] According to the existing scholarship on Rowan County apprentices, only one female was apprenticed to learn a trade: in November 1785 John Willson, Jr., took Catherine Steagle, age eleven, as an apprentice to "larn the art & mistry of spinning."[9] Most indentures for young girls did not mention any specific type of training, but only designated a length of time and the requirement that the master should "comply with the law." When the apprenticeship was completed, the girl usually received money and/or property of an amount agreed upon earlier, and a suit of clothes. For instance, in 1755 Mary McCafferty was bound to Hugh Shearer for fifteen years and ten months, and he was to "Providd [her] with Sufficent Meats, Drink and Apperrel . . . and Shall Also Teach the sd Orphan to reed English. And to Give Sd Orphan Such freedom Dues As by Law appointed."[10]

In Rowan County, Catherine Steagle may have been the only girl specifically apprenticed to learn spinning, but the indentures for twenty-three female apprentices stipulated that they receive a spinning wheel when finished. For a woman to receive a spinning wheel as part of her freedom dues parallels the indentures of boys, who usually were given "the tools of their trade" when they completed their apprentice training so they would be prepared to become journeymen. Of the seventy-five young women who were apprenticed, Catherine Steagle and the twenty-three others were to learn how to spin; since they received spinning wheels, presumably they could have continued spinning when their indentures expired. (See Table

5.) Fifty-one other female apprentices may or may not have learned how to spin during their terms, but without wheels they were not immediately prepared to spin afterwards.[11]

In the extant records of the counties later formed from Rowan, forty-nine apprentice indentures specified that young girls learn the art of the spinster, while others learned only housewifery.[12] Since all female apprentices in Rowan County did not receive spinning wheels upon completion of their indentures, and because other counties clearly distinguished between apprenticeships to learn spinning and apprenticeships to learn housewifery, knowledge and skill of spinning apparently were not necessarily part of the housewifery apprenticeship and, hence, may not have been among the common housewife's chores. In fact, unlike traditionally male skills, the difference between housewives and professional spinsters or any female artisans was not necessarily the skills they possessed, but rather the time they devoted to the task, the amount of work they produced, and the amount of payment (if any) they received for their work.

The classification of the female apprentice's spinning wheel as a "tool of the trade" can be substantiated further in the court records of Rowan County. In March 1767, spinster Isabella Moore asked the Salisbury District Superior Court to release her from jail, where she sat for a forty shilling debt to Robert Johnson. Moore petitioned the court to release her and discharge her debt on the basis that she was not worth the money owed "in any worldly substance working tools [i.e., her spinning wheel] and wearing appearel excepted."[13]

In Rowan County, as elsewhere in colonial America, the fact that many wills and inventories did not mention spinning equipment indicates that not all women spun and demonstrates that spinning equipment was financially important to professional spinsters.[14] Only approximately 35 percent of the wills written in Rowan County before 1790 contain specific references to spinning equipment.[15] Males wrote most of the wills mentioning spinning equipment, and they usually left spinning wheels to their wives or their daughters. In a few wills females left spinning equipment to daughters, daughters-in-law, or granddaughters. The only record of spinning equipment being left to a man occurred when John Owen willed Philip Dowell a "Wolen Wheel and [a] Linnen Wheel."[16]

Although men were the *de jure* owners of the spinning equipment in a household, women were the *de facto* owners: the ones who really possessed, and used, the wheels. For instance, James McLaughlin left his daughter Mary "her spinning wheel and Check reel and also [a] brass hatchel" and his other daughter Eleanor "her spinning wheel and a coars hatchel."[17] The fact that men legally had to will their wives' and daughters' property back to them shows women's low legal and economic status in eighteenth-cen-

Table 5. Women Artisans in Rowan County

Female master	Apprentice	Trade	County and date*
Baker, Anna	Nansey Jolley	weaver/ spinner	Surry 1782
Barrs, Sarah		spinner	Rowan 1768
Boone, Mary		spinner	Rowan 1756
Buttner, Sarah		weaver	[Moravian] 1786
Crosby, Ann		seamstress	Rowan n.d.
Dennis, Rachel	Elizabeth Dennis	spinner	Randolph 1786
Elrod, Mary		weaver	[Moravian] 1786
Fergison, Jean		spinner	Rowan 1770
Flood, Mary		weaver	[Moravian] 1786
Goetje, Mary Elisabeth Krause		glovemaker	[Moravian] 1780
Hogston, Anne		spinner	Rowan 1785
Holshouser, Hannah		spinner	Rowan 1784
King, Mary		milliner	Rowan 1772
Lock, Ann		spinner	Rowan 1770
McBroom, Mrs. James		spinner	Rowan 1769
McCartney, Elizabeth		weaver	Rowan 1785
McCrerry, Mary		spinner	Rowan 1769
McHarg[ue], Margaret		spinner/ weaver	Rowan 1780
McHenry, Elinor		spinner	Rowan 1792
McHenry, Gennat [Janet]		spinner	Rowan 1792
McLaughlin, Eleanor		spinner	Rowan 1779
McLaughlin, Mary		spinner	Rowan 1779
Means, [Margaret]		spinner	Randolph 1783
Mock, Mrs. DeWalt		spinner	Rowan, n.d.
Moore, Elizabeth		spinner	Rowan 1795
Moore, Isabella		spinner	Rowan 1768
Moore, Mary		spinner/ weaver	Rowan 1795
Moore, Susanna Jennings		weaver	Rowan 1798
Morr, Susanna		potter	Rowan 1784
Morrison, Mary		spinner	Rowan 1779
Myers, Mary		spinner/ weaver	Rowqn 1784
Newberry, Annas		spinner	Rowan 1770
Newfang, Anna Mary		spinner	Rowan 1775
Oliphant, Elizabeth		spinner	Rowan 1785
Orton, Jane		spinner	Rowan 1766
Orton, Rachel		spinner	Rowan 1766
Osbrough, Agnes		spinner	Rowan 1761

Table 5, Cont.

Female master	Apprentice	Trade	County and date*
Page, Mary		weaver	Rowan 1771
Parks, Margaret		spinner	Rowan 1761
Pincer, Sarah		spinner	Rowan 1768
Poston, Elizabeth		spinner	Rowan 1784
Poston, Margret		spinner	Rowan 1784
Ramsey, Jean		spinner	Rowan 1783
Rees, Ann		spinner	Rowan 1775
Riggs, Ann		spinner	Rowan 1787
Robinson, Ann [mother]		weaver	Rowan 1785
Robinson, Ann [daughter]		spinner	Rowan 1785
Rosebrough, Margaret		spinner	Rowan 1785
Rosebrough, Mary		weaver	Rowan 1777
Rutledge, Elenor		spinner	Rowan 1774
Sewel, Elizabeth		spinner/ weaver	Rowan 1789
Sharp, Mary	Elner Gibins	spinner	Randolph 1789
Shirts, Catherine	Bolley Colley	spinner	Randolph 1787
Smith, Elizabeth	Elizabeth Smith	spinner	Wilkes 1791
Snap, Christian		spinner	Rowan 1768
Snap, Elizabeth		spinner	Rowan 1768
Hauser [Spoenhauser], Elizabeth		weaver	[Moravian] 1773
Stamon, Sarah		spinner	Rowan 1768
Standley, [Elizabeth]	Mary Richerson	spinner	Guilford 1789
Steele, Elizabeth	Allen Campbell	weaver	Rowan 1781
	Elizabeth Campbell	spinner	Rowan 1781
Stewart, Elizabeth		spinner	Rowan 1778
Storey, Martha		spinner	Rowan 1762
Thompson, Martha		spinner	Rowan 1774
Todd, Sarah		spinner	Rowan 1777
Tomblin, Sarah		spinner	Rowan 1786
Wensel, Barbara		spinner	Rowan 1789
Walker, [Mary]	Sarah Brandon	spinner	Surry 1785
Wilson, Joan		spinner	Rowan 1769

(Cont.)

Table 5, cont.

Master	Female apprentice	Trade	County and date
Joseph Hickman	———, Esther	weaver	Rowan 1781
Benjamin Johnson	Aldrig, Jemima	spinner	Wilkes 1784
Robert Martin	Armstrong, Sarah	spinner	Wilkes 1787
John Johnston	Baker, Amelia	spinner	Rowan 1774
Thomas Whitticor	Baker, Ann	mantua maker	Surry 1775
John Clayton	Brabbin, Sarah	spinner	Surry 1787
John Church	Burch, Rachal	spinner	Rowan 1767
Robert Kimmins	Burnet, Tabitha	spinner	Guilford 1785
Hugh Jinkins	Callahan, Rosannah	spinner	Rowan 1766
James Gray	Cartwright, Hannah	spinner	Wilkes 1778
Isham Harvill	Cast, Winnifred	spinner	Wilkes 1785
James Williams	Childress, Pattie	spinner	Wilkes 1782
Philip Snider	Critzwitcher, Mary	spinner	Surry 1786
Michael Peeles Jr.	Cummins, Chatley	spinner	Rowan 1788
Michael Teague	Deetz, Ann Mary	mantua maker	Surry 1778
Major Loggins	Dinkins, Sarah	spinner	Stokes 1790
Robert Ayers	Durham, Lucretia	spinner	Wilkes 1792
Thomas Addeman	Engram, Shelley	spinner	Surry n.d.
Martin Miller	Eury, Esther	spinner	Rowan 1774
John Brown	Fowel, Sally	spinner	Randolph 1785
Tinch Carter	Gibbins, Susannah	spinner	Randolph 1790
John Dongan	Gibins, Betsey	spinner	Randolph 1789
Ashley Johnson	Gibson, Catharine	spinner	Surry 1785
John Love	Gibson, Mary	spinner	Surry 1785
Daniel Huff	Gibson, Phebe	spinner	Surry 1785
Robert Ayers	Gibson, Sarah	spinner	Wilkes 1789
Francis Ross	Greer, Agnes	spinner	Rowan 1777
Thomas Hill	Greer, Priscilla	spinner	Rowan 1777
Philip Hoodinpaff	Halcomb, Sarah	spinner	Burke 1788
William Beard	Ham, Betty	spinner	Rowan 1779
James Wallace	Ham, Jean	spinner	Rowan 1779
David Beard	Ham, Nancy	spinner	Rowan 1779
William Bell	Harlan, Mourning	seamstress	Randolph 1790
John Hammond	Harvey, Elizabeth	spinner	Randolph 1790
Benjamin Cutbirth	Hill, Elender	spinner	Wilkes 1789
Isaac Norman	Jackaway, Mary	spinner/weaver	Wilkes 1786
Will Davis	Johnson, May	spinner	Rowan 1770
Isaac Low	Jolley, Jemima	spinner	Wilkes 1783
John Burch	King, Mary	spinner	Surry n.d.
John Stephenson	McCoy, Isabella	spinner	Rowan 1777
Andrew Baker	Martin, Elizabeth	spinner	Wilkes n.d.
Peter Fulps	Moore, Anna	spinner	Surry 1787

Table 5, cont.

Master	Female Apprentice	Trade	County and date
Alexander Moore	Motts, Mary	spinner/ seamstress	Surry 1782
David Cowin	Murphy, Sarah	spinner	Rowan 1783
William Nelson	Nelson, Lidia	spinner	Rowan 1772
John Riddick	Odean, Mary (Adam)	spinner	Randolph 1787
Jesse McAnally	Parford, Rachel	spinner	Surry 1786
George Sevets, Jr.	Pellum, Ruth	spinner	Rowan 1783
William Raglin	Porter, Elizabeth	spinner	Wilkes 1784
William Temple Coles	Quin, Nancey	spinner	Rowan 1772
Charles Bookout	Rains, Sarah	spinner	Randolph n.d.
Benjamin Herndon	Redman, Amy	spinner	Wilkes 1783
Jeffrey Johnson	Redman, Lettice [mot]	spinner	Surry 1774
Benjamin Herndon	Redman, Lettice [dau]	spinner	Wilkes 1783
Thomas Robins	Robins, Elizabeth	spinner	Wilkes 1787
William McConnell	Sawyers, Mary	spinner	Rowan 1766
Christian Luther	Sewell, Persilla	spinner	Randolph 1790
William Clark	Simmons, Persilla	spinner	Randolph 1785
Ozwell Smith	Smith, Elizabeth	spinner	Wilkes 1789
John Lowry	Stapleton, Anne	spinner	Rowan 1777
James Bailey	Stapleton, Avis	spinner	Rowan 1777
Hugh Cathey	Stapleton, Hannah	spinner	Rowan 1777
John Willson, Jr.	Steagle, Catherine	spinner	Rowan 1785
John Johnston	Sumner, Elizabeth	spinner	Randolph 1785
John Murdock	Sumner, Mary	spinner	Randolph 1785
Francis Reynolds	Tailor, Phawney	spinner	Wilkes 1784
Thomas Dixon	Thornton, Rachell	spinner	Wilkes 1783
James White	Tobin, Margret	spinner	Rowan 1779
James Fletcher	Walters, Christian	spinner	Wilkes 1784
Robert King	Warnor, Polley	spinner	Wilkes 1787
James McKnight	Williams, Agnes	spinner	Rowan 1774
William McKnight	Williams, Rebecca	spinner	Rowan 1774

*County and date = county where earliest reference to artisan was found and the date of that reference.

SOURCES: Lynne Howard Fraser, "'Nobody's Children': The Treatment of Illegitimate Children in Three North Carolina Counties, 1760-1790 (master's thesis, College of William and Mary, 1987), 80-95; Kathi R. Jones, "'That Also These children May Become Useful People': Apprenticeships in Rowan County, North Carolina, from 1753-1795" (master's thesis, College of William and Mary, 1984), 70-94; apprentice bonds and records for Burke, Randolph, Surry, and Wilkes counties; Minutes of Court of Pleas and Quarter Sessions for Guilford, Randolph, Stokes, Surry, and Wilkes counties.

tury North Carolina. However, the informal matrilineal descent of such objects also may have provided the daughters with a sense of female identity.[18] Spinning equipment was also among the property consistently willed to a woman regardless of her future marital status, an indication of its potential importance to the woman's economic well-being. John Oliphant willed his wife the use of the front room of his house, a slave, a good horse, a saddle, a bridle, her bed and furniture, her apparel, and her spinning wheel during her widowhood; but she received only her horse, saddle, and bridle, her bed, her clothes, and her spinning wheel if she remarried.[19]

The spinning equipment left to women in wills included hatchels, reels, spinning wheels, and occasionally cards. All of these objects process the raw material of the fiber, usually flax or wool, into thread or yarn. Once flax has been broken, or the stalks crushed, the flax is beaten against a hatchel, a board with protruding metal spikes, to separate the fibrous part from the brittle coating and to reduce the fiber to a size that can be spun into thread. Hatchels came in various sizes, from coarse (with larger spikes spread farther apart) to fine (with smaller spikes closer together), to beat the flax more efficiently and to offer different grades of flax so different qualities of linen could be woven.

Cards serve a similar purpose to hatchels in the processing of wool. Cards are smaller boards with handles covered with curved pieces of wire to separate and align wool fibers. Like hatchels, they also come in assorted sizes to produce a wide range of wool yarn. Once the fibers were cleaned and separated, the spinster used a wheel to draw them out into thread or yarn; flax was spun on a small wheel to produce a fairly condensed thread, and wool was spun on a large wheel at a slower pace to yield a more loosely-spun yarn.

Determining that a few women worked as professional spinsters in the backcountry and that not all backcountry women may have known how to spin is significant for examining the consequences of the gender bias of spinning and the importance of spinning in the production of cloth in Rowan County. Philip Dowell and his two spinning wheels notwithstanding, the legal records of Rowan County have identified only women as spinsters. Spinning was not considered a male activity in the North Carolina backcountry, or anywhere else in the colonies, for that matter. Even the Moravian brethren in Wachovia, who usually were anxious to accomplish any task to please God, did not spin.[20]

A list of crafts practiced in Rowan County in 1759 shows that weaving was the single most widely practiced trade in the backcountry. Eighteenth-century sources estimate that it took seven spinsters to supply one weaver adequately with yarn or thread. The women identified as spinsters in legal documents must have supplied the local weavers. Not only did these female artisans have a monopoly on the craft of spinning—making them a vital link in the production of cloth in Rowan County—but they also comprised the largest single group of artisans in the county.

So why do spinsters not appear in the official records more often? The short answer comes from southeastern Pennsylvania, from where many people migrated to the North Carolina backcountry. Brief notations in household account books indicate that spinsters (usually teenage girls) hired out to different households for various lengths of time to do the spinning and other chores.[21] In these cases, the sex and age of the spinsters kept them out of the "official records" as artisans.

The longer answer points to a clear case of gender bias, evident in that the male-dominant society could not accept the work of these women artisans as professional in the eighteenth and twentieth centuries. Historian Allan Kulikoff alludes to this problem in explaining the "transition to capitalism" in early America. By assuming that the woman's traditional place of work, the household, is the most fundamental and elementary unit of social and class organization and that all family members contributed to this indivisible economic unit, most historians have ignored the production of individual household members. Some social historians have argued that early America had a household or domestic economic system, in which households in local communities made exchanges outside of commodity markets and without a true market price. Kulikoff points out that this argument denies the importance of commercial exchange in early America and ignores the relation of noncommercial exchange to the expansion of capitalism. By characterizing the household as a single economic unit and disregarding the gender roles associated with various household processes, the concept of a domestic economic system paints a romanticized view of a non-commercial world. And, finally, this concept precludes the very likely possibility that any household member, especially women, produced goods for consumption, exchange, or sale. In fact, wives probably engaged in such informal nonmarket trade more often than men.[22]

The household economic system theory has numerous problems, not the least of which is its tacit acceptance of the self-sufficiency of early America. More troubling, however, is the theory's assumption that all women participated in the household economic system in the exact same manner and for the same reasons. To refuse to recognize women's separate identities, even in examining what they frequently produced and traded, is to deny women their full place in early America.

English historian Pamela Sharpe rejected this "family economy" theory of domestic production in her study of Colyton, England, in the seventeenth and early eighteenth centuries, stating that "women's work was not a corollary of men's, nor a complement," but, "rather, it promoted the independence of women as wage earners in their own right." She found that far from being "supplements to the family economy," women used their domestic skills to support themselves financially.[23] Many of the same conclusions can be reached in examining the activities of women artisans in Rowan County.

As married women, the majority of women artisans in Rowan County were legally subsumed by their husbands' identity; these women's names often do not appear in the historical records. Unfortunately, their absence has led some historians to incorrect conclusions about the economic behavior of married women. For example, more historians than one have concluded that only unmarried women participated in their own right in the public economy of early America.[24] Historians have based this interpretation on the scant appearances of women (usually widowed or single) in account books and the assumption that merchants dealt with married women only on special terms.[25]

A cash account book kept by Salisbury merchant and tavernkeeper William Steele (and husband of Elizabeth Steele) sheds new light on women's participation in the public economy in Rowan County. Thirty-six women appear in Steele's book as having accounts with him. Twenty-seven are identified only by their name (no salutation), and nine have a descriptor (widow) or title (Mrs.) before their name. One woman, a close friend (and later wife) of Steele, is referred to only by her first name, "elisabath." While the marital status of the women without descriptors is difficult to determine, the majority of them were probably single.

Even so, the most important information in the account book may be about married women such as Catherin [*sic*] Smith. In September 1760, Steele's account book shows that Smith purchased some textiles and notions, a knife and "sundrys pr yr husband." She paid for them, as well as an earlier debt for "sundrys," with cash.[26] This entry challenges many of the assumptions about married women's participation in the economy: they could (and did) have accounts to buy items for themselves and other family members from merchants who would extend them credit.

The account book does not indicate where women obtained the money to pay their debts. Three women can be identified as artisans, which means they had an income of their own. However, in accounts where women were not the only individuals doing the buying, apparently the fruits of their labors helped pay for the purchases. Most of Steele's customers paid their accounts in cash, but on various occasions men's debts were satisfied with goods such as "22 yds of linen cloth @ 2/ per yd," "2 shirts," or "1 pr stockins."[27] The women who had accounts with Steele also often paid their bill with goods. Widow Donaldson used cash and "cloath" to pay for a bedgown, two cloaks, a silk gown, two handkerchiefs, a pair of mitts, fabric, a hat, an apron, ribbon, and a book. Catherine Gibson paid for fabric, notions, and a pattern for a gown with cash and "30 3/4 yds of cloth @ 2/ a yd," and Sarah Moran bought a new pair of stays with "cloth 13 1/4 yd @ 2/3" and cash.[28]

Court records show that women, especially those who spun, fulfilled an independent and expanding role in the market economy of Rowan County. Only one woman is identified as a spinster in the records in 1759, less than 1 percent of the artisan population for that time.[29] By 1770, the records identified twenty women as spinsters in Rowan County, almost 7 percent of the entire artisan population. Between 1753 and 1790, women artisans in Rowan County and the counties formed from it accounted for almost 15 percent of all artisans in the area.[30]

Whether they had formal training or not, eventually women artisans helped fulfill the backcountry demand for spinsters, weavers, seamstresses, milliners, knitters, and mantua (dress) makers. In Salisbury, seamstress Ann Crosby made dresses for Elizabeth Steele, and milliner Mary King used her knowledge of sewing and fashion to create Steele's hats. (Interestingly, King charged more for a single hat than Crosby asked to make an entire dress.)[31] Stocking knitter Mary Gayley used her account at John Nisbet's store, northwest of Salisbury, to keep supplied with knitting needles and then paid her account in the finished product.[32] More specialized training became available, for the wills in Surry County (formed from Rowan in 1771) record that Ann Baker and Ann Mary Deetz apprenticed to Thomas Whitticor and Michael Teague to learn the art of mantua making.[33] In Salem, a young woman named Mary Elizabeth Krause took additional training with the tanner and shoemaker, Br. Fritz, and learned how to make gloves.[34]

In addition to these few known women artisans, an untold number of anonymous Rowan County women most likely used their needlework skills to bolster the craft production of their artisan husbands, fathers, or brothers. Shoemaking, hatmaking, and saddle and harness making, to name but a few, required some sewing on the product. These women have never received credit for their work in male-oriented crafts because it is impossible to distinguish in the historical record or on the object itself the labor of the woman from that of the man.[35]

Weaving was the second largest craft in which Rowan women artisans participated. At least seventeen women worked as weavers in the backcountry up to 1790. Women were the occasional recipients of weaving equipment such as looms, gears, reeds, and tackling from male decedents in Rowan County wills. Weaving gear did not appear with the same frequency as spinning wheels, nor was it usually given in conjunction with spinning equipment. Mary Myers wrote an unusual will with references to weaving equipment in 1784, when she left her spinning wheels and weaver's reeds to her daughters and granddaughters.[36] While she was still alive, Myers evidently gained some discretionary income from selling her work; her name also appears in William Steele's account book. Using the account of Martha Myers, possibly a relative, Myers twice purchased sundries from Steele's store.[37]

The will and accounts of Mary and Martha Myers also offer a rare glimpse into the products of women weavers in Rowan County. The output of other female artisans such as spinsters, mantua makers, or milliners, while rarely found in the extant records (such as Elizabeth Steele's transaction with Ann Crosby), is fairly obvious. With weaving, the possibilities for the form and fiber of the final product are extensive. However, along with the spinning and weaving equipment listed in Mary Myers's will, her specific mention of a "counterpain [*sic*]", a "Read [*sic*] Spotted Coverlid [*sic*]," "My Black Spotted Coverlid [*sic*]," and "some Cotten yarn" strongly suggests that these objects were the fruits of her labor.[38] Since coverlets and counterpanes do not appear for sale in any of the store account books, evidently Mary Myers's skills and products filled a void in the backcountry textile market.

Martha may have filled a similar but smaller gap for specialized goods in the local textile market. Backcountry merchants imported large amounts and varieties of textiles from England to sell at their stores. The comparatively few "rough" or "common" fabrics among the imports indicate that Rowan County weavers focused their energies on producing textiles with common weaves and fibers for everyday wear, rather than specialized fabrics. In June 1761, along with some notions and fabric (silk, taffeta, and persian), Martha purchased "1 pasteboard" from William Steele.[39] Placing a pasteboard between folds of fabric (usually wool) and applying heat and pressure gave the fabric a "glazed" or smooth, almost glossy finish; patterns could also be produced.[40] While glazed textiles such as calimanco, durant, and stuff for clothing and bedding were available in Rowan County, Martha may have received a special request that a merchant could not fulfill.

Four women weavers, one of whom also worked as a tailor, appear in the extensive records of the Moravians between 1753 and 1790. Mary Elrod, Mary Flood, Elizabeth Hauser, and the aforementioned Mary Elizabeth Krause all originally plied their trades for the Single Sisters' *Oeconomy*.[41] The Single Sisters lived together as a family in their own house. They were responsible for supporting themselves, which they did through a variety of business ventures. The Single Sisters' income came primarily from doing laundry and sewing; however, they were always eager to branch out into new avenues.[42] They established a weaving operation in the 1770s by accepting Elizabeth Hauser, a local teenager who knew how to weave, into the Single Sisters after an attempt to get a weaver from Pennsylvania had failed.[43] Mary Elrod and Mary Flood kept the operation going in the following decade.[44]

The female Moravian artisans were not limited to the Single Sisters. If a person, regardless of sex, was competent in a trade, the Moravians usually had no objections to their setting up in business for themselves. After her husband's death five years earlier, Sarah Buttner in 1786 chose to move to Salem from Rowan County to work as a weaver.[45] Buttner's talents were not limited to weaving, however. When she asked the *Aufseher Collegium* for a girl to help with her growing tailor shop in 1797, the board decided not to allow her to expand her business and reminded her that she was only to do sewing "for her own livelihood."[46] Apparently, the *Collegium* did not want Buttner to become too successful.

Two more women weavers stand out among backcountry artisans. In 1781, Joseph Hughes of Salisbury bound out a "certain Mulattoe Girl named Ester, a slave" to Joseph Hickman "for . . . Two years and five months . . . to Learn the art and Mistery of a weaver." Four years later Hickman's son, Joseph Jr., appeared before Justices of the Peace Michael Brown and Valentine Beard and swore to the completion of Ester's apprenticeship and her knowledge of weaving.[47] A survey of orphans' court and apprenticeship indentures indicates that Ester may have been the only non-white in Rowan County apprenticed to learn a trade. She is the only slave artisan positively identified in the official records.[48]

Although not a slave, Ann Baker found herself in an equally interesting situation following the death of her husband Michael in 1776. Instead of taking the path of instant remarriage, which many widows with underage children chose, Baker chose to create her own financial security by expanding her spinning and weaving operation with at least one apprentice, Nansey Jolley. In 1782, with one son grown and gone from home, Baker was doing well enough to be among a handful of women on the Surry County Tax List; when the census taker came in 1790, she headed a household that included two males over sixteen, six males under sixteen, and two other females.[49] No doubt some members of Baker's household were her employees.

Like their male counterparts, women artisans spanned the economic scale. In fact, Elizabeth Maxwell Steele, Salisbury's wealthiest female resident in the eighteenth century, was probably a spinster and a weaver. Steele is also the best documented woman artisan in the entire backcountry. According to her unpublished biography by Archibald Henderson, the Maxwell family emigrated to the North Carolina backcountry in the second quarter of the eighteenth century. Elizabeth Maxwell was born in 1733.

Around 1750 she married Robert Gillespie, a merchant, who ran an ordinary/store in Salisbury with a partner, Thomas Bashford, beginning in 1756.[50] They had two children. While returning home to Salisbury from Fort Dobbs during the Indian uprising of 1759, Robert was slain and scalped by Cherokees.[51]

Robert Gillespie owned extensive tracks of land and left his widow financially secure. In 1760 she bought land, and probably a house, from William Williams, a hatter, in the north square of Salisbury to operate her own tavern.[52] Elizabeth did well enough in the tavern business to continue buying land in Salisbury and Rowan County, purchases that historian Ramsey feels showed her to be a shrewd, capable woman.[53] In 1763 she married for the second time, taking neighbor William Steele, the tavernkeeper and merchant in Salisbury who was a native of Lancaster, Pennsylvania, as her husband.[54] A 1761 entry for elisabath [*sic*] in William Steele's Cash Account book that shows neither prices nor cash paid for the items listed indicates that their relationship had been close for some time.[55] Elizabeth had two more children by William, and their marriage lasted until his death in 1773.

Although no authorities have referred to Elizabeth Steele as an artisan, the evidence is compelling. The inventory taken of the portion of her estate that was not bequeathed after her death in 1791 mentions four spinning wheels, two for wool and two for linen, cards, and a flax hackle; she also owned five sheep and a pair of sheep shears.[56] Clearly, wool and flax were being processed and spun in her household.

More interesting, however, is that Elizabeth Steele took Allen Campbell, orphan of Collin Campbell, as an apprentice to learn the trade of weaver in August 1781.[57] No weaving equipment was mentioned in her inventory because she probably agreed to give it to Allen when he completed his indenture. However, the inventory does list "a quantity of home spun cloth," another sign that cloth was being woven at the Steeles'. Further evidence comes from an invoice to the estate from William Watt, a clothier, who charged Elizabeth Steele sixteen shillings for the "Dressing of 16 1/2 yds of cloth."[58] Dressing, which consisted of washing the fabric to clean it and size it, was the last step in processing cloth before it could be made into anything. In addition, earlier invoices from tailor Arthur Erwin and an anonymous tailor charge only for making clothes (and not for supplying the fabric), which indicates that the family supplied the material from which they were made.[59]

Elizabeth Steele owned at least five slaves, and the possibility exists that the slaves did the spinning and perhaps the weaving. However, since she grew up on the North Carolina frontier in the second quarter of the eighteenth century, chances are great that Elizabeth Steele learned how to spin, weave, and sew with great proficiency. This knowledge undoubtedly helped her to supervise the work of her slaves and convince the Rowan County Orphan's Court that she could adequately provide for Allen Campbell's instruction in weaving. Finally, Elizabeth Steele had strong ties to the artisan community of Rowan County. Invoices and receipts document her business with Tobias Forror, blacksmith; Henry Barroth, potter; Ann Crosby, seamstress; Jonathan Boone, joiner; John Lewis Beard, tanner; and Arthur Erwin, tailor. These records show not only that Steele patronized local artisans but that a local market existed for the artisans' skills.[60]

Elizabeth Steele was not a typical female artisan. Her wealth and her continued control over her finances after she married William Steele, her appearances in the public record, and her wealth characterize her as highly unusual.

As married women or widows with control over their finances, Elizabeth Steele and Ann Baker had a distinct advantage over single women artisans: they had the respect of society. Not all women artisans were models of industry and propriety, but the court records show that single female artisans ran afoul of the law more frequently than other women. Rowan County criminal action papers reveal spinsters who were involved in adulterous relationships (sometimes resulting in illegitimate children), stealing, and slander, and who were victims of violent crimes. Ironically, these women were not the criminal misfits of Rowan County they appear to be, but rather social outcasts whose "crime" was attempting to remain in control of their economic destiny. Instead of getting married (or remarried) and being subsumed by their husband's identity, a handful of women in Rowan County chose to retain their own identity by remaining unmarried and financially independent. Single women tended to postpone marriage and remain independent wage earners, especially during prosperous economic periods.[61]

By remaining single, these women violated the social expectations for women to marry. Even worse by eighteenth-century moral standards, the decision not to marry did not stop at least three women artisans from behaving as if they were married. For trying to express their sexuality while remaining in control of their finances, Sarah Barrs and Joseph Thomas, Sarah Pincer and Francis Metcalf, and Sarah Stamon and William Watson were summoned before the Court because "divers times . . . [they] did criminally copulate and cohabit and live together in the constant habitual practice of Fornication against the decency and good order of Society an evil example to all others."[62]

Single professional women had more at risk in backcountry society than being found guilty of copulation and cohabitation. Because they were unmarried, risked possible public knowledge of any sexual liaisons, and maintained control over their incomes, they were easy targets for society's wrath, manifested in many different forms: possible beatings, rape, and accusations of stealing. Spinsters Agnes Osbrough, Catherine Ervington, Isabella Moore, and Mary Osbrough filed charges in the Rowan Court of Pleas and Quarter or Salisbury District Superior Court for being physically assaulted by men; Ervington also claimed that William Nettle raped her.[63]

These women may have been the victims of fellow artisans who were not accustomed to dealing with women on a professional basis. Three of the men charged with assault against women artisans were male artisans: William Williams, a hatter who was accused twice, James Townsley, a tinsmith, and John Lewis Beard, a tanner and butcher. For Williams and Beard, who practiced trades in which they had occasion to interact with female artisans, the possibility of friction with female professionals becomes greater.

Another possible explanation for the sometimes frequent appearance of women artisans in the records is that women artisans held grudges against those individuals whom they perceived to treat them unfairly. John Johnston accused Ann Lock of stealing six pewter spoons, and James Hemphill accused Agnes Osborough of taking a peck of meal.[64] Lock was later accused of unspecified charges and taken to trial by the king's prosecutor in the Court of Pleas and Quarter but found not guilty.[65] Agnes Osborough's luck did not improve, however. During the next two years she went to court against James Osborough and Matthew Long and lost each case.[66] Agnes and her sister Mary both brought assault charges against tanner John Lewis Beard on the same day.[67]

While these women all seem to have had sporadic brushes with the law, Isabella Moore made a virtual career of it. A spinster, Isabella Moore had a distinct advantage over most of the women in Rowan County in that she was a property owner. A deed for purchasing lot 4 in the southeast square of Salisbury from Andrew Bailie in 1763 marked her first appearance (out of ten) in the Rowan County legal records.[68] However, most of the times that Moore showed up in the records, the consequences were far more serious than closing a land deal. An anonymous Rowan County lawyer recorded in his account book that in March 1765 Robert Johnston, a Salisbury hatter, took Moore all the way to Superior Court for slander. Whatever she said must have been rather powerful, as Johnston paid his lawyer five pounds to try the case.[69] Moore may have accused Johnston of being the father of her six-month-old illegitimate child. However, when the Rowan County Orphan's Court took away the baby and put him under the guardianship of John Johnson four months later, Moore said he was the son of James Craige.[70]

Isabella Moore's penchant for trouble continued into later years. She entered "a plea of Trespass, Assault, and Battery &c.," against tinsmith James Townsley for damages in the amount of twenty pounds proclamation money in July 1767.[71] Only nine months later, Moore was charged with stealing a shift and a handkerchief from Eleanor Morris, and at the trial in April she was found guilty and sentenced "to receive 30 lashes on her bare back at the public whipping post at 3 o'clock this afternoon."[72]

In *Women's Life and Work* Spruill wrote, "Superior women in frontier settlements were strong, daring, and self-reliant, as well as skillful and industrious."[73] Ester, Ann Baker, and even Isabella Moore are just a few examples of that statement's truth. However, Ester, Baker, and Moore were more than superior women on the frontier; they were artisans who spun, wove, and sewed in addition to their normal household chores. Because of the exploitation of married women's economic lives by their husbands, the actual number of Rowan County women who produced thread, cloth, and clothing, or who contributed their needlework skills to their husband's craft, will never be known. The identification of a few female artisans through occasional legal documents and evidence that not all women practiced these skills as part of housewifery show that the reinterpretation of artisans working in the southern backcountry needs to include female artisans as well.

Although acknowledging the additional economic roles women filled in the eighteenth and nineteenth centuries, previous authors for numerous reasons have not formally called these women artisans. As Mary H. Blewett notes in the introduction to her book *Men, Women and Work*, women's work and labor experiences have always been interpreted in the context of the male paradigm.[74] Historians have portrayed the female work experience in terms of the numerous differences from rather than the obvious similarity to the male model: both resulted in production. In many recent studies of artisans in urban areas on the cusp of industrialization, women seamstresses are portrayed not as skilled artisans who enter the work force because of economic forces beyond their control, but as interlopers who willingly undercut male journeyman tailors to get jobs.[75]

The differences between women and men artisans include training, work locations, and economic reality. Although in Rowan County many orphaned girls learned how to spin or weave through apprenticeships identical to the boys in the county, in New England and the Middle Colonies large manufactories or spinning schools were a favorite mode of "poor relief" that provided women with a skill.[76] Nevertheless, women's training did not include the unspoken expectations, which served as the foundation of all male apprenticeships and journeyman positions, that age, experience, and hard work could lead them to the highest economic level as a self-employed master.[77]

In *Out to Work* Alice Kessler-Harris points out that training in skills associated with housewifery offered none of the economic protection of the traditional apprenticeships. Even though occupations such as spinster or weaver could be quite lucrative, they were taught to women as future wives with household subsistence, not full-time employment, in mind.[78] The fact that most women artisans worked within their homes and used their profits to run the household rather than expand businesses did not lessen their skill, however.

The recognition of women working as spinsters and weavers in Rowan County and the research concerning the household mode of production should also help destroy the "superwoman" myth of the colonial housewife who cooked and preserved everything the family ate; reared the children; spun, wove, and dyed the material out of which she sewed the family's clothes and linens and knitted their stockings; took care of the garden; worked the fields when her husband and sons were unable; and served as nurse and midwife to her family and community.[79] Perpetuated by the Centennial celebration of 1876 and the subsequent colonial revival movement, the myth continues due to the lack of serious research on colonial women in the South. Perhaps the knowledge that women worked as professional artisans in the southern backcountry rather than simply augmenting the skills of the backwoods housewife, will result in wider recognition of the existence of colonial women artisans.

SEVEN

Artisans, the Regulator Crisis, and Politics in Rowan County

Artisans played a profound role in the economic transformation of Rowan County, but they were less important in political affairs. Other studies of artisans in early America—which have focused on urban areas—have shown that when artisans had an intense interest in economic issues that directly affected them, these artisans frequently became involved in political organizations with similar agendas. As previous chapters have shown, backcountry artisans cared about economic issues that affected them personally, such as the development of a market economy with merchants and a good road system that tied them into a trans-Atlantic network. However, no group participation in politics occurred among Rowan County artisans as a result of the economic development of the county. The reason for this difference appears to be two-fold: their geographical location in the backcountry removed Rowan County artisans from the immediacy of the colonial politics experienced by their urban counterparts, and, because of the developing nature of the society they lived in, politics simply was *not* a priority for them; economic success at their craft *was*.

This chapter will begin with an examination of artisan participation in the most important political event in colonial North Carolina, the War of the Regulators. While the artisans as a group did not take sides during the crisis, quite a few artisans were drawn into the crisis on an individual basis. The remainder of the chapter will take a look at artisans who found themselves in the public eye for reasons other than politics—usually financial or criminal activity.

Artisans who were prominent in Rowan County politics often filled offices such as sheriff or justice of the peace, and many others took lesser roles such as constable or jury duty. The majority of artisan studies have focused on the effect of local and national politics and economics on artisans and their subsequent activism as a group to influence those matters. Rowan County did not have a mechanic population with a common conscience, and artisans in the county never acted as a group. Even though Rowan County had merchants and artisans who operated within the bounds of a market economy that had ties to large urban areas and the trans-Atlantic community, their participation was not so great, nor their community so large, as to be unduly affected by the same forces which threatened those professions in larger colonial urban areas. An absence of group political activism on the part of artisans does not mean political activism was completely absent from the county, however. When a group of disgruntled backcountry residents challenged rampant corruption in local government, the War of the Regulation brought the backcountry briefly to its knees. Some Rowan County residents were Regulators and others were corrupt government officials; however, the county's geographic location west of the Yadkin River considerably lessened the effects of the Regulator crisis on its population. The Rowan County artisans who did participate in politics, such as Andrew Allison and Edward Hughes, did so as individuals and not as representatives of the region's artisans.

Artisans were an integral factor in backcountry society since its inception. Most of these men considered, and identified, themselves primarily as craftsmen.[1] Yet they decided to supplement their work as artisans with farming when they helped settle Rowan County in the 1740s. These artisan-farmers lived in a geographically isolated, rural area with an economy clearly based in agriculture. A market economy eventually evolved in Rowan County in which artisans and merchants provided goods and services to the local populace. In addition, the merchants also possessed crucial ties to larger economic markets in South Carolina, Pennsylvania, and even England. The existence of artisans practicing a wide variety of trades and merchants able to order goods from England reveals that Rowan County residents had a substantially higher standard of living available to them than previously thought.

Salisbury, the county seat of Rowan County, also became its economic center when merchants and artisans moved there to profit from the potential customers the courts and legal system brought to the town. Bethabara and Salem, the towns the Moravians settled on the Wachovia Tract, also served as commercial enclaves for the county, although their control by the church in Pennsylvania retarded their economic development.

In addition to the economic activity in Rowan County, the county also fell on the fringes of the backcountry area which hosted the War of the Regulators. In 1766 backcountry residents of Orange, Rowan, and Anson counties realized they had lost control of their local government to courthouse rings. These officials either set abnormally high tax rates, defrauded, and charged illegal rates for government services, or they were generally incompetent and ignored the presence of these crimes. Between 1754 and

1768, county officials in Orange, Rowan, and Anson counties embezzled public funds and taxes while county registrars and clerks extorted unfair fees from the population they represented. Sheriffs frequently seized the property of individuals who could not pay their taxes; these officials later sold the property to their cronies for less than its actual value.

As the behavior of millwright James Carter demonstrates, while on the periphery of the actual crisis, Rowan County did experience such conduct from some of its officials. A politically successful artisan and multiple officeholder, Carter was the chief agent of corruption in Rowan County. Born in Southampton township, Bucks County, Pennsylvania, during the second decade of the eighteenth century, Carter left his home before 1736 and relocated in the Appoquinimink Creek district on the border between Pennsylvania (now Delaware) and Maryland. Caught in a dispute over land and religion with the authorities in Maryland, Carter found himself a prisoner in the Cecil County jail for debt in 1740. Later the same year, William Rumsey, a prominent Marylander, intervened in Carter's case and obtained his release from jail. Rumsey became Carter's patron and friend, lending him vast sums of money to build mills and teaching him the formal craft of surveying. In return, Carter witnessed Rumsey's will, which was probated in 1743.

Following Rumsey's death, Carter moved to Augusta County, Virginia, where he built a mill and lived for approximately three years before moving on to the Yadkin River in 1747.[2] Carter owned more than a thousand acres of land throughout Rowan County, but instead of going into land speculation or devoting himself full time to his trade, he quickly became involved in local politics as a multiple officeholder. Carter certainly had a base of support on which to draw: he knew at least seven of the founding families of Rowan while they were still in Pennsylvania and may well have become their voice in local government during the early years of settlement. In addition to witnessing innumerable land grants, in 1753 Carter became a justice of the peace, a commissioner to supervise the building of the courthouse, a commissioner to purchase legal books for the Court of Pleas and Quarter, a member of the surveying team responsible for running the dividing line between Rowan and Orange counties, and the Rowan County registrar of deeds. The court also granted him a license to run a tavern.[3]

More responsibility came to Carter the following year when, in his role as Granville's deputy-surveyor, he held the warrant for the 640-acre tract of land destined to become the county seat.[4] On February 11, 1755, the town of Salisbury was formally created when William Churton and Richard Vigers, Granville's agents, granted "635 acres of land for a township" to James Carter and Hugh Forster, trustees.[5]

As if Carter did not already have enough offices to fulfill, Gov. Matthew Rowan appointed him to the Assembly on February 27, 1754, and (probably with the outbreak of Indian hostilities) had him commissioned a major in the colonial militia. In May when some Rowan County residents complained "that a party of Indians suspected to be Catawbor have Committed several gross abuses on the White People of Rowan and Anson Countys," Carter and his fellow justice of the peace and militia officer, Alexander Osborne, were requested to investigate the situation and report back to the Assembly.[6] Carter proposed, and received (with John Brandon), a sum of five hundred pounds to be used "to purchase arms and ammunition for the defense of the frontier province."[7]

Carter had come a long way from debtor's prison in Maryland to his exalted status in Rowan County. However, his former incarceration may have made a lasting impression on him never to be without funds again, and the combination of offices he held made it too easy to get rich quickly. By 1756 Carter knew he had overstepped legal boundaries; in order to avoid losing his property, he deeded his home, his slaves, and all his belongings to his daughter and son-in-law, Mary and Jonathan Boone, as well as some land to his granddaughter, Abigail.[8]

In the May 1757 session of the provincial Assembly, John Starkey, the public treasurer for the southern district, moved that Carter answer charges that he never purchased the arms and ammunition for which the Assembly had allotted him five hundred pounds three years earlier.[9] When Carter failed to answer the charges of the Assembly by the fall, the House followed through on the Council's recommendation and expelled him from his seat and stripped him of his commission in the militia.[10] Meanwhile, back in Rowan County, Sheriff David Jones sold 350 acres of Carter's land on Crane Creek to pay a debt he owed Sabinah Rigby, William Rumsey's widow.[11] Carter's troubles still had not ended, however. Four years later the Assembly found Carter, in his office as the Registrar of Deeds, guilty of "exacting and extorting considerable sums of Money from several Persons" without providing them with the surveys and deeds they required.[12] This last episode with illegal activity forced Carter out of public life forever, although he continued to live quietly in Salisbury until his death in 1765.

The impressive extent of Carter's officeholding notwithstanding, people abused other county offices more easily for profit. The most important officer in local government was the sheriff, whose duties mainly served the Court of Pleas and Quarter. Appointed by the governor, the sheriff had to be a freeholder residing in the county and backed by a bond for one thousand pounds sterling in order "that he should faithfully discharge the duties of that office and account for and pay all publick and private moneys by him received as sheriff." The sheriff spent the majority of his time in office fulfilling duties of law enforcement such as serving and executing all writs and processes (for which he received a commission), administrating the county jail, imprisoning criminals, inflicting corporal punishment, attending executions, viewing dead bodies (a duty later passed on to the newly created office of coroner), holding elections for vestrymen and assemblymen, and calling up jurors. Beyond a doubt, the collection of public duties was the most important aspect of the sheriff's job, as well as the one which tempted even the most honest man. Furnished with a list of taxables in the county, the sheriff collected the public or provincial poll tax along with the county tax. The sheriff could continue in office indefinitely, as long as every two years he could provide certificates or receipts from the treasurer proving that he had collected and turned in the public taxes.[13]

Eight men served as sheriff in Rowan County between 1753 and 1770; half of them were artisans. All four artisans—weaver David Jones, millwright Edward Hughes, carpenter Francis Lock, and tailor Andrew Allison—became players in the Regulator drama.

David Jones was a prime example of incompetence in county government. Originally from Haverford township in Chester County, Pennsylvania, Jones moved to Oley township in the same county in 1733. Six years later his name showed up on a petition in Prince Georges County, Maryland, asking Governor Samuel Ogle to divide the county in order to have a courthouse located closer to the settlement in which Jones lived. Evidently the petition was successful, as subsequent references to Jones in Maryland are found in the Frederick County records. By 1754 Jones was living on a 220-acre tract in Rowan County adjoining Samuel Bryan, one of Morgan Bryan's sons.[14]

Jones became the first sheriff of Rowan County in 1753 based on his filing the provincial tax collection accounts in March 1754.[15] His reappointment to the office the following year and the Moravians' complimentary (albeit politically naive) observations showed Jones to be a conscientious, if not somewhat overworked, sheriff.[16] Kept extremely busy all over the county collecting taxes and supervising elections, Jones occasionally failed to fulfill all his duties: once he neglected to attend Orphans Court and another time he did not return a bail bond on time.[17]

In the summer of 1756, Jones began to fall behind in settling his tax accounts with the Court of Pleas and Quarter.[18] While local officials continued to ask him for the records, they did not perceive Jones's lack of recordkeeping as a serious problem, and they recommended him for another term as sheriff. When Jones failed to reply to the court's request, the justices finally turned the inept sheriff over to Attorney General Robert Jones, who promptly filed suit against him for £1205, the balance of taxes he owed the county.[19] What Jones did with the money, if he even had it, remains a mystery. Not surprisingly, he kept a low profile in the county following his departure from office, witnessing a few deeds and even serving on jury duty. Records indicate that Jones did not have large sums of money to spend, which may explain why he never paid the government the £1205 8s. 7d. officials said he owed them.[20]

With officials such as Carter and Jones all too common throughout the region, in 1766 backcountry residents, under the leadership of Herman Husband, decided to "regulate" their local government, beginning with the formation of the Sandy Creek Association. The Regulators' attempts to make government officials comply strictly and continuously with the public will on the local and colonial level fell victim to the far-reaching political ties of the courthouse rings. Finally, frustration gave in to anger, and the self-styled Regulators challenged the government to comply with their demands by withholding their taxes and committing sporadic acts of violence.

The failure of some Rowan County inhabitants to pay taxes drew the sheriffs, Francis Lock and Andrew Allison, directly into the crisis. Lock, a carpenter, originated from Derry or Paxtang township in Lancaster County, Pennsylvania, and settled in Rowan County by 1752; he lived in the Irish Settlement and took office as sheriff in 1764.[21] Lock did not become involved in local politics as quickly as his predecessors, but he soon cultivated friendships with powerful men in the county by conducting land transactions with them, witnessing deeds, and sitting on petit juries. By 1759 Lock received a commission as an ensign in the Rowan County militia, and two years later he served on the grand jury.[22]

Lock became sheriff of Rowan County just as the Regulator crisis commenced, and he must have sensed trouble ahead. Instead of beginning his term by complaining about the insufficiency of the jail, as had previous sheriffs, he contracted with workmen "to repair & make the Gaol Sufficient to retain prisoners therein."[23] Lock's first two years as sheriff were relatively benign, he even settled his tax accounts for 1764 within a few months of the end of the term.[24] Because of the mounting Regulator problems in 1766, Lock did not file the settlement of his 1765 tax accounts until the spring of 1767.[25] In fact, his tax accounts for 1766 preoccupied Lock even before the year had ended, since more than a third of the taxables in the county refused to pay their taxes. Lock told the Court "that the 1833 persons mentioned in the above account were delinquents, insolvents, or insurgents Mob or such who generally refuse to pay their taxes and rescue on distress."[26] The year before there were only 292 delinquent taxables.

Lock had financial motivation to settle those tax accounts: the county would not pay him his commission until final receipt of the tax money. Lock earned a commission only on the taxes he collected successfully. Needless to say, the Regulators seriously reduced the income Lock expected to make in his role as tax collector. Undaunted, he continued to try to collect the taxes even after he was out of office, but backcountry tensions were high, and Lock soon ran into problems. According to his sworn statement of October 14, 1768, eight days earlier Lock demanded that James Dunlap pay his county taxes for 1764, 1765, and 1766. When Dunlap "obstantly Refused to pay the saime [*sic*] or any part thereof," Lock seized his horse, a sorrel gelding, for back payment. Dunlap gathered fifteen of his friends and they "unjustly unlawfully and violently Rescued" the gelding from Lock.[27]

Three weeks later the situation had not improved, and Lock reported to the Court of Pleas and Quarter that he had "used particular Endavours to Collect the Said Tax" from the remaining delinquents, "but was Violently Opposed in the Execution of the Said Office particullary by those Who have Lately Styled themselves Regulators, by which Means he Declares he is rendered in cupable of Making a further Settlement."[28] Lock returned to Court in 1769 to repeat his description of the circumstances surrounding his non-collection of taxes.[29]

Lock was not alone in his predicament. None of the sheriffs who served after him until the Battle of Alamance could collect all the county taxes, either. The last artisan to serve as sheriff before 1770 was Andrew Allison, a tailor. Originally from Coletrain township in Lancaster County, Allison came to Rowan County in 1751 and helped form the Fourth Creek Settlement.[30] Allison was no political novice. An early arrival to the backcountry and a settlement organizer, he commanded enough respect to be named one of the first justices of the peace for Rowan County. Appointed sheriff in 1768, Allison, a stable force in politics, had an even more difficult time collecting taxes than Lock: only 205 people paid their taxes, 87 fewer than had paid Lock. In a statement to the court Allison explained, "Owing to a Refractory disposition of a Sett of People calling themselves Regulators Refusing to pay any Taxes or other Public money to a Sheriff or any other Officer whatsoever by which means many Well disposed People neglects to discharge their Public dues as the Burden must Consequently fall very heavy on the well meaning Few & desires to be Recommended to his Excellency the Governor Councill & Generall Assembly for Such Redress as they in their Wisdom Shall Seem Meet."[31]

The failure to collect taxes placed Allison and Lock (as well as other sheriffs, including Griffith Rutherford and William Temple Coles) in a precarious political as well as financial situation. As political appointees of the governor, they wanted to make sure their intention to collect taxes while sheriff was taken seriously. Above all, they did not want to appear to be Regulator sympathizers by not collecting the taxes due the county. To prove their attention to duty and their intent to collect back taxes, in December 1771 Francis Lock, Andrew Allison, Griffith Rutherford, and William Temple Coles asked the Assembly for permission to collect the arrearages of taxes and file their settlements.[32] The scheme worked for Lock, Allison, and Rutherford; two years later "An Estimate of the Balances due from the Several Sheriffs and Collector of Public Taxes, to the Public of North Carolina" listed amounts owed by all four of the pre-Regulator sheriffs (including David Jones and Edward Hughes) and William Temple Coles.[33] Both Lock and Allison filed their final tax accounts as sheriffs on November 7, 1772. Lock eventually collected from 2800 taxables, leaving 359 delinquents, and Allison ultimately solicited taxes from 4040 individuals, leaving 618 delinquents.[34]

Andrew Allison had an even greater reason to dislike the Regulators than just their refusal to pay taxes: they inadvertently destroyed the political career of his son Adam. Gov. Tryon appointed Adam to succeed his father as sheriff of Rowan County for 1769. The timing was ill-fated, however; even though Adam showed "his readiness and earnest desire to accept the said office of sheriff for said County," he could not procure the securities required by law for the faithful execution of the office from his friends because "they doubted not either of his integrity or honesty but the confused state and present disturbances together with the scarcity of circulating money in this county."[35]

Francis Lock and Andrew Allison continued to be active in Rowan County politics following their demanding tenure as sheriffs. Lock filled a series of lesser offices in the county, such as road overseer, special commissioner to evaluate the quality of a recently constructed bridge, and county coroner, before he found lasting fame as a colonel in the North Carolina militia during the Revolution.[36] Although he kept a lower political profile, Andrew Allison returned to duty as Justice of the Peace, an office he held until his death in 1780.[37]

Regulator committees in Rowan, Anson, and Orange counties continued their attempt to make county government accountable to the freeholders. In 1768 citizens of Rowan and Orange counties petitioned the House of Representatives for help in the matter.[38] As time progressed but a solution to the backcountry's problems did not, Rowan County officials decided to mediate with the rebels to bring an end to the crisis. In March 1771, officials met with local Regulators "to Settle and pay unto any and Every Person within the County Any and all such Sums or claims of Money as we or our Deputies have taking through Inadvertancy or otherwise over and Above what we Severally ought to have taken for fees."[39]

Further east in Orange County, the movement remained more radical. In the fall of 1770 a group of Regulators embarked on a serious spree of violence at Hillsborough Superior Court. After a mob vandalized the courthouse and attacked some individuals, anxious anti-Regulators persuaded Gov. Tryon to lead military forces into the backcountry to put down the Regulators. Lacking the military discipline and training of the royal troops, the Regulators succumbed at the Battle of Alamance on May 16, 1771, ending the movement.[40]

A rather strange Rowan County footnote to the Regulator crisis involved David Jones's successor as sheriff, millwright Edward Hughes. Originally from Philadelphia County, Pennsylvania, Hughes arrived in Rowan County (via two years in the Valley of Virginia) in 1748 and settled near his friends James Carter, Morgan Bryan, and Squire Boone in the Bryan Settlement. Hughes very well may have been *the* first resident on the northwest Carolina frontier; he certainly owned one of the highest income-producing tracts of land in the entire backcountry. Situated on the east bank of the Yadkin, the Great Wagon Road ran right through his 314 acre estate, making his ferry and his ordinary highly profitable enterprises.[41]

Like James Carter, Hughes quickly became involved in local affairs. He was named justice of the peace at the county's formation, and the 640-acre grant from Granville for the town of Salisbury was registered in Hughes's name as trustee for the county.[42] As a result of his location east of the Yadkin River, Hughes served as one of the justices for the Wachovia Tract, and he often accompanied Sheriff David Jones on his visits to the Moravians. Hughes had a mutually beneficial relationship with the Moravians on a personal and official level. At the start of the Seven Years' War, the brethren warned Hughes of impending Indian attacks for which he was able to prepare. The cause of the alarm turned out to be just some hungry Cherokees from a fort near the Haw River, whom he fed and sent to another fort.[43] In return, Hughes accepted the brethren's refusal to sign a petition pertaining to military affairs in the county and noted their offer to contribute money or provisions to the frontier defense.[44] In the spring of 1759, Hughes notified the brethren that his house was surrounded by Indians and he needed help. A group of brethren responded by riding to Hughes's home, scaring off the Indians, and saving the family.[45]

Gov. Dobbs named Hughes Sheriff of Rowan County in July 1758. Six months into his term, Attorney General Jones summoned Hughes to the Supreme Court in Salisbury to execute an action of debt against him. Hughes (among others) had posted a security bond when the Assembly granted James Carter the money to purchase arms and ammunition for the frontier defense. After Carter embezzled the money, the attorney general tried to get the colony's money back, but Carter and the other securities were insolvent, leaving only Edward Hughes. Fortunately for Hughes, no judgment could be served against him while he filled the office of sheriff; unfortunately, his alignment with Carter probably cost him his job the next year.[46] When the Court held elections to recommend a sheriff for 1759 to the governor, Hughes apparently won over John Brevard, who was also involved with Carter, and Benjamin Milner, who was not. The Court later reconsidered, scratched out the results of the first vote, and the governor appointed Benjamin Milner high sheriff for the following year.[47]

Hughes remained active in county politics as a justice and a member of the committee appointed to help Benjamin Milner settle his tax accounts as sheriff.[48] After being called into court and warned in 1760, Hughes presented his complete tax accounts for the county in 1763.[49] Thrown out of office and spurned by the leadership elite over the Carter affair, Hughes became irascible. Angry over the lack of support he received from the Moravians (who did their best to stay out of politics) and his friends when he felt he needed it most, he became increasingly bitter toward them. He began by harassing guests at the Moravians' Tavern in Bethabara; as a justice Hughes would arrest people the brethren thought were innocent and defend the ones found guilty.[50] Then he began making slanderous statements about his former friends.[51]

Hughes's campaign against the Moravians climaxed in March 1771, just as the county resolved its differences with the Regulators. Nonetheless, Hughes came to the tavern with a group of men claiming to be Regulators and demanded to see Frederick Marshall, Jacob Bonn, and Traugott Bagge, the recognized leaders of the brethren outside of Wachovia. After listening to Hughes's wild accusations, the brethren calmly informed him that any questions concerning land would have to be answered by Granville's agents or church officials in Pennsylvania. (See Appendix B.) When his threats as a pseudo-Regulator did not frighten the Moravians, Hughes tried to drive away their business by posting notices along the banks of the Yadkin River that Indians were about to invade the backcountry and attack Bethabara.[52] This episode marked one of Hughes's last appearances in the public records, even though he lived into the nineteenth century.

The conditions that caused the conflict and motivated the Regulators and the anti-Regulators have long been a subject of historical debate. Most historians analyzing the Regulation have interpreted it as either a sectional conflict or a class conflict. Seizing upon the geographic and economic differences between the eastern Tidewater plantation-based economy and the western Piedmont agrarian economy, historians endorsing the sectional approach portrayed the backcountry as a remote, isolated region, governed by corrupt officials, that the eastern-dominated provincial government ignored and left underrepresented. Beset by economic problems, over-taxation, and corrupt officials with no relief in sight, westerners revolted. This theory, pioneered by John Spencer Bassett at the end of the nineteenth century, has continued to gain support from historians.[53] Proponents of the class conflict theory such as Kay and Cary have used quantitative analysis of tax assessments to highlight substantial differences in the economic situations of the opposing factions, depicting the anti-Regulators as members of the wealthy, governing class and the Regulators as an oppressed, lower class.[54]

More recently, however, other historians have attributed the Regulator movement to the general chaos caused by the great migration of settlers into the backcountry during the third quarter of the eighteenth century. In *"Poor Carolina,"* Ekirch theorizes that the massive influx of people into the backcountry created a fluid society devoid of a traditional political power structure. Instead, backcountry leaders were recent arrivals, without ties to the area, who had an opportunistic view of the region and went into politics not to serve the community out of a sense of duty, but to exploit the situation and personally benefit. Ekirch argues that this corruption was the fundamental cause of the Regulator disturbances. The legitimacy of a group of officials with an already tenuous claim to authority was undermined, and new backcountry residents who were unfamiliar with their leaders became instantly suspicious of them when reports of malfeasance arose.[55]

In "Planters, Merchants, and Lawyers," Whittenburg maintains that almost all of the first emigrants to the backcountry were farmers, and until the late 1750s they lived in an overwhelmingly agricultural society. Later arrivals to the backcountry in the 1760s included a professional class of lawyers and merchants (with ties to the provincial government) who took over the political and social leadership roles previously held by planters. Angry at their displacement by corrupt outsiders, the planters rebelled.[56] In a later quantitative study of settlement patterns in the backcountry, Whittenburg refined his argument to identify a "burnt-over district" in the center of the backcountry that included the south-central and western portions of Orange County, the portion of Rowan which fell east of the Yadkin River, and northeastern Anson County. According to Whittenburg, a diverse mixture of ethnic and religious inhabitants, along with problems patenting land claims (because of the closing of the Granville District land office in 1763), added to, if not created, the chaos and turmoil (including the Regulator Movement) that occurred in western North Carolina.[57]

Although one contemporary observed that "the merchant, the lawyer, the tavernkeeper, the artisan, and court officials, adventurers in the perennial pursuit of gain" were among the recent arrivals to the backcountry, this characterization does not hold true for Rowan County.[58] By virtue of its location mainly west of the Yadkin River on the frontier, Rowan County was much more susceptible to the problems caused by the French and Indian War, which actually decreased immigration to the region in the late 1750s and early 1760s. While a disproportionately large number of artisans appeared in Rowan County in 1759, and the average rate of annual artisan immigration increased by approximately one-third between the 1750s and 1760s, the vast majority of these later artisans did not practice trades which promised a "perennial pursuit of gain." In fact, a significant portion of those later artisans were Moravians, who would not have actively participated in politics, including the Regulation.

As the cases of James Carter, Edward Hughes, and David Jones show, Rowan County was not completely devoid of political problems. A single announcement in the Court of Pleas and Quarter minutes illustrates that Rowan County experienced at least some of the "professionalization" which occurred in other backcountry counties. On April 21, 1768, the court "Ordered that anyone making a motion to the court must address it by an attorney unless expressly directed otherwise by the court."[59] Evidently, enough lawyers had arrived in Rowan County to force the court to follow proper legal etiquette and make the residents pay their fees.

The problems with corruption and embezzlement that occurred elsewhere in the backcountry also occurred in Rowan County, but clearly not to the same extent. Certain factors—the settlement of Rowan before 1763, the ethnic and religious profile of its population, its location mainly west of the Yadkin River—meant that fewer people became agitated to the point of rebellion. Of those who did rebel or react, artisan participation in the Regulation was apparently negligible; no extant documents show artisans, as a group, organized to play any role in the crisis.

Quantitative analysis of those Rowan County artisans who could be associated with the Regulation in any manner supported the lack of discernable behavior among the group. In fact, fewer than 15 percent (49) of the 328 artisans working in Rowan County can be tied to the Regulation at all. From those names, 21 (6.4%) artisans can be identified as Regulators or sympathetic to the Regulation; 20 (6%) artisans came out against the Regulation; and 8 (2.4%) names appeared on both lists.[60] (See Tables 6 and 7.) The two groups do not reflect any definite patterns with regard to any of the various interpretations of the Regulation's causes. Similar complements of artisan types were involved on either side; comparable numbers of artisans on both sides were early and late arrivals to the backcountry. Wealth was impossible to measure because of the county's incomplete tax lists. When slave ownership was used as an indicator of wealth, the tax list indicated that only one artisan out of forty-nine was a slaveholder, and he was a Regulator, blacksmith Benjamin Merrill.[61] As for political office, four Regulators were constables; two anti-Regulators were constables and two

Table 6. Rowan County Artisans Involved in the Regulator Crisis

Regulators	Anti-Regulators
Adams, James, weaver	Alexander, Moses, blacksmith
Allin, John, carpenter	Allison, Andrew, tailor sheriff
Barton, William, cooper	Baxter, German, silversmith
Billingsley, James, carpenter C	Beck, John, cabinetmaker/gunsmith
Boone, Jonathan, joiner	Bradley, John, carpenter
Bullin, John, cooper	Cook, William, Jr., tanner
Clark, John, wagonmaker	Ernst, Johann, tanner
Cowan, John, gunsmith C	Henly, Derby, weaver
Graham, James, Sr., blacksmith C	Holder, Charles, saddler/carpenter
Hall, Thomas, weaver	Holder, George, carpenter/surveyor
McCuiston, John, blacksmith	Johnson, Robert, Jr., hatter
Merrill, Benjamin, blacksmith*	Lock, Francis, carpenter sheriff
Morrison, James, tailor	Marshall, George, joiner
Ramsey, James, shoemaker	Mitchell, John, wheelwright
Ryan, Edward, weaver	Moore, William, weaver
Smith, David, blacksmith	Patterson, James, blacksmith C
Smith, Thomas, weaver	Rodgers, John, saddler
Stuart, James, weaver C	Smith, Samuel, blacksmith C
Thompson, James, cooper	Strehorn, Gilbert, tailor
White, Thomas, tailor	Wilson, William, carpenter
Woods, Robert, carpenter/ weaver/cooper	
Names appearing on both lists	
Barr, James, weaver C	
Brown, William, millwright C	
Davis, James, carpenter C	
Mebane, William, weaver C	
Patterson, John, skinner C	
Smith, John, blacksmith C	
Thompson, John, cooper/shoemaker C	
Williams, William, hatter	

C: constable

*Slave owner

Source: Data base of individuals involved in Regulator movement compiled by James P. Whittenburg.

Table 7. Artisan Arrival Dates in Rowan County

Year	Regulator	Anti-Regulator[1]	Total[2]
1750	2	2	14
1751	1	0 (1)	3
1752	2	2	8
1753	0	0 (2)	20
1754	0	0	7
1755	0	0 (1)	17
1756	0	0 (1)	13
1757	1	0	10
1758	0	1	12
1759	4	4 (1)	35
1760	1	0 (1)	8
1750-1760	**11**	**9** (7)	**147**
1761	0	0	10
1762	1	0	14
1763	3	0	11
1764	0	1	8
1765	3	2	15
1766	0	3	29
1767	3	1 (1)	17
1768	1	1	29
1769	0	1	25
1770	1	1	23
1761-1770	**12**	**10 (1)**	**181**

[1]Numbers in parentheses are artisans whose names appeared on both lists.

[2]Total number of artisans arrived in county

Sources: Names of Regulators and Anti-Regulators supplied by James P. Whittenburg; artisan arrival dates compiled from data base of artisans in Rowan County in dBase III+ sorted by year of arrival.

were sheriffs, the aforementioned Francis Lock and Andrew Allison. But neither Lock nor Allison were recent arrivals to the county, Lock having arrived by 1752 and Allison by 1749.

This lack of group behavior on the part of Rowan County artisans in the Regulator crisis is mirrored in artisans' irregular holding of county offices. As some profiles of artisans who were active in public life will show, in addition to learning a craft during their apprenticeships, these men received an education in reading, writing, and mathematics so they would have the skills to operate their own shops one day. Such knowledge was in short supply on the northwestern Carolina frontier during the eighteenth century, and, in Rowan County at least, those individuals who possessed such skills soon became the rudiments of local government.

The level of education was probably the only common element among these artisans. Such lack of political organization and commonality of purpose in both the Regulator crisis and local officeholding demonstrates that politics was not a priority for rural artisans. However, an examination of the political inertness of Rowan County artisans begs a comparison to their well-organized and very active urban counterparts. As indicated earlier in the chapter, the rural environment appears to be the decisive variable in explaining the failure of Rowan County artisans to organize politically. Conversely, the urban environment may best explain the urban artisans' success at political organization.

Urban artisans typically made up a large percentage of a city's population. They usually lived in the same part of the city, with the populations of neighborhoods frequently determined by their trades and/or wealth. The urban location made artisans completely dependent on their craft for their livelihood. In the confines of the city, these artisans enjoyed close social and familial relationships, frequent contact with other tradesmen, access to recent news, membership in political groups and craft guilds, and regular attendance at the local tavern and maybe even church. All of these institutions provided craftsmen with many opportunities to form a common understanding of the world around them. This shared ideology, defined by Nash as an "awareness of the surrounding world . . . and reasoned reactions to the forces impinging upon one's life," led these mechanics to represent the interests of their class by holding political offices and to act or react as a group to political and economic events that endangered their well-being.[62] In short, the crucial element behind the political organization of urban artisans were the urban environment and the gathering of artisans in one location, not the artisans or their crafts.

If the urban environment provided the basis for group participation of artisans in politics, then the lack of such an environment, especially in the southern colonial backcountry, meant that rural artisans did not have the same opportunity to organize politically. In Rowan County, artisans formed a small percentage of the population, they lived far apart (by urban standards), and they did not depend completely on their craft for their livelihood: most of them also farmed. Few, if any, of the occasions that existed for artisan interaction in urban areas were present in Rowan County (especially among artisans practicing the same craft) because it was an overwhelmingly agrarian society. As a result of this isolation, when Rowan County artisans developed an "awareness of the surrounding world . . . and reasoned reactions to the forces impinging upon one's life" to the point of becoming involved in politics, they did so on an individual basis, not as representatives of an occupational group, as the rest of the chapter will show.

The only political office in Rowan County that artisans came close to monopolizing was the office of sheriff. Of the eight men who served as sheriff between 1753 and 1770, four were artisans: the aforementioned David Jones, 1753-1757; Edward Hughes, 1758; Francis Lock, 1764-1766; and Andrew Allison, 1767. These men held more than their education in common; all four of them came from Pennsylvania and were among the earliest settlers in Rowan County. While the records of all four men reveal that maintaining accurate accounts of tax revenues was just as difficult as actually collecting the taxes, each sheriff handled his office, and his subsequent problems, differently.

Unlike the one-year terms of sheriffs, justices of the peace were appointed by the governor during good behavior, which for all practical purposes meant life. Together the justices made up the Court of Pleas and Quarter, which administered civil and criminal law in the county. For their knowledge of the law and power to enforce it, justices found respect as dignified, honorable, and important men in the county.[63] Fifty-three men served as justices of the peace in Rowan County between 1753 and 1770, and six of them were known artisans. In addition to Andrew Allison, James Carter, and Edward Hughes, the justices included tanner George Henry Berger, carpenter John Ford, and blacksmith William Lynn.[64] These three men became justices quite a few years after Allison, Carter, and Hughes, and they represent how the leadership of the county changed to include a more accurate representation of the people who lived in Rowan.

William Lynn became a justice in 1761, approximately eight years after his arrival in Rowan County.[65] Evidence suggests that Lynn may have been from Talbot or Queen Anne's County, Maryland, and that he came to Rowan County via the Shenandoah Valley with his brothers John, James, and Andrew Lynn in the early 1750s.[66] Since William Lynn does not appear in the land records until 1762, but he lists "goods and Chattels Lands and Tenaments" as security for James Stewart to show up in court in March

1754, one of his brothers probably gave him some land in 1753 when they registered their deeds.[67] Lynn had no experience as a public official before he was sworn in as justice. In fact, his appearances before the court were limited to administering an estate and acting as guardian for an orphan, serving as a juror, and standing security for other people's debts.[68] Michael Miller, a cooper, in his record of these debts, hints that Lynn and farmer David Dayes did business with him. Perhaps Lynn forged the bands that held together Miller's barrels, used to store and transport Dayes' crop.[69]

Unlike many of his predecessors, Lynn did not make a career of politics. He did not own much land or witness a lot of other people's land transactions (as did other officeholders), and consequently his name rarely surfaces in the official records. The only other public position Lynn held was the office of road commissioner in 1774.[70] When he died fifteen years later, Lynn called himself a yeoman but left his blacksmithing tools to his son Israel.[71]

Carpenter John Ford probably did not arrive in Rowan County until the early 1760s. His immediate acquaintance with such powerful backcountry residents as land speculator Henry McCulloh, Salisbury land trustees James Carter and Hugh Forster, justice William Temple Coles, and his own neighbor John Frohock, coupled with his swift rise through the political ranks, suggests that Ford may have been one of the "adventurers in the perennial pursuit of gain" who relocated in the backcountry prior to the Regulator crisis.[72] Named an overseer of roads by the court in 1763 (the first year he appears in the records), less than two years later Gov. Tryon appointed him a justice of the peace.[73]

Outside of his identification as a carpenter in a 1767 deed, Ford's trade never entered the public record. Like many other artisans, though, he was financially diversified: Ford also owned a tavern and a public mill.[74] Ford's political career in Rowan County slowed down considerably following the Battle of Alamance, and he disappeared from Rowan County records altogether when his land was annexed to Surry County in 1773, which became part of Stokes County in 1789. He died in Stokes County in 1795.[75]

George Henry Berger represents another facet of the Rowan County population that gradually entered the public arena. Berger's background and activities in Rowan County are difficult to document because he was German. Not only did the non-Moravian German people live apart from the English people in Rowan County, the language barrier often kept German people out of the records, or English clerks anglicized their names beyond recognition. Ramsey notes in *Carolina Cradle* that a few German people were among the earliest settlers in Rowan County (although the majority of them came after 1752), but their ignorance of the English legal system and the language discouraged them from obtaining deeds to their lands, registering their stock marks, or becoming active in county affairs.[76] The German residents of Rowan County focused their attention on their family, their church, and their ethnic community. However, court records suggest that, like the Moravians, they selected a few bilingual individuals to act as their liaison with local government and to help with legal and financial matters.

George Henry Berger was one of these individuals. Berger probably came to Carolina as a young man from Germany via Pennsylvania in the 1750s, but he did not legally acquire a Rowan County land grant until 1761.[77] Once he became a freeholder, Berger fulfilled his civic obligations, such as jury duty, and his knowledge of the legal system and the language made him an indispensable resource in the German community. In the 1760s Berger's name appears in the court records witnessing documents between German parties, providing security for the administrators of Germans' estates and German tavernkeepers, and even giving testimony in civil and criminal cases involving Germans.[78] Gov. Tryon appointed Berger a justice of the peace in 1769, a move probably calculated to win political support for the governor from the backcountry Germans. Located west of the Yadkin River along Dutch or Second Creek and the various branches of Crane Creek, and fairly oblivious to the nuances of Anglo politics, the German community was staunchly anti-Regulator. Berger's appointment as justice provided the German settlers of Rowan County with an official voice in government in exchange for their support of the king.

Berger became more active in politics as time progressed. In addition to his responsibilities as a justice, during the 1770s Berger became a road commissioner, a captain in the militia, a town commissioner, and a member of the Rowan Committee of Safety.[79] By the last quarter of the eighteenth century, Berger was a respected and influential leader throughout Rowan County, and his presence was necessary to insure the success of any public endeavor in the region.[80]

Not all the Germans who became active in public life did so for their community. Johann Ludwig Barth arrived in Philadelphia from Rotterdam aboard the ship *Patience* in 1749. Six years later John Lewis Beard shows up in the Rowan County Deed Book witnessing the sale of a Salisbury town lot to Theodoras Feltmatt.[81] A butcher by trade, Beard established himself in business on four adjoining lots in Salisbury so his butchering would not interfere with the ordinary he ran in his dwelling house.[82] Beard intended to become an active and vital part of the backcountry community from the moment he arrived. While he, like Berger, occasionally helped his fellow countrymen when circumstances warranted, Beard had much larger career goals than just being a liaison between the German and Anglo communities: he wanted to become an entrepreneur. To achieve his goal Beard knew he could not limit himself to the German community, he needed to take advantage of the economic opportunities available throughout the backcountry.

Beard was a natural born businessman. His business prospered, and he purchased some land outside of town to expand his enterprises. He may have missed the commercial action of Salisbury, though, and obtained four more town lots there in 1761.[83] Beard's growing financial empire was not enough to achieve his goal; he needed to maintain a high profile in Rowan County's official circles as well. He frequently could be found at the courthouse serving on juries, taking part in cases as plaintiff and witness, witnessing legal documents for others, obtaining his tavern licenses, and finalizing his many land transactions.[84]

Unlike George Henry Berger, Beard rarely demonstrated a sense of selfless public spirit. For instance, he hardly ever provided security for individuals to settle estates or pursue political office. This behavior and a few clues point to a darker side of Beard's personality. In April 1762, spinster Agnes Osborough had the Court of Pleas and Quarter issue a civil writ for Beard's arrest for owing her damages in the amount of forty pounds. Two months later the court issued another writ for Beard's arrest, but this time for criminal charges. According to the writ, Beard "assaulted . . . beat, wounded and evilly [*sic*] treat" Osborough "so that her Life was Disparied of and he then did other injuries to her."[85] Records do not show what happened to the case. However, because of his wealth, Beard could count some of the most powerful people in Rowan County among his friends: clerks of court, justices of the peace, land agents, constables, and officers of the local militia. Since he does not disappear from the records at this time, apparently Osborough could not make her charges against Beard stand, or he was found innocent. Beard's legal problems with Osborough were not a singular occurrence. Both court records and an anonymous lawyer's account book indicate that Beard was constantly in court fighting over land, money, and even an accusation of slander.[86]

Beard realized the advantages of having friends in powerful positions, which may have helped him out of some of his legal predicaments, but his aim was to consolidate his own economic power. Towards this end, Beard applied amazing foresight and vision. As a butcher in the German community (but who lived in Salisbury), Beard, not surprisingly, had business relationships with tanners Conrad Michael, George Henry Berger, and James Carson. Recognizing the economic advantages to processing a whole animal at one location over dividing up the butchering and tanning at different locations, Beard may have gone into partnership with Conrad Michael, purchasing Michael's tannery in 1762 and leaving Michael as the master tanner, as records suggest. Subsequent land purchases in the next two years indicate that the tannery probably expanded (possibly buying out Berger as well, who may have gone to work for Beard), and in 1764 it came solely under Beard as senior partner when Michael decided to return to Germany to visit relatives.[87]

In addition to operating his butchery/tannery, Beard continued to run a tavern in Salisbury, a main outlet, no doubt, for the products of his butcher shop. Beard realized that his success depended primarily on the economic well-being of the community; consequently, he patronized the local craftspeople with whom he was acquainted. Public records show that Beard knew hatters James Bowers, Casper Kinder, and William Williams, tailor Henry Zevily, millwright Henry Grubb, potter Michael Morr, spinster Isabella Moore, weaver Christopher Rendleman, saddler Hugh Forster, joiner James Kerr, wheelwright Michael Brown, and tin- and silversmith James Townsley.[88]

As with any entrepreneur, economic expansion was continually on Beard's mind. Approximately ten years after his acquisition of the tannery, records indicate that Beard had begun catering outside of his tavern, providing thirty-two pounds of beef and thirty dozen "bisquits" for William Steele's wake.[89] The Steeles were customers of Beard's tannery, as well, purchasing hides and sole leather from him and having a calfskin specially tanned and curried there.[90] The Steele family papers also reveal that once again Beard had enlarged his business at the tannery at this time to include a shoemaker as well.[91] Business at the tannery complex may have been stiff competition for the Moravians on the other side of the river.

Ultimately, between his quest for wealth and his less-than-perfect life, John Lewis Beard was probably more than less typical of most backcountry settlers. Although he sometimes ran afoul of the law, his wealth provided him with the respect necessary to serve as a town commissioner, a trustee for the Salisbury Academy, and a member of the Committee of Safety in 1775.[92] Beard conducted business with his fellow Germans, as well as other county residents like the Steeles, with profit as the primary motive. Occasionally he helped out worthwhile causes; after the death of his daughter, Beard gave the land for the German Reformed Church in Salisbury.[93]

A great number of artisans served the county in lesser roles than sheriffs or justices of the peace. Between 1753 and 1770 Rowan County had 363 constables, who attended to various law enforcement duties for the sheriff (helping to collect the tax, notifying individuals of jury duty, serving warrants) in districts throughout the county. They also assisted the court when it met. Fifty-three constables were artisans (see Table 8), for most it was the highest political office they ever attained. Because most of a constable's duties occurred within his immediate community rather than the entire county, more Germans (including two Moravians) served as constables than

Table 8. Rowan County Artisans Who Served as Constables, 1753-1770

Name	Craft	Year
Allison, Thomas	joiner	1753
Barr, James	weaver	1757
Berry, James	blacksmith	1756
Billingsley, James	carpenter	1769
Brown, Jacob	wheelwright	1766
Brown, Michael	wheelwright	1766
Brown, William	millwright	1769
Bryan, Joseph	saddler	1767
Carson, James	tanner	1759
Cathey, George	millwright	1764
Cook, Thomas	tailor	1754-1755
Cowan, John	gunsmith	1764
Cowan, William	carpenter	1770
Cunningham, John	tanner	1761
Davis, James	carpenter	1757
Dobbins, John	blacksmith	1768-1769
Dunham, Hugh	hatter	1757
Elrod, Robert	weaver	1756
Findley, John	cooper	1754
Fletcher, James	weaver	1769
Garrison, Isaac, Jr.	weaver	1770
Gillespie, Matthew	cordwainer	1756
Graham, James, Sr.	blacksmith	1761
Graham, Richard	saddler	1759
Grant, William	weaver	1753
Hooser, Peter	weaver	1764
Hughey, Henry	weaver	1754
Ireland, William	cordwainer	1770
Johnston, John	carpenter	1761
Leonard, Valentine	tailor	1762
Lewis, Daniel	weaver	1769
Luckey, Robert	wheelwright	1765
Mebane, William	weaver	1764
Morr, Michael	potter	1770
McCulloh, James	bricklayer	1754
McConnell, John	weaver	1758
O'Neal, Arthur	tailor	1760-1763, 1765, 1767-1768

(Cont.)

Table 8, cont.

Name	Craft	Year
Patterson, James	blacksmith	1768
Patterson, John	skinner	1762
Patton, John	blacksmith	1769
Reed, Samuel	cordwainer	1763
Shore, Henry	carpenter	1763
Skidmore, Elijah	cordwainer	1761, 1763
Smith, John	blacksmith	1760
Smith, Samuel	blacksmith	1767
Stephenson, William	carpenter	1767
Stuart, James	weaver	1767
Thompson, John	cooper or shoemaker	1769
Watt, William	clothier	1755, 1764
Woods, Samuel	weaver	1761, 1764
Zevily, Henry	tailor	1770

SOURCE: Data base of Rowan County office holders compiled from Rowan County, Minutes of the Court of Pleas and Quarter Sessions (Raleigh: North Carolina Department of Archives and History) in dBase III+.

any other political office. At least one German artisan, Michael Brown, used the office of constable to help his fellow countrymen and to gain entry into the political ranks. For some other artisans, the situation was the reverse: James Carson, who was already prominent, may have become constable to give something back to the community. These artisans frequently appear in the public sphere not because of their political activity but as a result of their financial status.

Wheelwright Michael Brun was born in Ruschberg, Germany, in 1732 and migrated to America with his parents six years later. After arriving in Philadelphia, the family probably spent the next twenty years in Lancaster County, Pennsylvania, where Brown and his older brother Jacob learned the trade of wheelwright and wagonmaker.[94] In April 1758 "Michael Brown" surfaced as a juror in the Rowan County Court of Pleas and Quarter.[95] His presence on a jury indicates that Brown must have owned land in the county, although the first extant deed to him for 274 acres on the south side of the middle fork of Crane Creek is dated 1760, the same year his brother arrived.[96] A year later Brown succeeded John Smith as constable for militia captain Conrad Michael's district, which was presided over by Justice Alexander Cathey.[97]

Brown and his brother arrived in Rowan County just as the overland trade to the East was expanding, and they both profited handsomely from the increased demand for wagons. Over the next few years Brown became more involved in the larger German community by serving as constable again and overseeing the road system; he also helped the German settlers on a personal level by witnessing deeds and posting security for estate administration and tavern licenses.[98] For all of the good his community service achieved, Brown gained more notoriety in the county when he built a large cut-stone house in 1766. An impressive structure accentuated with double casement windows, the house conveyed a message of material success and knowledge of style understandable in any language. Not surprisingly, Brown's fame soared. Through hard work and service to others he achieved a reputation as a stable, dependable force in the German community, and he earned a similar respect from the rest of the county by displaying that success through architecture.[99]

In the years following the construction of his house, Brown became a naturalized Englishman, a trustee of the German Lutheran Church in Salisbury, and a captain in the militia.[100] The number of appearances in local court as an estate administrator and road commissioner, and in Superior Court as a grand juror, increased appreciably, and in 1777 he was named a justice of the peace.[101] As the court records and the Steele family papers document, Brown remained active as a justice until his death in 1807.[102]

James Carson gained a prominent place in Rowan County when he co-founded the Trading Settlement in 1753. Originally from East Nottingham township in Chester County, Carson was a prosperous tanner who probably relocated to the backcountry to invest in inexpensive land, according to Ramsey.[103] After obtaining a 640-acre tract located on either side of Crane Creek, Carson set to work establishing his tannery.[104] By virtue of his early arrival and his financial situation, Carson became an informal member of Rowan County's leadership. Over the course of his career, Carson kept his official duties limited to jury duty, witnessing documents, and serving as constable and road commissioner.[105] Yet records reveal that he knew the most influential men in Salisbury: trustees James Carter and Hugh Forster; sheriffs David Jones and William Nassery; justices Andrew Allison, William Buis, and John Dunn (his neighbor); constables James Allison (Andrew's brother), William Robinson, Samuel Reed, Henry Chambers, Richard King, Lawrence Snapp, Matthew Gillespie, and James McCulloh; and Granville agent Francis Corbin, among others.[106] Serving as constable in 1759 certainly did not advance Carson's political standing in the county. Although constable was the highest political office he held, the informal power he wielded as a landowner and businessman surpassed his responsibilities as constable many times over.

As in the cases of John Lewis Beard and James Carter, some Rowan County artisans found themselves on the opposite of the law. Unlike Beard and Carter, most of these artisans found themselves in trouble with the law for less fortunate reasons than politics and greed. Records from the Rowan Court of Pleas and Quarter and the Salisbury District Superior Court indicate that approximately forty artisans found their way into the public sphere through their involvement in cases that named them as either a defendant or plaintiff. Most of these cases involved relatively minor civil offenses such as trespassing, debt, or broken contracts.[107] However, some Rowan County artisans found themselves accused or the victims of a wide range of criminal activity as well. The most common criminal complaint involving artisans was stealing, including money, clothes, food, and animals. Sometimes these were non-violent crimes, as when joiner Oliver Wallace was found guilty of felony horse stealing, or Samuel Holloway stole nine pounds proclamation money from hatter William Williams.[108] Less frequently, the stealing occurred with violence, as when planter David Hall injured hatter Robert Johnston in the process of stealing a peck of malt.[109]

More disturbing, however, are the signs of violent crime in Rowan County. Accounts of murder, assault, and sexual deviance can all be found. In September 1763 the Superior Court heard the case of Henry Horah (probably a weaver), William McConnell Jr., and tailor Thomas Cook, who stood accused of murdering "Negro Ceasor." The three pled not guilty, and one of them was found guilty of a lesser charge.[110] As shown in the previous chapter, assault was the most common form of violence on men and women, and complaints for the crime can be found in criminal and civil action papers. Millwright James Carter complained that Dr. Andrew Cranson assaulted him in 1756, and eleven years later Thomas Hendry swore in a deposition that clothier William Watt assaulted him near William Beatty's house "by taking him [by] the throat and using a great many threatening expressions."[111]

Fortunately, the two descriptions of sexual deviance in Rowan County fall into the realm of bizarre rather than violent behavior. The first account is really the denouncement of a rumor supposedly credited to blacksmith James Berry in January 1756. According to Berry, "it is publickly reported that I have said I saw James Carter in bed with James Keleys wife and fucken with her and he saw Wm Mact at the same time Lying under a blanket with Margret Carter." He then declared the report "entire false" and stated specifically that he never saw Carter with Kelly's wife. Whether the report was true or not (and with Carter's track record it probably was), Berry stood to lose a lot from being associated with it. As already shown, Carter was a corrupt but powerful man in Rowan County who could have ruined Berry easily. Berry obviously knew that and tried to make peace with the millwright. His efforts were not entirely successful, and in June 1756 Carter summoned Berry to Superior Civil Court on a charge of trespass.[112]

The other episode of sexual deviance comes from a Superior Criminal Court jury, finding Salisbury hatter Robert Johnston guilty of having "a veneral [*sic*] affair" with "one black cow" in 1765. What may be more interesting than the charge and verdict is the fairly detailed description (see Appendix G) of exactly what transpired between Johnston and the cow "to the great displeasure of Almighty God, [and] to the great Scandal of all human kind."[113]

The migration patterns from the Middle Colonies down the Great Wagon Road into the backcountry and the creation of the early settlements by groups of acquaintances show that the artisans of Rowan County, like the rest of the county's residents, made a conscious decision to live in the southern backcountry even though their economic survival in the region (especially in the early years of settlement) depended on supplementing the income they derived from their trades with farming. In contrast to urban artisans in colonial America, Rowan County artisans did not develop a group consciousness to combat the economic problems which they faced, nor did they turn to group participation in politics to improve them. Consequently, when Rowan County artisans appear in the public sphere, at least in the extant records, they do so as the direct result of their individual actions, usually in political, financial, or criminal endeavors.

The absence of artisans in group political participation in Rowan County does not mean that all backcountry residents acted alone. The Regulator movement proved that backcountry residents could and would organize and act collectively when outsiders threatened their traditional position in society and politics. For numerous reasons, however, the problems that caused the Regulation did not directly affect all Rowan County artisans and therefore, they did not respond as a group.

Those artisans who did participate in the civic affairs of Rowan County did so in a number of offices and a variety of levels. Their knowledge of reading, writing, and arithmetic made them highly sought after commodities for political office in the backcountry. Four of the eight sheriffs, the highest law enforcement officers in the county, who served before 1770 were artisans. Almost 15 percent of the men who assisted them as constables were also artisans. And artisans counted for 11 percent of the justices of the peace, the men who administered justice throughout the county.[114] Other artisans helped with the development of the county by acting as road commissioners.

Nevertheless, the vast majority of artisans in Rowan County never held any political office: jury duty at the Court of Pleas and Quarter was the extent of their involvement in public life. Instead, these artisans channeled their energy into improving their economic situation. John Lewis Beard did not fill a political office in Rowan County until 1770, when he became a Salisbury commissioner, he devoted his time to becoming a backcountry entrepreneur instead. James Carson, one of the wealthiest men in the county, served only as a constable. Nonetheless, they appear in the records repeatedly as a result of their economic status.

Other artisans were unwilling participants in the public sphere of Rowan county, dragged there by their participation in or roles as victims of illegal activity. While few artisans became criminals in Rowan County (the possible result of having a trade and an income), the scope of violent crime in which they were involved was fairly broad.

Unlike his counterparts in densely populated urban areas, from the moment the artisan decided to move to Rowan County, his individual initiative, whether it be in politics or trade, became the definitive force in shaping his life.

APPENDIX A

Andrew Kremser's Indenture to Frederick Jacob Pfeil, Shoemaker

This INDENTURE made the Sixth Day of February in the Year of Our Lord One thousand seven hundred and Sixty Nine, WITNESSETH, That Andrew Kremser, Son of the late Andrew Kremser of Friedensthal in the County of Northampton in the Province of Pennsylvania, Yoeman, HATH, of his own voluntary Will placed and bound himself Apprentice to Frederick Jacob Pfeil of Bethabara in the County of Rowan in the Province of North Carolina Shoemaker, to be taught in the Trade Science or Occupation of a Shoemaker, and with him as an Apprentice to serve from the Day of the Date hereof till the Seventh Day of March which will be in the year of our Lord One thousand Seven hundred and Seventy four; during all which Term the said Apprentice his said Master well & faithfully shall serve, his Secrets keep, and his lawfull Commands gladly do, and behave in all Respects as a faithful Apprentice ought to do both to his Master and all his.

And the said Master his said Apprentice the said Trade which he now useth as a Shoemaker, with all Things thereunto belonging, shall & will teach and instruct, or cause to be well and sufficiently taught and instructed, after the best Manner he can; and shall and will also find & allow unto his said Apprentice Meat, Drink, Washing, Lodging and Apparel, both Linnen & Woolen, & all other Necessaries fit and convenient for such an Apprentice, during the Term aforesaid, & at the End of the said Term shall & will give to the said Apprentice One new Suit of Apparell.

In Witness whereof the Parties above named have to these Presents interchangeably set their Hands & Seals the Day & Year first above written.

Done before me one of His Majesty's Justices of the Peace for the County of Rowan, The Day & Year above mentioned.
Jacob Loesch

( )
Frederick Jacob Pfeil
( )

KNOW ALL YE MEN by these Presents
That I Jacob Pfeil of Bethabara in Rowan County in the Province of North Carolina Shoemaker, am held & firmly bound unto Frederick Marshall of Bethabara aforesaid, in the Sum of One hundred Pounds of current Money of this Province, to be paid to the said Frederick Marshall, his certain Attorney Executors

Administrators or Assigns: To which Payment well and truly to be made I bind myself, my heirs Executors and Administrators and every one of them firmly by these Presents. Sealed with my Seal and dated the Sixth Day of February in the Year of Our Lord One thousand Seven hundred and Sixty Nine and in the Ninth year of His Majesty's Reign.

THE CONDITION of this Bond is, that if the said Frederick Jacob Pfeil doth not remove his Apprentice Andrew Kremser this Day bound to him out of the Brethren's Settlements of Bethabara or Salem, nor bind him to any other Master, without the consent of the said Frederic Marshall or his Heirs previously obtained. AND during the whole Time of his Apprenticeship lodgeth and boards him the said Andrew Kremser, in the Single Brethren's house, according to the Custom of the United Brethren. AND if the said Apprentice should turn out to be of such Life and Manners, that according to the Rules of the Brethren he could not be tolerated amongst them, and in that Case at the Request of the said Frederic Marshall or his Heirs the said Frederick Jacob Pfeil shall bind out his said Apprentice to an other Master not residing at the Settlement aforesaid. OR, if the said Frederick Jacob Pfeil himself should remove from the said Settlements, and shall than bind out his said Apprentice to an other Master residing at Salem, and in both the last Cases shall content himself with such Sum or Satisfaction as he shall be able to get of the said Apprentice's new Master THEN the above Obligation to be void or else to be and remain in full Force and Virtue.

Sealed & delivered in the ( )
Presence of Frederick Jacob Pfeil (Seal)

Jacob Loesch
Nicholas Lorenz Bagge

SOURCE: *RM* 2:608-9.

APPENDIX B

Edward Hughes's Last Meeting with the Moravians

According to the Wachovia Diary, March 16, 1771.
". . . for this afternoon the part of Regulators from the Yadkin appeared as they had said and summoned the Brn. Marshall, Bonn and Bagge to the Tavern. They were told if they had any thing to say they might come to Br. Marshall's room, so a dozen of them came, with Edward Hughes, who acted as spokesman. His first complaint was that the Stewards had been unjustly treated, in that Br. Jacob Loesch had measured for himself a piece of land on which their father had paid a sum of money, —the amount not stated—to Carter, at the time County Clerk; and that Br. Jacob Loesch had then sold the land to his brothers, George and Adam, —of whom the former was present, —and that they had settled on it. As all these transactions took place before the arrival in Wachovia of the three Brethren above mentioned, they answered that the only thing to be done would be to summon Jacob Loesch to North Carolina to meet and settle with the Stewards, and that they would have to send the call themselves. The other complaint Hughes made on his own account, saying that he had paid a certain sum of money to Mr. Corbin for the land on which Bethabara stands; he could show no written proof of this, but demanded £30, saying many harsh and untrue things about Br. Joseph [Bishop Spangenberg], who had taken this land from him, etc. In short, the trumped-up complaint of these people was only groundless babbling, but they were answered politely and seriously, and they and their unfounded pretentions were referred to the persons concerned, and with that they left. They may have wanted to try whether the terrifying name of Regulator would not frighten us into giving them what they wanted."

SOURCE: *RM* 1:452.

APPENDIX C

Definitions of Craftsmen and Terms

Definitions are taken from the *Oxford English Dictionary* unless otherwise noted. Date in parentheses refers to the earliest appearance of the written word.

Blacksmith: A smith who works in iron or black metal, as distinguished from a "whitesmith," who works in tin or white metal. (1483)

Bricklayer: One who lays the bricks in building. (1485)

Brickmaker: One who makes bricks as his trade. (1465)

Cabinetmaker: One whose business it is to make cabinets and the finer kind of joiner's work. (1681)

Carpenter: "An artificer in wood"; as distinguished from a joiner, cabinetmaker, etc., one who does the heavier and stronger work in wood, as the framework of houses, ships, etc. (1325)

Clothier: One engaged in the cloth trade: a. A maker of woollen cloth; b. esp. One who performs the operations subsequent to the weaving; c. A fuller and dresser of cloth (U.S.); d. A seller of cloth and men's clothes. (1362)

Cooper: A craftsman who makes and repairs wooden vessels formed of staves and hoops, such as casks, buckets, tubs. (1415)

Cordwainer: [Originally meant a dealer or maker of cordovan leather; then a worker in this type leather; a shoemaker] Now obsolete as the ordinary name, but often persisting as the name of the trade-guild or company of shoemakers, and sometimes used by modern trade unions to include all branches of the trade. (1100)

Gunsmith: One whose occupation it is to make and repair small firearms. (1588)

Gunstocker: One who fits the stocks of guns to the barrels. (1689)

Hatter: A maker of or dealer in hats. (1389)

Joiner: A craftsman whose occupation it is to construct things by joining pieces of wood; a worker in wood who does lighter and more ornamental work than that of a carpenter, as the construction of the furniture and fittings of a house, ship, etc. (1386)

Mantua-maker: One who makes mantuas; later, a dress-maker. (1694)

Mason: A builder and worker in stone; a workman who dresses and lays stone in building. (1205)

Milliner: a. A vendor of "fancy" wares and articles of apparel, esp. of such as were originally of Milan manufacture, e.g. "Milan bonnets," ribbons, gloves, cutlery.

b. In modern use, a person (usually a woman) who makes up articles of female apparel, esp. bonnets and other headgear. (1530)

Millwright: An engineer or mechanic whose occupation it is to design or set up mills or mill machinery. (1481)

Potter: A maker of pots, or of earthenware vessels. (1100)

Saddler: One who makes or deals in saddles or saddlery. (1389)

Saddletree: The framework which forms the foundation of a saddle. (1411)

Seamstress: A woman who seams or sews; a needlewoman whose occupation is plain sewing as distinguished from dress or mantle-making, decorative embroidery, etc. (1644)

Shoemaker: One whose trade it is to make shoes. (1381)

Silversmith: A worker in silver; one who makes silverware. (1000)

Spinster: 1. A woman (or, rarely, a man) who spins, esp. one who practices spinning as a regular occupation. (1362) 2. Appended to names of women, originally in order to denote their occupation, but subsequently (from the 17th century) as the proper legal designation of one still unmarried. (1380)

Tailor: "One whose business is to make clothes"; a maker of the outer garments of men, also sometimes those of women, esp. riding habits, walking costumes, etc. (1297)

Tanner: One whose occupation is to tan hides or to convert them into leather by tanning. (975)

Tinner: 2. One who works in tin; a tin-plater, tinman, tinsmith. (1611)

Tinsmith: A worker in tin; a maker of tin utensils; a whitesmith. (1858)

Turner: One who turns or fashions objects of wood, metal, bone, etc., on a lathe. (1400)

Wagon[maker]: [One who builds] strong, four-wheeled vehicles designed for the transport of heavy goods. (1523)

Wheelwright: A man who makes wheels and wheeled vehicles. (1281)

Whitesmith: a. A worker in "white iron"; a tinsmith. b. One who polishes or finishes metal goods, as distinguished from one who forges them; also, more widely, a worker in metals. (1302)

Wicar: 1. A maker of wicks for candles. 2. A maker of baskets.

APPENDIX D

Moravian Artisans Working on the Wachovia Tract, 1753-1770

Name	Craft	Arrival Date
Aust, Gottfried	potter	1755
Bagge, Lorenz	joiner	1766
Beck, John Fredrich	cabinetmaker	1766
Beck, John Valentine	gunstocker	1764
Broesing, Andreas	joiner	1765
Buttner, Sarah	weaver	1765
Christ, Rudolph	potter	1766
Culver, Charles	brickmaker	1766
Enerson, Enert	cabinetmaker	1764
Ernst, Johann Jacob	tanner	1766
Feldhausen, Heinrich	shoemaker	1754
Flex, Johannes Samuel	weaver	1766
Fockel, Gottlieb	tailor	1766
Goetje, Maria Elisabeth Krause	glovemaker	1766
Hauser, Daniel	blacksmith	1765
Hauser, George	blacksmith	1755
Hauser, Georg Peter	weaver	1762
Hauser, Michael, Sr.	weaver	1753
Hauser, Michael, Jr.	tanner	1758
Heckenwalder, Christian	mason	1766
Herbst, Johann Heinrich	tanner	1762
Holder, Charles	saddler	1766
Holder, George	carpenter	1766
Hurst, James	weaver	1766
Ingebretsen, Erich	millwright	1753
Kapp, Jacob	turner	1756
Kastner, Johan Anton	blacksmith	1768
Koffler, Adam	clockmaker	1762
Krohn, Peter	cooper	1769
Martin, Johnson	carpenter	1768
Mau, Johann Samuel	bricklayer	1762
Moeller, Ludwig	potter	1766

Name	Craft	Arrival Date
Mueller, Joseph	gunsmith	1766
Mueller, Joseph	potter/mason	1766
Nissen, Tycho	gravestone cutter/ wheelwright	1770
Oesterlein, Mattheus	blacksmith	1766
Peterson, Hans	tailor	1753
Pfeil, Frederick Jacob	shoemaker	1753
Praezel, Gottfried	weaver	1766
Rasp, Melchoir	bricklayer	1755
Reuter, Christian Gottlieb	surveyor	1763
Rominger, David	carpenter	1769
Schaub, Johannes Fredrich	cooper	1755
Schill, Bernhard	weaver	1766
Schmid, Heinrich	blacksmith	1769
Schmidt, Johann Christoph	brickmaker	1755
Schmidt, Johann George	blacksmith	1754
Schober, Gottlieb	tailor	1768
Schor, Johann Heinrich	carpenter	1759
Spoenhauser, John Henry	cooper	1755
Stauber, Paul Christian	saddler	1768
Steup, John Christian	blacksmith	1760
Stotz, Peter	brickmaker	1762
Strehle, Christian Gottlieb	tanner	1770
Strehle, Christian Rudolph	carpenter	1770
Tesch, Johannes	saddler	1765
Triebel, Christian	carpenter	1755
van der Merk, Jacob	millwright	1756
Wolff, William Adam	carpenter	1769

Source: *RM* and data base of artisans in Rowan County in dBase III+ sorted by name and location (Wachovia).

APPENDIX E

Rowan County Artisans, 1753-1770

Name	Craft	Beg./End Dates	
Adams, James	weaver	1767	1790
Adams, John	potter	1755	1790
Alexander, Daniel	joiner	1763	1790
Alexander, Moses	blacksmith	1752	1790
Allin, John	carpenter	1763	1778
Allison, Andrew	tailor	1751	1780
Allison, Thomas	joiner	1753	1780
Atkins, Joseph	carpenter	1770	1778
Baker, Henry	wagonmaker	1757	1772
Barr, James	weaver	1753	1788
Barrs, Sarah	spinster	1768	1768
Bartleson, Richard	chairmaker	1764	1787
Barton, William	cooper	1770	1772
Baxter, German	silversmith	1765	1774
Beard, John Lewis	tanner	1755	1789
Bell, William, & wife	seamstress	1766	1790
Berger, George Henry	tanner	1761	1805
Beroth, Henry	potter	1766	1800
Berry, James	blacksmith	1756	1758
Betty, Charles	shoemaker	1758	1764
Betz, Andreas (Andrew)	gunsmith	1766	1795
Bickerstaff, John	weaver	1763	1776
Biles, Thomas	wheelwright	1761	1784
Billingsley, James	carpenter	1765	1790
Blith, Samuel	turner	1753	1774
Boise, Bostian	tailor	1757	1758
Bondrick, Nicholas	carpenter	1761	1761
Bones, William	tailor	1769	1790
Boone, Jonathan	joiner	1756	1778
Boone, Mary Carter	spinster	1756	1765
Bowder, Benjamin	tailor	1762	1762
Bowers, James	hatter	1756	1778
Bradley, John	carpenter	1770	1794

Name	Craft	Beg./End Dates	
Brandon, John	tailor	1768	1768
Brock, Elias	carpenter	1753	1767
Brown, Jacob	wheelwright	1760	1808
Brown, Michael	wheelwright	1758	1807
Brown, William	millwright	1767	1787
Bruner, George	gunsmith	1757	1793
Bryan, Joseph	saddler	1759	1790
Bullin, John	cooper	1767	1795
Buntin, John, Sr.	weaver	1762	1790
Carson, James	tanner	1753	1784
Carson, Samuel	shoemaker	1767	1777
Carter, James	millwright	1752	1765
Cathey, Andrew	shoemaker	1749	1790
Cathey, George	millwright	—	—
Cavet, James	carpenter	1769	1790
Clark, John	wagonmaker	1765	1789
Cook, Robert	tailor	1753	—
Cook, Thomas	tailor	1750	1790
Cook, William, Jr.	tanner	1769	1812
Cooper, Samuel	blacksmith	1770	1782
Coulter, Martin	tailor	1758	1758
Coulter, Samuel	saddler	1760	—
Courtney, William	mason	1769	1771
Cowan, John	gunsmith	1759	1789
Cowan, William	carpenter	1759	1791
Cox, Zachariah	cooper	1759	1761
Craig, Archibald	carpenter	1756	1756
Crosby, Ann	seamstress	—	—
Cunningham, John	tanner	1755	1762
Davenport, William	saddler	1759	1803
Davidson, George	tanner	1749	1790
Davis, James	carpenter	1759	1765
Denny, Edmond	cooper	1770	1790
Dickey, John	gunsmith	1762	1808
Dickie, Thomas	millwright	1768	1807
Dickson, Joseph	blacksmith	1769	1801
Dickson, Michael	weaver	1756	1756
Dills, Henry	saddler	1769	1795
Divist, Andrew	cordwainer	1770	—
Dobbin, Alexander, Sr.	shoemaker	1755	1798
Dobbins, James	blacksmith	1759	1791
Dobbins, John	blacksmith	1769	1800
Donnell, John	wheelwright	1767	1792

(Cont.)

Name	Craft	Beg./End Dates	
Doub, John	tanner	1763	1810
Douthid, John, Sr.	weaver	1759	1784
Dry, George	cordwainer	1769	1769
Dunham, Hugh	hatter	1763	1792
Elrod, Robert	weaver	1759	1790
Endsley, Alexander	shoemaker	1770	1790
Enyart, Abram	weaver	1770	1791
Ervin, Robert	carpenter	1759	1778
Erwin, Arthur	tailor	1766	1790
Erwin, James, Jr.	saddletree maker	1766	1790
Evington, Catherine	spinster	1770	1770
Ewing, Nathaniel	saddler	1770	1778
Farillow, John	wheelwright	1758	1767
Fergison, Jean	spinster	1769	1769
Ferguson, Andrew	carpenter	1764	1797
Findley, John	cooper	1754	1790
Fletcher, James	weaver	1754	1824
Forbus, Arthur	weaver	1764	1764
Ford, John	carpenter	1767	1795
Forster, Hugh	tanner	1755	1762
Foster, Joseph	blacksmith	1770	1811
Frazier, John	millwright	1759	1794
Frey, George	blacksmith	1766	1812
Gambell, James	shoemaker	1759	1794
Garrison, Isaac	weaver	1767	1792
Gauntt, Zebulon	wheelwright	1757	1757
Gillespie, John	cooper	1759	1790
Gillespie, Matthew	cordwainer	1753	1759
Goss, Frederick	cooper	1759	1804
Goyer, Jacob	saddler	1770	1770
Graham, James	blacksmith	1751	1790
Graham, Richard	saddler	1751	1779
Grant, William	weaver	1768	1804
Graves, Conrad	blacksmith	1767	1820
Gray, George	tailor	1769	1805
Grob, Heinrich (Henry Grubb)	millwright	1763	1763
Hall, David	blacksmith	1762	1790
Hall, Thomas	weaver	1762	1790
Hauser, George	blacksmith	1755	1796
Hauser, Martin	carpenter	1754	1761
Henly, Derby	weaver	—	1808
Hill, John	weaver	1769	1794
Hodgin, Robert	weaver	1763	1780

Name	Craft	Beg./End Dates	
Hogden, John	blacksmith	1766	1766
Hord, John	carpenter	1769	1769
Hughes, Edward	millwright	1748	1786
Hughes, John	tailor	1767	1790
Hughey, Henry	weaver	1752	1791
Hughey, Samuel	blacksmith	1769	1834
Ireland, William, Sr.	cordwainer	1758	1790
Johnson, John	carpenter	1766	1790
Johnston, Gideon, Sr.	shoemaker	1765	1807
Johnston, Peter	carpenter	1768	1768
Johnston, Robert, Jr.	hatter	1757	1777
Johnston, Thomas	hatter	1757	1816
Jones, David	weaver	1753	1795
Kerr, David	weaver	1759	1804
Kerr, James	joiner	1756	1804
Kerr, Nathaniel	tanner	1765	1790
Keylaygler, John	blacksmith	1758	—
Killpattrick, Hu[gh]	tailor	1768	—
Kinder, Caster	hatter	1768	1785
Knox, John	blacksmith	1758	1810
Lash, Adam	blacksmith	1759	1771
Leonard, Valentine, Sr.	tailor	1759	1782
Lewis, Daniel	weaver	1759	1801
Little, Peter	tanner	1770	1774
Lock, Ann	spinster	1770	1770
Lock, Francis	carpenter	1752	1796
Long, Matthew	weaver	1755	1764
Luckey, John, Jr.	hatter	1762	1789
Luckey, Robert	wheelwright	1756	1772
Luckey, Samuel	tanner	1756	1798
Lycans, Hance [Hans]	blacksmith	1759	1790
Lynn, Hugh	cooper	1770	1785
Lynn, William	blacksmih	1753	1758
Mackie, William	tanner	1755	1755
Marshall, George	joiner	1767	1778
Martin, Moses	blackmith	1759	1793
McAdow, James	shoemaker	1761	1790
McBroom, Mrs. James	spinster	1769	1769
McCleland, William	cooper	1770	1781
McConnahey, James	shoemaker	1767	1804
McConnell, John	weaver	1752	1791
McCrerry, Mary	spinster	1769	1769
McCuiston, John	blacksmith	1765	1769

(Cont.)

Name	Craft	Beg./End Dates	
McCulloch, James	saddler	1755	1792
McCullough, James	bricklayer	1770	—
McDowell, David	joiner	1760	1761
McHenry, Henry	tailor	1758	1771
McMackin, Andrew	blacksmith	1768	1768
McPheeters, Daniel	cooper	1757	1793
Mebane, William	weaver	1753	1759
Merrill, Benjamin	blacksmith	1740	1771
Michael, Conrad	tanner	1756	1788
Milakin, Joseph	weaver	1752	1757
Miller, Frederick	tanner	1768	1785
Miller, John	cooper	1757	1807
Miller, Michael	cooper	1753	1774
Mitchell, John	wheelwright	1759	1790
Mock, Mrs. Dewalt	spinster	—	—
Montgomery, John	weaver	1770	1790
Moore, Isabella	spinster	1768	1768
Moore, William	weaver	1759	1784
Morr, Michael	potter	1765	1784
Morr, Susanna	potter	1760	1784
Morrison, James	tailor	1763	1790
Neal, William	weaver	1758	1790
Newberry, Andrew	blacksmith	1769	1770
Newberry, Annas	spinster	1769	1769
Newberry, William	carpenter	1769	1769
Ogle, Hercules	blacksmith	1765	1766
O'Neal, Arthur	shoemaker	1768	1778
Orton, Jane	spinster	1766	1766
Orton, Rachel	spinster	1766	1766
Osbrough, Agnes	spinster	1760	1760
Parks, Margaret	spinster	1761	1761
Patterson, James	blacksmith	1759	1790
Patterson, John	skinner	1760	1771
Patton, John	blacksmith	1761	1800
Penny, Alexander	cooper	1761	1790
Philips, Aventon	blacksmith	1753	1782
Pincer, Sarah	spinster	1768	1768
Porter, Thomas	cooper	1765	1789
Price, William	blacksmith	1768	1790
Prichard, James	tailor	1767	1790
Quine, Francis	tailor	1762	1790
Ramsey, James	shoemaker	1767	1790
Randleman, Christopher	weaver	1761	1778
Raper, William	shoemaker	1759	1798

Name	Craft	Beg./End Dates	
Reed, Samuel	cordwainer	1753	1790
Reynold, Francis	shoemaker	1756	1784
Roarke, James	shoemaker	1767	1768
Robinson, Benjamin	weaver	1761	1777
Rodgers, John	saddler	1768	1787
Rodgers, Robert	tailor	1768	—
Rodsmith, Paul	blacksmith	1770	1790
Rogers, Robert	blacksmith	1765	1765
Ross, Joseph	blacksmith	1768	1790
Ruddack, John	saddler	1761	1802
Ryan, Edward	weaver	1759	1790
Schmidt, George	blacksmith	1754	1791
Sevitz, George	millwright	1768	1778
Shinn, Samuel	mason	1759	1762
Simison, James	turner	1764	1778
Simison, Robert	wheelwright	1757	1790
Skidmore, Elijah	cordwainer	1759	1769
Smiley, James	weaver	1767	1767
Smith, David	blacksmith	1759	1787
Smith, John	blacksmith	1756	1800
Smith, Samuel	blacksmith	1765	1765
Smith, Thomas	weaver	1752	1783
Snap, Christian	spinster	1768	1768
Snap, Elizabeth	spinster	1768	1768
Spreaker, George	blacksmith	1769	1790
Stamon, Sarah	spinster	1768	1768
Steel, Andrew	joiner	1766	1790
Steel, Ninian	wheelwright	1768	1793
Steele, Elizabeth Gillespie	weaver	1733	1791
Stogdon, John	blacksmith	1767	1767
Storey, Martha	spinster	1762	1762
Strehorn, Gilbert	tailor	1758	1790
Stuart, James	weaver	1752	1798
Thom(p)son, James	cooper	1760	1781
Thom(p)son, John	cooper	1755	1760
Thompson, John	cordwainer	1753	1774
Townsley, James	tinsmith	1768	1791
Tuck(er), Enoch	wicar	1767	1778
Walker, Mary (& Robert)	spinster	1768	1790
Wallace, Oliver	joiner	1764	1766
Walton, Richard	tanner	1762	1790
Wasson, Archibald	cordwainer	1759	1785
Wasson, Joseph	shoemaker	1763	1790

(Cont.)

Name	Craft	Beg./End Dates	
Watson, Samuel	shoemaker	1758	1758
Watt, William	clothier	1753	1790
Weatherspoons, John	weaver	1759	1781
Wheeler, John	tailor	1768	1769
White, Thomas	tailor	1759	1801
Whitsett, John	carpenter	1753	1753
Wiley, John	wheelwright	1764	1790
Williams, William	hatter	1758	1783
Wilson, Joan	spinster	1769	1769
Wilson, William	carpenter	1759	1803
Woods, Robert, #1	carpenter	1757	1766
Woods, Robert, #2	weaver	1768	1803
Woods, Robert, #3	cooper	1767	1767
Woods, Samuel	weaver	1754	1781
Woodson, David	silversmith	1769	1816
Work, Henry	carpenter	1765	1795
Wright, Abraham	weaver	1770	1770
Zevely, Henry	tailor	1759	1790
Zimmerman, Christian	weaver	1759	1790

SOURCE: Data base of artisans in Rowan County in dBase III+ sorted by name and location (Rowan).

APPENDIX F

Road Building in Rowan County, 1753-1770

Total Number of Roads per Year

1753	3	1762	0
1754	1	1763	3
1755	1	1764	3
1756	1	1765	5
1757	2	1766	3
1758	0	1767	5
1759	1	1768	2
1760	0	1769	5
1761	0	1770	4

SOURCE: *Rowan Court Abstracts*

APPENDIX G

Court Account of Robert Johnston and His Cow

[September 23, 1765] The Jurors for our sovereign Lord the King upon their oath present that Robert Johnston late of the Town of Salisbury in the County of Rowan, Hatter, not having the fear of God before his eyes nor regarding the order of Nature but being moved and seduced by the instigation of the Devil on the tenth day of May 1765 with force and arms . . . in and upon one black cow which the said Robert Johnston then and there had feloniously did make an assault and then and there feloniously wickedly diabolically and against the order of Nature had a veneral affair with the said Cow and then and there carnally knew the said Cow, and then and there feloniously, wickedly, diabolically and against the order of Nature, did committ and perpetuate that detestable and abominable crime of Buggery (not to be named among Christians) to the great displeasure of Almighty God, to the great Scandal of all human kind . . . .

SOURCE: Salisbury District Superior Court Criminal Action Papers, NC DAH.

Notes

Abbreviations

Burke Apprent.	Burke County Apprentice Bonds and Records, 1784-1873. NC DAH.
CR	William L. Saunders, Walter Clark, and Steven B. Weeks, eds. *The Colonial Records of North Carolina*. 30 vols. Raleigh: NC DAH, 1886-1941.
Guilford CPQS	Guilford County Court of Pleas and Quarter Sessions Minutes, 1781 1811. Microfilm. NC DAH.
MASP	Moravian Archives, Southern Province. Winston-Salem, North Carolina.
NC DAH	North Carolina Department of Archives and History, Raleigh.
Randolph Apprent.	Randolph County Apprentice Bonds and Records, 1779, 1780, 1781, 1783-1805. NC DAH.
Randolph CPQS	Randolph County Court of Pleas and Quarter Sessions Minutes, 1779-1782, 1787-1794. Microfilm. NC DAH.
RM	Adelaide L. Fries, Douglas LeTell Rights, Minnie J. Smith, and Kenneth G. Hamilton, trans. and ed. *The Records of the Moravians in North Carolina*. 11 vols. Raleigh: North Carolina Historical Commission, 1922-1969.
Rowan Apprent.	Rowan County Apprentice Bonds and Records, 1777-1804. NC DAH.
Rowan Civ. Act.	Rowan County Civil Action Papers, 1755-1774. NC DAH.
Rowan Court Abstracts	Jo White Linn. *Abstracts of the Minutes of the Court of Pleas and Quarter Sessions, Rowan County, N.C.* Vol. 1, *1753-1762, Abstracts of Books 1-2*. Vol. 2, *1763-1774, Abstracts of Books 2-4*. Salisbury: Mrs. Stahle Linn, Jr., 1977, 1979. [Cited by book.]
Rowan CPQS	Rowan County Court of Pleas and Quarter Sessions Minutes, 1753-1772, 1773-1899. Microfilm. NC DAH.
Rowan Crim. Act.	Rowan County Criminal Action Papers. NC DAH.
Rowan Deed Abstracts	Jo White Linn. *Rowan County, North Carolina, Deed Abstracts*. Vol. 1, *1753-1762: Abstracts of Books 1-4*. Vol. 2, *1762-1772: Abstracts of Books 5-7*. Salisbury: Mrs. Stahle Linn, 1972. [Cited by book.]
Rowan Estates	Rowan County Estates Records. NC DAH.
Rowan Will Abstracts	Jo White Linn. *Abstracts of Wills and Estates Records of Rowan County, North Carolina, 1753-1805, and Tax Lists of 1759 and 1778. Salisbury: Mrs. Stahle Lin, Jr., 1980. Rowan County, North Carolina, Will Abstracts, 1805-1850: Abstracts of Books G-K, 1850.* Salisbury, N.C.: Mrs. Stahle Linn, Jr., 1971.
Rowan Wills	Rowan County Wills, 1762-1804. NC DAH.

Salisbury Civ. Act.	Salisbury District Superior Court Civil Action Papers, 1756-1763, 1770-1773, 1778-1783. NC DAH.
Salisbury Crim. Act.	Salisbury District Superior Court Criminal Action Papers. NC DAH.
Salisbury Crown	Salisbury District Superior Court Crown Docket, 1767-1779, DAH.
Salisbury Execution	Salisbury District Superior Court Execution Docket, 1755-1767, 1767-1769, 1770-1772. NC DAH.
Salisbury Misc.	Salisbury District Superior Court Miscellaneous Records, 1754-1807. NC DAH.
Salisbury Ref.	Salisbury District Superior Court Reference Docket, 1767-1769. NC DAH.
Salisbury Trial	Salisbury District Superior Court Trial and Minute Docket, 1761-1776. Supreme Court Trial and Minute Docket, 1776-1790. NC DAH.
1790 U.S. Census	U.S. Government. *Heads of Families at the First Census of the United States Taken in the Year 1790: North Carolina*. Washington, D.C.: Government Printing Office, 1908; reprint, Baltimore: Genealogical Publishing Co., 1966.
SHC	Southern Historical Collection. Special Collections. University of North Carolina, Chapel Hill.
Stokes CPQS	Stokes County Court of Pleas and Quarter Sessions Minutes, 1790-1793. Microfilm. NC DAH.
Stokes Wills	Stokes County Wills. NC DAH.
Surry Apprent.	Surry County Apprentice Bonds and Records, 1779-1921. NC DAH.
Surry CPQS	Surry County Court of Pleas and Quarter Sessions Minutes, 1779-1802. Microfilm. NC DAH.
Surry Will Abstracts	Jo White Linn. *Surry County, North Carolina, Will Abstracts*. Vols. 1-3, *1771-1827*. Salisbury, N.C.: Mrs. Stahle Linn, Jr., 1974.
Wilkes Apprent.	Wilkes County Apprentice Bonds and Records, 1778-1908. NC DAH.
Wilkes CPQS	Wilkes County Court of Pleas and Quarter Sessions Minutes, March 1778-July 1790, Oct. 1790-May 1797. Microfilm. Microfilm. NC DAH.

Chapter 1. Artisans and the Backcountry

1. Hugh T. Lefler and Albert R. Newsome, *North Carolina: The History of a Southern State*, 3d ed. (Chapel Hill: Univ. of North Carolina Press, 1973), 122.

2. Carl Bridenbaugh, *The Colonial Craftsman* (Chicago: Univ. of Chicago Press, 1961); idem, *Cities in the Wilderness: The First Century of Urban Life in America 1625-1742* (New York: Knopf, 1955); idem, *Cities in Revolt: Urban Life in America, 1743-1776* (New York: Oxford Univ. Press, 1955); and idem, *Myths and Realities: Societies of the Colonial South* (New York: Atheneum, 1976).

3. For a definition of the "inarticulate" with regard to artisans, see James H. Hutson, "An Investigation of the Inarticulate: Philadelphia's White Oaks," *William and Mary Quarterly*, 3d ser., 28 (Jan. 1971): 3-26. Lemisch quote from Jesse Lemisch, "The American Revolution from the Bottom Up," in Barton Bernstein, ed., *Towards a New Past: Dissenting Essays in American History* (New York: Pantheon, 1968), 3-45; see also Jesse Lemisch

and John K. Alexander, "The White Oaks, Jack Tar, and the Concept of the 'Inarticulate,'" with a note by Simeon J. Crowther and a rebuttal by James H. Hutson, *William and Mary Quarterly*, 3d ser., 29 (Jan. 1972): 109-42.

4. Jackson Turner Main, *The Social Structure of Revolutionary America* (Princeton, N.J.: Princeton Univ. Press, 1965).

5. Howard B. Rock, *Artisans of the New Republic: The Tradesmen of New York City in the Age of Jefferson* (New York: New York Univ. Press, 1984), vii.

6. Sean B. Wilentz, *Chants Democratic: New York City and the Rise of the American Working Class, 1788-1850* (New York: Oxford Univ. Press, 1984); Rock, *Artisans*.

7. Charles S. Olton, *Artisans for Independence: Philadelphia Mechanics and the American Revolution* (Syracuse, N.Y.: Syracuse Univ. Press, 1975); see also idem, "Philadelphia's Mechanics in the First Decade of the Revolution, 1765-1776," *Journal of American History* 59 (1972): 311-26; Gary B. Nash, *The Urban Crucible: Social Change, Political Consciousness, and the Origins of the American Revolution* (Cambridge, Mass.: Harvard Univ. Press, 1979); see also idem, "Artisans and Politics in Eighteenth-Century Philadelphia," in Ian M.G. Quimby, ed., *The Craftsman in Early America* (New York: Norton for Winterthur, 1984), 62-88.

8. Charles G. Steffen, *The Mechanics of Baltimore: Workers and Politics in the Age of Revolution, 1763-1812* (Urbana: Univ. of Illinois Press, 1984); Tina H. Sheller, "Artisans, Manufacturing, and the Rise of a Manufacturing Interest in Revolutionary Baltimore Town," *Maryland Historical Magazine* 83 (Spring 1988): 3-18.

9. Sharon V. Salinger, "Artisans, Journeymen, and the Transformation of Labor in Late Eighteenth-Century Philadelphia," *William and Mary Quarterly*, 3d ser., 40 (Jan. 1983): 62-84; see also idem, "'Send No More Women': Female Servants in Late Eighteenth-Century Philadelphia," *Pennsylvania Magazine of History and Biography* 107 (Jan. 1983): 29-48; idem, *"To Serve Well and Faithfully": Labor and Indentured Servants in Pennsylvania, 1682-1800* (New York: Cambridge Univ. Press, 1987); Charles G. Steffen, "Changes in the Organization of Artisan Production in Baltimore, 1790-1820," *William and Mary Quarterly*, 3d ser., 36 (Jan. 1979): 101-17; and Susan E. Hirsch, *Roots of the American Working Class: The Industrialization of Crafts in Newark, 1800-1860* (Philadelphia: Univ. of Pennsylvania Press, 1978).

10. Gary B. Nash, "Poverty and Poor Relief in Pre-Revolutionary Philadelphia," *William and Mary Quarterly*, 3d ser., 33 (Jan. 1976): 3-20; Billy G. Smith, "The Material Lives of Laboring Philadelphians, 1750-1800," *William and Mary Quarterly*, 3d ser., 38 (April 1981): 163-202; Bruce Laurie, *Artisans into Workers: Labor in Nineteenth-Century America* (New York: Noonday Press, 1989).

11. Bridenbaugh, *Colonial Craftsman*, 7-20. Thomas W. Wertenbaker actually preceded Bridenbaugh in his assessment of the southern artisan's situation in his 1942 book *The Old South: The Foundation of American Civilization* (reprint, New York: Cooper Square, 1963), 226-27, 269-70.

12. Jean B. Russo, "Self-Sufficiency and Local Exchange: Free Craftsmen in the Rural Chesapeake Economy," in Lois Green Carr, Philip Morgan, and Jean B. Russo, eds., *Colonial Chesapeake Society* (Chapel Hill: Univ. of North Carolina Press for the Institute of Early American History and Culture, 1988), 390-91.

13. Russo, "Self-Sufficiency", 395, 405.

14. Jean B. Russo, "Free Workers in a Plantation Economy: Talbot County, Maryland, 1690-1759" (Ph.D. diss., Johns Hopkins Univ., 1983).

15. Russo, "Free Workers," iii; Christine Daniels, "'WANTED: A Blacksmith Who Understands Plantation Work': Artisans in Maryland, 1700-1800," *William and Mary Quarterly*, 3d ser., 50 (Oct. 1993): 743-67.

16. Lefler and Newsome, *North Carolina*, 110.

17. Richard J. Hooker, ed., *The Carolina Backcountry on the Eve of the Revolution: The Journal and Other Writings of Charles Woodmason, Anglican Itinerant* (Chapel Hill: Univ. of North Carolina Press, 1953), 7.

18. Bridenbaugh, *Myths and Realities*, 143.

19. Lefler and Newsome, *North Carolina*, 122.

20. Julia Cherry Spruill, *Women's Life and Work in the Southern Colonies* (1938; reprint, New York: Norton, 1972), 81; and Rolla Milton Tryon, *Household Manufactures in the United States, 1640-1860* (1917; reprint, Johnson Reprint Corp., 1966), 49.

21. Charles G. Sellers, *The Market Revolution: Jacksonian America, 1815-1846* (New York: Oxford Univ. Press, 1991), 5.

22. John McCusker and Russell Menard, *The Economy of British America, 1607-1789* (Chapel Hill: Univ. of North Carolina Press for the Institute of Early American History and Culture, 1985); Thomas Doerflinger, *A Vigorous Spirit of Enterprise: Merchants and Economic Development in Revolutionary Philadelphia* (Chapel Hill: Univ. of North Carolina Press for the Institute of Early American History and Culture, 1986); Carville Earle and Ronald Hoffman, "Staple Crops and Urban Development in the Eighteenth-Century South," *Perspectives in American History* 10 (1976): 7-78; Jacob Price, "Economic Function and the Growth of American Port Towns in the Eighteenth Century," *Perspectives in American History* 7 (1974): 121-86; Paul E.G. Clemens, *The Atlantic Economy and Colonial Maryland's Eastern Shore: From Tobacco to Grain* (Ithaca, N.Y.: Cornell Univ. Press, 1980).

23. Carole Shammas, "How Self-Sufficient Was Early America?" *Journal of Interdisciplinary History* 13 (Autumn 1982): 252-53; idem, *The Pre-Industrial Consumer in England and America* (Oxford: Clarendon Press, 1990), 53-75.

24. Bettye Hobbs Pruitt, "Self-Sufficiency and the Agricultural Economy of Eighteenth-Century Massachusetts," *William and Mary Quarterly*, 3d ser., 41 (1984): 333-35.

25. Joyce Appleby, "Commercial Farming and the 'Agrarian Myth' in the Early Republic," *Journal of American History* 68 (1982): 836.

26. James A. Henretta, "Families and Farms: *Mentalité* in Pre-Industrial America," *William and Mary Quarterly*, 3d ser., 35 (1978): 3-32; and James T. Lemon, *The Best Poor Man's Country: A Geographical Study of Early Southeastern Pennsylvania* (Baltimore: Johns Hopkins Univ. Press, 1972).

27. Allan Kulikoff, "The Transition to Capitalism in Rural America," *William and Mary Quarterly*, 3d ser., 46 (1989): 125. Kulikoff was not the first historian to use the "transition" model. Steven Hahn and Jonathan Prude (eds.) examined various aspects of the changing rural economy during the nineteenth century in *The Countryside in the Age of Capitalist Transformation* (Chapel Hill: Univ. of North Carolina Press, 1985).

28. Allan Kulikoff, *The Agrarian Origins of American Capitalism* (Charlottesville: Univ. Press of Virginia, 1992), 3.

29. Bridenbaugh, *Myths and Realities*, 143-44.

30. Bridenbaugh, *The Colonial Craftsman*, 29, 24.

31. Paraphrased in Jack Greene, "Independence, Improvement, and Authority: Toward a Framework for Understanding the Histories of the Southern Backcountry during the Era of the American Revolution," in Ronald Hoffman, Thad W. Tate, and Peter J. Albert, eds., *An Uncivil War: The Southern Backcountry During the American Revolution* (Charlottesville: Univ. Press of Virginia for the U.S. Capitol Historical Society, 1985), 9-10. Greene drew heavily upon Richard R. Beeman, "Social Change and Cultural Conflict in Virginia: Lunenburg County, 1746 to 1774," *William and Mary Quarterly*, 3d ser., 35 (1978): 455-76, esp. 457, 468, 478.

32. Albert H. Tillson, "The Southern Backcountry: A Survey of Current Research," *Virginia Magazine of History and Biography* 98 (July 1990): 387.

33. Bridenbaugh, *Myths and Realities*, 122.

34. Not just the South but the entire colonial American backcountry lived in different stages of development at the same time. For more information see Gregory H. Nobles, "Breaking into the Backcountry: New Approaches to the Early American Frontier, 1750-1800," *William and Mary Quarterly*, 3d ser., 46 (Oct. 1989): 641-70.

35. Greene, "Independence, Improvement, and Authority," 3; Bridenbaugh, *Myths and Realities*, 120; Richard R. Beeman, *The Evolution of the Southern Backcountry: A Case Study of Lunenburg County, Virginia, 1746-1832* (Philadelphia: Univ. of Pennsylvania Press, 1984), 12.

36. Tillson, "Southern Backcountry," 397.

37. Beeman, "Evolution of the Southern Backcountry," 11, 26; Warren Billings, John Selby, and Thad W. Tate, *Colonial Virginia: A History* (White Plains, N.Y.: KTO Press, 1986), 209.

38. For more differences between the backcountries of the southern colonies see Tillson, "Southern Backcountry," 387-422.

39. Beeman, *Evolution of the Southern Backcountry*, 10-12.

40. Ibid., 27, 30, 34, 99, 102.

41. David Hackett Fischer, *Albion's Seed: Four British Folkways in America* (New York: Oxford Univ. Press, 1989), 6-7, 605-782.

42. A. Roger Ekirch, "'A New Government of Liberty': Hermon Husband's Vision of Backcountry North Carolina, 1755," *William and Mary Quarterly*, 3d ser., 34 (1977): 632-46; Marvin L. Michael Kay, "The North Carolina Regulation, 1766-1776," in Alfred F. Young, ed., *The American Revolution: Exploration in the History of American Radicalism* (DeKalb: Northern Illinois Univ. Press, 1976), 71-123; Marvin L. Michael Kay and Lorin Lee Cary, "Class, Mobility, and Conflict in North Carolina on the Eve of the Revolution," in Jeffrey J. Crow and Larry E. Tise, eds., *The Southern Experience in the American Revolution* (Chapel Hill: Univ. of North Carolina Press, 1978); John S. Bassett, "The Regulators of North Carolina," American Historical Association, *Report for the Year 1894* (Washington, D.C., 1895), 142-212; and James P. Whittenburg, "Planters, Merchants, and Lawyers: Social Change and the Origins of the North Carolina Regulation," *William and Mary Quarterly*, 3d ser., 34 (April 1977): 215-38; idem, "'The Common Farmer (Number 2)': Herman Husband's Plan for Peace between the United States and the Indians, 1792," *William and Mary Quarterly* 3d ser., 34 (1977): 647-50.

43. Hoffman, Tate, and Albert, eds., *Uncivil War*; Crow and Tise eds., *Southern Experience*.

44. Daniel B. Thorp, *The Moravian Community in Colonial North Carolina* (Knoxville: Univ. of Tennessee Press, 1989), 1-2; Beeman, *Evolution of the Southern Backcountry*; and Robert D. Mitchell, *Commercialism and Frontier: Perspectives on the Early Shenandoah Valley* (Charlottesville: Univ. Press of Virginia, 1977).

45. H. Roy Merrens, *Colonial North Carolina in the Eighteenth Century: A Study in Historical Geography* (Chapel Hill: Univ. of North Carolina Press, 1964), 162.

46. Beeman, *Evolution of the Southern Backcountry*, 61-63.

47. Mitchell, *Commercialism and Frontier*, 235-37.

48. Joseph Ernst and H. Roy Merrens, "'Camden's turrets pierce the skies!': The Urban Process in the Southern Colonies during the Eighteenth Century," *William and Mary Quarterly*, 3d ser., 30 (1970): 549-74.

49. Merrens, *Colonial North Carolina*, 146-66.

50. Daniel B. Thorp, "Doing Business in the Backcountry: Retail Trade in Colonial

Rowan County, North Carolina," *William and Mary Quarterly*, 3d ser., 48 (July 1991): 387-408.

51. Robert W. Ramsey, *Carolina Cradle: The Settlement of the Northwest Carolina Frontier, 1747-1762* (Chapel Hill: Univ. of North Carolina Press, 1964); James Brawley, *The Rowan Story, 1753-1953: A Narrative History of Rowan County, North Carolina* (Salisbury: Rowan Printing Co., 1953); idem, *Old Rowan: Views and Sketches* (Salisbury: Rowan Printing Co., 1959); idem, *Rowan County... A Brief History* (Raleigh: NC DAH, 1974); Jethro Rumple, *A History of Rowan County, North Carolina* (1881; reprint, Baltimore: Regional Publishing Co., 1978); Fred Burgess, *Randolph County, Economic and Social* (reprint; Randolph County Historical Society, 1969); and Lindley S. Butler, *Rockingham County: A Brief History* (Raleigh: North Carolina Dept. of Cultural Resources, DAH, 1982).

52. *RM*; J.H. Clewell, *History of Wachovia in North Carolina: The Unitas Fratrum or Moravian Church in North Carolina during a Century and a Half, 1752-1902* (New York: Doubleday, Page, 1902); and Levin T. Reichel, *The Moravians in North Carolina: An Authentic History* (1857; reprint, Baltimore: Geneaological Publishing Co., 1968).

53. Christopher Hendricks, "The Planning and Development of Two Moravian Congregation Towns: Salem, North Carolina, and Gracehill, Northern Ireland" (master's thesis, College of William and Mary, 1987); William J. Murtaugh, *Moravian Architecture and Town Planning* (Chapel Hill: Univ. of North Carolina Press, 1967); Daniel B. Thorp, "The City That Never Was: Count von Zinzendorf's Original Plan for Salem," *North Carolina Historical Review* 56 (Jan. 1984): 36-58; John Larson, "A Mill for Salem," *Three Forks of Muddy Creek* 9 (1983): 17-25; Johanna Carlson Miller, "Mills on the Wachovia Tract, 1756-1849" (master's thesis, Wake Forest Univ., 1985); Johanna Miller Lewis, "The Salem Congregational Mill," *Three Forks of Muddy Creek* 13 (1988): 39-46; and idem, "The Use of Water Power on the Wachovia Tract of North Carolina by the Moravians during the Eighteenth Century," *Communal Studies* 9 (1989): 10-22.

54. Johanna Miller Lewis, "A Social and Architectural History of the Girls' Boarding School Building at Salem, North Carolina," *North Carolina Historical Review* 66 (April 1989): 125-48; Jon Sensbach, "A Separate Canaan: The Making of an Afro-Moravian World in North Carolina, 1763-1836" (Ph.D. diss., Duke Univ., 1991); and Jerry L. Surratt, *Gottlieb Schober of Salem: Discipleship and Ecumenical Vision in an Early Moravian Town* (Macon, Ga.: Mercer Univ. Press, 1983); idem, "The Moravian as Businessman: Gottlieb Schober of Salem," *North Carolina Historical Review* 60 (Jan. 1983): 1-23; and Daniel B. Thorp, "Assimilation in North Carolina's Moravian Community," *Journal of Southern History* 52 (1986): 19-42.

55. Michael Hammond, "Garden Archaeology at Old Salem," in *Earth Patterns* ed. William Kelso (Charlottesville: Univ. Press of Virginia, 1990); idem, "New Light on Old Salem," *Archaeology*, Nov./Dec. 1989, 37-41; idem, "The Archaeological Investigations of the Charles Alexander Cooper House, Lot 41"; "An 1840's Barn, Lot 71"; "The John Ackerman House, Lot 91, Old Salem, N.C.," three mss. on file at Old Salem, Inc., 1984, 1986; idem, "Archives and Archaeology," *Three Forks of Muddy Creek* 12 (1987): 28-36; L. McKay Whatley, "The Mount Shepard Pottery: Correlating Archaeology and History," *Journal of Early Southern Decorative Arts* 6 (May 1980): 21-57.

Chapter 2. The Early History and Settlement of Rowan County

1. John A. Lawson, *A New Voyage of Carolina*, ed. Hugh T. Lefler (Chapel Hill: Univ. of North Carolina Press, 1967), 51.

2. *RM* 1: 40, 38.

3. Lawson, *New Voyage*, 52.

4. Ibid., xiii-xiv, 92.

5. Billings, Selby, and Tate, *Colonial Virginia*, 209.

6. William G. Boyd, ed., *William Byrd's Histories of the Dividing Line Betwixt Virginia and North Carolina* (New York: Dover, 1967), 304.

7. Ibid., 66.

8. A. Roger Ekirch, *"Poor Carolina": Politics and Society in Colonial North Carolina, 1729-1775* (Chapel Hill: Univ. of North Carolina Press, 1981), 31.

9. Jack P. Greene, *Pursuits of Happiness: The Social Development of Early Modern British Colonies and the Formation of American Culture* (Chapel Hill: Univ. of North Carolina Press, 1988), 125, 127; Lemon, *Best Poor Man's Country*, 222.

10. Merrens, *Colonial North Carolina*, 32-35.

11. Ibid., 37-41, 46-47.

12. Lefler and Newsome, *North Carolina*, 156-57; Samuel J. Ervin, Jr., *A Colonial History of Rowan County, North Carolina*, James Sprunt Studies in North Carolina History, vol. 16, no. 1 (Chapel Hill: Univ. of North Carolina, 1917), 5; Ramsey, *Carolina Cradle*, 6; *CR* 5: 355.

13. Rumple, *History of Rowan County*, 29.

14. Ervin, *Colonial History*, 5-6.

15. Merrens, *Colonial North Carolina*, 48.

16. Ramsey, *Carolina Cradle*, 7-8.

17. James S. Brawley, *Rowan County*, 2-3; Ramsey, *Carolina Cradle*, 7.

18. Bernard Bailyn, *Voyagers to the West* (New York: Knopf, 1986), 14-15; James G. Leyburn, *The Scotch-Irish: A Social History* (Chapel Hill: Univ. of North Carolina Press, 1962), 220; Merrens, *Colonial North Carolina*, 66-67. In *Myths and Realities* (130), Bridenbaugh maintains that the Great Wagon Road also followed the old Indian trails and "was only made possible by the Iroquois at the Treaty of Lancaster in 1744 to permit the use of their Great Warrior's Path through the Shenandoah Valley, and in North Carolina it took the course of the Cherokee Trading Path" beyond Salisbury. When the South Carolina Piedmont opened up for settlement the road continued through the upcountry and thence southward to reach its terminus just across the Savannah River in Augusta, Georgia.

19. Brawley, *Brief History*, 4; Ramsey, *Carolina Cradle*, 17.

20. Merrens, *Colonial North Carolina*, 8, 12; Ramsey, *Carolina Cradle*, 10-22.

21. Merrens, *Colonial North Carolina*, 64.

22. Ramsey, *Carolina Cradle*, 10-22, 175; Leyburn, *Scotch-Irish*, 189-90, 213-15.

23. Ramsey, *Carolina Cradle*, 30, 33.

24. Mikle Dave Ledgerwood, "Ethnic Groups on the Frontier in Rowan County, 1750-1778" (master's thesis, Vanderbilt Univ., 1977), 2.

25. Ramsey, *Carolina Cradle*, 32.

26. *Rowan Deed Abstracts*, 6:337 (Jan. 13, 1767); 2:244-45 (June 2, 1757); Ramsey, *Carolina Cradle*, 32, 209.

27. Ramsey, *Carolina Cradle*, 32, 36, 45.

28. Ibid., 36; *Rowan Deed Abstracts*, 6:212 (Sept. 7, 1765); 4:319, 320 (Dec. 25, 1753); 3:66-68 (Jan. 22, 1756); *Rowan Court Abstracts*, 2:680 (Jan. 16, 1767), 470 (July 13, 1763).

29. Ramsey, *Carolina Cradle*, 45; *Rowan Deed Abstracts*, 6:128, 129 (Feb. 13, 1765); *Rowan Court Abstracts* 4:53 (Nov. 5, 1774); 3:197 (May 10, 1770).

30. Ramsey, *Carolina Cradle*, 95.

31. *Rowan Deed Abstracts*, 4:727-731 (July 13, 1762); 1:19-22 (June 19, 1753); *Rowan Court Abstracts*, 1:174 (April 21, 1757); Rowan CPQS, May 7, 1788.

32. Ramsey, *Carolina Cradle*, 107, 116; *Rowan Deed Abstracts* 4:866-68; 6:254, 255; Rowan Crim. Act., Oct. 4, 1758.

33. Ramsey, *Carolina Cradle*, 108-9; artisan figure derived from computer data base of artisans in Rowan County prior to 1770.

34. *CR* 5:24.

35. Bailyn, *Voyagers*, 15.

36. David Leroy Corbitt, *The Formation of the North Carolina Counties, 1663-1943* (Raleigh: NC DAH, 1950), 185.

37. Rowan CPQS, June 1753 session; *Rowan Court Abstracts*, 1:1-6.

38. Daniel B. Thorp, "Moravian Colonization of Wachovia, 1753-1772: The Maintenance of Community in Late Colonial North Carolina" (Ph.D. diss., Johns Hopkins Univ., 1982), 18-19.

39. *RM* 1:12-13, 496.

40. Vernon Nelson, "The Moravian Church in America," in *Unitas Fratrum: Moravian Studies*, ed. Mari P. Van Buijtenen, Cornelius Dekker, and Huib Leeuwenberg (Utrect: Rijksarchief, 1975), 145-46. For more information see Adelaide L. Fries, *The Moravians in Georgia, 1735-1740*, Winston-Salem: n.p., 1945.

41. Nelson, "Moravian Church," 146-48.

42. Gillian L. Gollin, *Moravians in Two Worlds: A Study of Changing Communities* (New York: Columbia Univ. Press, 1967), 17-18, 143.

43. Frances Griffin, *Less Time for Meddling: A History of Salem Academy and College, 1772-1866* (Winston-Salem: Blair, 1979), 18-19.

44. Clewell, *History of Wachovia*, 2.

45. *RM* 1:14.

46. Ibid., 32-33.

47. Nelson, "Moravian Church," 150; Clewell, *History of Wachovia*, 6-8.

48. *RM* 1:59-60.

49. Ibid., 65; *Rowan Deed Abstracts*, 6:1-17. According to Gwynne S. Taylor in *From Frontier to Factory: An Architectural History of Forsyth County* (Raleigh: Division of Archives and History, Dept. of Cultural Resources, 1981, 1), today the Wachovia Tract constitutes over 37 percent of the 419 square miles of Forsyth County.

50. Thorp, *Moravian Community*, 30.

51. *RM* 1:15; this interpretation also appears in Merrens, *Colonial North Carolina*, 60.

52. Thorp, *Moravian Community*, 24; idem, "Moravian Colonization," 35-36.

53. Gollin, *Moravians in Two Worlds*, 148.

54. Spangenberg to Rev. White, Jan. 17, 1754, quoted in Thorp, "Moravian Colonization," 21.

55. Thorp, "Moravian Colonization," 21-22, 36.

56. Ibid., 43.

57. Thorp, *Moravian Community*, 33.

58. Spangenberg quoted in Thorp, "Moravian Colonization," 52.

59. *RM* 1:73.

60. According to Gollin (*Moravians in Two Worlds*, 143), the *Oeconomy* was not opposed to the sanctity of private property in theory, although in practice it incorporated a communism of property, production, labor and consumption that could destroy the very foundations for a system of private property.

61. Thorp, *Moravian Community*, 40-41; Gollin, *Moravians in Two Worlds*, 142.

62. Nelson, "Moravian Church," 150.

63. *RM* 1:73.

64. Mitchell, *Commercialism and Frontier*, 53.

65. *RM* 1:78.

66. Ibid., 2:528.
67. Ibid., 82-85.
68. Murtaugh, *Moravian Architecture*, 112.
69. Ernst and Merrens, "'Camden's turrets,'" 560.
70. *RM* 1:101, 106.

Chapter 3. The Development of Rowan County

1. *RM* 1:80.
2. Ibid., 39.
3. Jacob Loesch in Bethabara to Peter Boehler in Bethlehem, April 27, 1754, MASP.
4. *RM* 1:343-44, 485; Reichel, *Moravians in North Carolina*, 38.
5. *RM* 1:107, 112.
6. Ibid., 107, 123.
7. Ibid., 485-86.
8. Supply Order to Bethlehem from Jacob Loesch at Bethabara, July 26, 1756, MASP.
9. *RM* 1:149.
10. Thorp, *Moravian Community*, 135.
11. Spangenberg to brethren at Bethabara, Dec. 6, 1756, trans. Kenneth G. Hamilton, MASP.
12. *RM* 1:179. Lovefeasts were celebratory worship services that featured coffee and sweet rolls.
13. Joseph Spangenberg in Bethlehem to brethren in Bethabara, June 29, 1755, trans. Kenneth G. Hamilton, MASP.
14. Spangenberg to brethren and sisters at Bethabara, Oct. 18, 1757, trans. Kenneth G. Hamilton, MASP.
15. Thorp, *Moravian Community*, 112-15.
16. Ibid., 120.
17. *RM* 1:132-33, 156.
18. *RM* 1:122.
19. Thorp, *Moravian Community*, 120-21.
20. Joseph Spangenberg in Bethlehem to brethren in Bethabara, June 29, 1755, trans. Kenneth G. Hamilton, MASP.
21. Thorp, *Moravian Community*, 120-21.
22. *RM* 1:172, 160.
23. Ibid., 171, 182. Prior to this sale Aust had been selling clay pipes to local people and even shipping them to Bethlehem.
24. Ibid., 179-80, 241, 486, 488.
25. Forty people came to the mill in July 1756, and in December wagonloads of grain were brought from as far away as New Garden (a Quaker settlement, now Guilford College) and the Jersey settlement (now Linwood in Davidson County). *RM* 1:158, 173.
26. Jacob Loesch to Joseph Spangenberg, Nov. 3, 1756, MASP.
27. A bark mill reduced tanbark (usually from oak and hemlock trees) to a coarse powder which, when steeped in water, produced an astringent substance called tannin, or tannic acid. Tannic acid is the main chemical agent used in curing leather. Oil mills pressed out linseed oil from flax seeds. An important product to eighteenth-century Americans, this oil was used to make paint, preserve wood, fuel lamps, and even serve as medicine. For more information see Miller, "Mills on the Wachovia Tract."
28. Joseph Spangenberg to brethren at Bethabara, Dec. 6, 1756, trans. Kenneth G. Hamilton, MASP.
29. Br. Spangenberg to Br. Loesch, June 15, 1758, trans. Elizabeth Marx, MASP.

30. *RM* 1:484, 148, 344.

31. Thorp, *Moravian Community*, 135.

32. Spangenberg to Jacob Loesch at Bethabara, Feb. 6, 1758, trans. Kenneth G. Hamilton, MASP.

33. Rowan CPQS, 2:680; Ramsey, *Carolina Cradle*, 37.

34. *RM* 1:188. At least thirteen weavers (excluding the Moravians) were working in Rowan County by 1758 according to data from Rowan County deeds, wills, and minutes of the Court of Pleas and Quarter.

35. Bethania was settled by a mixture of church members and "strangers" who sought shelter at the Bethabara mill during Indian attacks in the backcountry. As Bethabara became overcrowded and the "strangers" expressed an interest in joining the church, during a visit to Wachovia in 1759 Br. Spangenberg decided that this was a unique opportunity to create a new village on the tract, owned and run by the church where Moravian sympathizers could live among the brethren. Bethania may have been a "safety valve" to keep Bethabara from becoming too crowded and too big, so that it would not compete with the future center of trade and manufacture.

36. Ramsey, *Carolina Cradle*, 191-92.

37. Rowan CPQS; Rowan Apprent.; Rowan Estates; Rowan Wills; Rowan Civ. Act.; Rowan Crim. Act.; Salisbury Civ. Act.; Salisbury Misc.; Salisbury Trial; Salisbury Crown; Salisbury Crim. Act.; Salisbury Execution; Salisbury Ref.; *Rowan Deed Abstracts*.

38. Lemon, *Best Poor Man's Country*, 7. Recent research by Judith Ridner at the College of William and Mary indicates that Lemon understated the number of artisans in Pennsylvania.

39. Rowan CPQS, April 16, 1767.

40. Figures derived from data on children bound in Rowan County in Lynne Howard Fraser, "'Nobody's Children': The Treatment of Illegitimate Children in Three North Carolina Counties, 1760-1790" (master's thesis, College of William and Mary, 1987), 80-95.

41. *CR* 23:70-71.

42. Ibid., 432, 510, 577-83; Kathi R. Jones, "'That Also These children May Become Useful People': Apprenticeships in Rowan County, North Carolina, from 1753 to 1795" (master's thesis, College of William and Mary, 1984), 23-25.

43. The numerical discrepancies between the number of apprentices and the number of apprenticeship agreements results from four children who transferred from one apprenticeship to another.

44. Figures derived from Fraser, "'Nobody's Children,'" 80-95; and Rowan CPQS.

45. Rowan CPQS, May 11, 1777, Aug. 6, 1787.

46. The survey of artisans working within the original boundaries of Rowan County by 1790 was compiled from Rowan CPQS; Rowan Apprent.; Rowan Wills; Rowan Civ. Act.; Rowan Crim. Act.; Burke Apprent.; Guilford CPQS; Randolph CPQS; Randolph Apprent.; Stokes CPQS; Surry CPQS; Surry Apprent.; Wilkes CPQS; Wilkes Apprent.; Museum of Early Southern Decorative Arts, *Index to Early Southern Artisans* (New York: Clearwater Publishing, 1985); 1790 U.S. Census.

47. Anonymous receipt, May 11, 1770, John Steele Papers, SHC; Rowan CPQS, 1783.

48. For more information on this topic see Salinger, "*To serve well and faithfully*"; and Harold B. Gill, *Apprentices in Colonial Virginia* (Salt Lake City: Ancestry Publishing, 1990).

49. Lemon, *Best Poor Man's Country*, 10.

50. Lefler and Newsome, *North Carolina*, 128; Marvin L. Michael Kay and Lorin Lee Cary, "A Demographic Analysis of Colonial North Carolina with Special Emphasis upon

the Slave and Black Populations," in *Black Americans in North Carolina and the South*, ed. Jeffrey J. Crow and Flora J. Hatley (Chapel Hill: Univ. of North Carolina Press, 1984), 77, table 3.1.

51. Rowan Apprent., April 15, 1781, March 1, 1785. For additional information on slavery in the backcountry see Sensbach, "Separate Canaan."

52. Lemon, *Best Poor Man's Country*, 12.

53. Salisbury Civ. Act., March 5, 1770.

54. Rowan CPQS, Feb. 16, 1770, Nov. 8, 1771.

55. Ramsey, *Carolina Cradle*, 110.

56. Rowan Crim. Act., Oct. 4, 1758.

57. Ibid.; Rowan Civ. Act.

58. *Rowan Deed Abstracts*, 3:338-40.

59. *CR* 7:120.

60. Rowan CPQS, 1782, and Aug. 3, 1774.

61. Rowan Wills, Sept. 7, 1777. In addition, Miligan did not own any land, which indicates that his sole profession was that of weaver.

62. Rowan Wills, Nov. 14, 1789.

63. *Rowan Will Abstracts*; Rowan Wills.

64. This is especially true for German artisans. As Ramsey notes in *Carolina Cradle*, since the Germans were a minority who did not speak English, they did not participate in the political process; hence they do not appear in the official records. The Germans rarely ventured into the English speaking areas of the county, and they generally handled their legal affairs among themselves.

65. Rowan CPQS, Oct. 10, 1765.

66. *Rowan Court Abstracts*, 3:86, 108, 127.

67. Lemon, *Best Poor Man's Country*, 2, 5.

68. Mitchell, *Commercialism and Frontier*, x.

69. Lemon, *Best Poor Man's Country*, 73-77; Mitchell, *Commercialism and Frontier*, 18, 46.

70. Mitchell, *Commercialism and Frontier*, 45, 52-53.

71. In "Transition to Capital," Kulikoff describes subsistence agriculture in its purest sense as an economic level achieved with an almost complete absence of exchange, whereas self-sufficient farms enjoyed almost total production of their food and clothing.

72. Mitchell, *Commercialism and Frontier*, 151-52.

73. Henretta, "Families and Farms," 15.

74. Mitchell, *Commercialism and Frontier*, 154-55.

75. *CR* 23:390.

76. William Conrad Guess, "County Government in Colonial North Carolina," *James Sprunt Studies in History and Political Science*, vol. 11, no. 1, 26; Paul M. McCain, "Magistrates Courts in Early North Carolina," *North Carolina Historical Review*, 48 (Jan. 1971): 23-24.

77. *Rowan Court Abstracts*, 1:2, 7, 11, 16; Rumple, *History of Rowan County*, 61.

78. *Rowan Court Abstracts*, 1:8-9.

79. Ibid., 21.

80. Ibid., 20.

81. Ramsey, *Carolina Cradle*, 161-62.

82. On Dec. 17, 1753, Carter purchased 640 acres of land from Corbin, Granville's agent. *Rowan Deed Abstracts*, 2:1, 2; *Rowan Court Abstracts*, 1:34.

83. Ramsey, *Carolina Cradle*, 154-57.

84. *Rowan Deed Abstracts,* 2:81-83.

85. Ramsey, *Carolina Cradle,* 158-59.

86. *CR,* 5:355.

87. Ramsey, *Carolina Cradle,* 158-60.

88. Ibid., 164. Henry Horah Sr. is not identified as a weaver in any of the primary sources consulted.

89. *Rowan Court Abstracts,* 4:22 (May 4, 1774); 3:264 (May 8, 1771).

90. Ernst and Merrens, "'Camden's turrets,'" 549-74.

91. Artisans' figures generated from data base of artisans in Rowan County in dBase III+ sorted by trade and year of arrival. Information on artisans on Rowan County 1759 tax list provided by James P. Whittenburg.

92. Invoice, Nov. 7, 1785, John Steele Papers, SHC; Anonymous Personal Account Book, 1791, Macay-McNeely Papers, SHC.

93. Henry M. Miller, "Colonization and Subsistence Change on the 17th Century Chesapeake Frontier" (Ph.D. diss., Michigan State Univ., 1984), 14-16.

Chapter 4. The Commercial Development of Rowan County

1. Ironically, the magnitude of the increase in the Rowan artisan population does not parallel the demographics of the entire county. The population of Rowan County grew rapidly from the county's creation, when there were 1,000 taxables (approximately 5,000 residents) until 1756, when the taxables had increased to 1,500. Indian problems throughout the backcountry led families to flee the region during the French and Indian War and the population eventually dropped over the next four years to fewer than 700 taxables. The population did not recover its prewar figures until the latter part of 1763. From that point on the population exploded to 2,600 taxables by 1765 and at least 4,000 by 1770.

Analysis of artisans' arrival dates in Rowan County and their last appearance in the records shows that during the French and Indian War no artisans left the county and the number of new artisans increased. From 1752 to 1755, an average of 5.75 artisans settled in Rowan County each year. Between 1756 and 1759, when the county's population was dropping, the average annual number of artisans entering the county rose to 12.5 as a result of 28 artisans who came to Rowan in 1759. Following the war, the artisan arrival rate settled back to its prewar level for a few years before it finally paralleled the population trends in the entire county by increasing to an average of 14 artisans arriving a year.

2. Lemon, *Best Poor Man's Country,* 27-30.

3. Robert Hogg Account Books (vol. 1, Invoices; vol. 2, Account Book for Wilmington and Cross Creek Store Individuals Accounts; vol. 3, Day Book that accompanies Account Book; vol. 4, Journal), SHC (hereafter cited as Hogg Account Books); General Merchandise Store Ledger, Nisbet Collection, SHC (hereafter cited as Nisbet Ledger); Account Book, 1784-1796, Rowan County, John Dickey Papers, Manuscript Collection, Perkins Library, Duke Univ. (hereafter cited as Dickey Account Book); Account Book, Alexander and John Lowrance Papers, 1749-1796, Manuscripts Collection, Perkins Library, Duke University (hereafter cited as Lowrance Account Book); William Steele Account Books (vol. 1, Memorandum Book... With a List of Balances; vol. 2, William Steel's [*sic*] Cash Account), John Steele Papers, SHC.

4. Lemon, *Best Poor Man's Country,* chap. 1; Mitchell, *Commercialism and Frontier,* 143, 152; Nobles, "Breaking into the Backcountry," 657.

5. Merrens, *Colonial North Carolina,* 143.

6. *Rowan Court Abstracts* 1:5, 2:146-47.
7. Ibid., 1:18, 2:280, 89.
8. *CR*, 5:355.
9. *Rowan Court Abstracts*, 2:146.
10. *Rowan Deed Abstracts*, 3:395-96.
11. Rowan Wills, C:129; *Rowan Deed Abstracts*, 3:522-25.
12. Thorp, "Doing Business," 387-89.
13. Ibid., 392.
14. Henry Wensel Will, Rowan Wills.
15. Nisbet Ledger.
16. Ibid.
17. Ibid.; William Steel's Cash Account.
18. Nisbet Ledger.
19. James M. Gaynor and Nancy L. Hagedorn, *Tools: Working Wood in Eighteenth Century America* (Williamsburg: Colonial Williamsburg Foundation, 1993), xiii.
20. Nisbet Ledger.
21. Ibid.; Dickey Account Book.
22. Nisbet Ledger, accounts of Nathaniel Ewing, Adam Simonton, William Bones, and David Hill; John Dickey Account Book, account of James Graham.
23. Nisbet Ledger; Dickey Account Book; Lowrance Account Book; William Steel's Cash Account.
24. Nisbet Ledger; William Steel's Cash Account.
25. Invoice of Items purchased from Wm Glen[ripped] by Wm Steel, 1760, Steele Papers.
26. Nisbet Ledger; Dickey Account Book.
27. Nisbet Ledger.
28. William Steel's Cash Account.
29. Nisbet Ledger.
30. Lowrance Account Book.
31. Nisbet Ledger.
32. William Steel's Cash Account.
33. Nisbet Ledger.
34. Lowrance Account Book.
35. Thorp, "Doing Business," 392.
36. Nisbet Ledger.
37. Account of the Estate of William Steele with Absolam Taylor, Feb. 1770-Sept. 21, 1775, Steele Papers.
38. Invoice and receipt from Joseph Atkins to Elizabeth Steele, May 20, 1775, Steele Papers.
39. The analysis of purchases was achieved by placing the entire contents of the Steele and Lowrance account books and samples from the Hogg and Nisbet books into a computerized data base using dBase III+. Purchases were divided into the following categories: stationery, tools, hardware, household accessories, cookware, dining equipage, drinking equipage, fabric, notions, clothing, fashion accessories, food, liquor, firearms and accessories, jewelry, and metal.
40. Invoices in Steele Papers.
41. Merrens, *Colonial North Carolina*, 144, 145, 153.
42. Ibid., 146. Bath, Beaufort, and Brunswick were seaports that had faded into insignificance by the late eighteenth century.
43. Ibid., 162.

44. Ibid., 155. Cross Creek was renamed Fayetteville in 1784 in honor of Lafayette; it later merged with Campbelltown.

45. *Rowan Court Abstracts*, 1:18.

46. Ibid., 2:486, 563, 564, 609, 647, 707, 733; 3:96.

47. Ibid., 2:733; 3:125.

48. Merrens, *Colonial North Carolina*, 159-61.

49. Robert Hogg emigrated to North Carolina in 1756 from Scotland and established a prosperous merchant firm in Wilmington with Samuel Campbell. For more information on Robert and his brother James, see Bailyn, *Voyagers*, 499-544.

50. Robert Hogg Account Book for Wilmington and Cross Creek Store Individuals Accounts. The Robert Johnston and William Williams listed in the store accounts may not be the same individuals who worked in Rowan County. According to Bailyn, the Hogg & Campbell "concern" in Cross Creek did not become a satellite store until 1774, when James Hogg opened it. Bailyn, *Voyagers*, 535.

51. Robert Hogg Day Book.

52. Robert Hogg Account Book, Invoices.

53. Ibid.

54. Ramsey, *Carolina Cradle*, 169.

55. *Rowan Deed Abstracts*, 3:293-95, 66-68.

56. Thorp, "Doing Business," 390. Stores required no license to operate in Rowan County and as a result, are difficult to identify.

57. Ramsey, *Carolina Cradle*, 166-68.

58. William Steel's Cash Account and William Steele's Memorandum Book with a list of balances [1768], Steele Papers. The men were Mr. Gamble, James Rusel, John Penel, John Scott, and Thomas Bagsham.

59. Thorp, "Doing Business," 393-94.

60. Nisbet Ledger; Dickey Account Book; Lowrance Account Book; William Steel's Cash Account.

61. *Rowan Deed Abstracts*, 6:145, 146, 147, 148, 542, 543; 7:458; 9:265; Bethabara Diary, Sept. 20, 1775, MASP.

62. Betz's father-in-law was George Bruner. *Rowan Deed Abstracts*, 6:450.

63. Ibid., 2:236, 237; 5:257, 258; 7:312; 2:396, 397.

64. Invoice from William Watt to the estate of Elizabeth Steele, June 19, 1792, and invoice from Tobias Forror to the estate of Elizabeth Steele, June 26, 1790, Steele Papers.

65. Invoice from Absolam Taylor to estate of William Steele, 1770-1773, Steele Papers; invoice from Paul Rodsmith to John Steele, paid Nov. 7, 1785; invoice from Joseph Atkins to estate of William Steele, paid May 20, 1775; invoice from Arthur Erwin to William Steele, paid Aug. 8, 1774; invoice from Salisbury Misc.

66. Thorp, *Moravian Community*, 116, 127, 140.

67. Bethabara Diary, Oct. 17, 1768, MASP, on loan to Old Salem, Inc.

68. Tuis Gap is located at the Clay-Macon County line; there are a number of Big Spring creeks, branches, and gaps in Clay, Macon, Mitchell, and Rutherford counties; and Stovertown was probably Stover's Gap in Avery County. Geographical information from William S. Powell, *The North Carolina Gazetteer* (Chapel Hill: Univ. of North Carolina Press, 1968).

69. *RM* 1:344, 489. A gunstocker carved and fitted custom gunstocks to their owners.

Chapter 5. Moravian Artisans on the Wachovia Tract

1. *RM* 1:206.
2. Ibid., 228.
3. Larry E. Tise, "Building and Architecture," in *Winston-Salem in History* (Winston-Salem: Historic Winston, 1976), 9:6.
4. *RM* 1:215.
5. Ibid., 265.
6. Ibid., 265, 282.
7. Winston-Salem Section, North Carolina, American Institute of Architects, *Architectural Guide, Winston-Salem, Forsyth County* (Winston-Salem, 1978), 15. For more information on the town planning of Salem see Hendricks, "Planning and Development"; and Thorp, "City That Never Was."
8. *RM* 1:295, 298, 320. Although the published records indicate that church leaders announced the name of the town to Wachovia residents in 1765, letters between various church boards show the name had been selected as early as 1763. *Vorsteher Collegium* in Bethlehem to *Aeltesten Conferenz* at Bethabara, Aug. 31, 1763, trans. Elizabeth Marx, MASP.
9. *RM* 1:282, 328, 344, 498, 490.
10. Spangenberg to Conference at Bethabara, Sept. 3, 1760, trans. Kenneth G. Hamilton, MASP.
11. Thorp, *Moravian Community*, 122-23.
12. *RM* 1:123, 124, 484.
13. Quoted in Thorp, *Moravian Community*, 190-91.
14. Spangenberg to Conference at Bethabara, Jan. 21, 1761, MASP.
15. The 1762 Inventory of Souls in Wachovia lists Schmidt as living in Bethabara with his wife and children. *RM* 1:254.
16. Gammern to Seidel, Mar. 9, 1763, MASP.
17. *RM* 1:300.
18. Draft of letter from Ettwein in Bethabara to F.W. Marshall, 1766, trans. Kenneth G. Hamilton, MASP; Matthew Schropp to Nathanael Seidel in Bethlehem, Oct. 5, 1766, MASP.
19. Ettwein in Bethlehem to Shropps, Graffs, and Lorenz in Bethabara, Aug. 23, 1767, MASP; *Aeltesten Conferenz Protocol*, Mar. 6, June 23, June 27, Aug. 6, Nov. 8, Nov. 14, and Nov. 23, 1768, and Jan. 17, 1769, MASP; *RM* 2:374, 378, 387.
20. *RM* 1:171-72.
21. Ibid., 237. For accounts of other sales see ibid., 287, 412.
22. Ibid., 412.
23. Ibid., 251, 275, 307.
24. Ibid., 269, 332.
25. Ibid., 287; 2: 759, 762-63.
26. *Aeltesten Conferenz Protocol*, Nov. 14, 1768, MASP; *RM* 2:714 (*Aufseher Collegium Protocol*, Jan. 14, 1772).
27. *RM* 1:486, 179-80.
28. Quoted in Thorp, *Moravian Community*, 190-91.
29. *RM* 1:254.
30. Spangenberg to Jacob Loesch, Nov. 25, 1761, trans. Kenneth G. Hamilton, MASP; Spangenberg to Conference at Bethabara, Nov. 26, 1761, trans. Kenneth G. Hamilton, MASP.
31. *RM* 1:241, 486, 488.

32. Lorenz Bagge in Bethabara to Nathanael Seidel in Bethlehem, Nov. 21, 1766, MASP.

33. *RM* 1:253-55. In the 1762 "Inventory of Souls in Wachovia" out of the thirty-two artisans, nine were farmer/artisans; in addition, the list included one apprentice.

34. Conference in Bethabara to Provincial Synod in Bethlehem, Apr. 14, 1766, MASP; Spangenberg to Conference at Bethabara, Mar. 2, 1762, MASP.

35. Spangenberg to Conference at Bethabara, Nov. 26, 1761, trans. Kenneth G. Hamilton, MASP.

36. Spangenberg to the Board in Bethabara, April 17, 1762, trans. Kenneth G. Hamilton, MASP.

37. *RM* 1:254, 485.

38. Ibid., 355; Lorenz Bagge in Bethabara to Nathanael Seidel in Bethlehem, Nov. 21, 1766, MASP.

39. *Aeltesten Conferenz Protocol*, Feb. 14, 1767. The *Aeltesten Conferenz*, or Elder's Conference, was the church board charged with overseeing all the other church boards in Wachovia as well as ruling on the personal matters or problems of congregation members.

40. Ettwein in Bethabara to Spangenberg, Feb. 1763, trans. Elizabeth Marx, MASP.

41. Gammern in Bethabara to Nathanael Seidel in Bethlehem, Mar. 9, 1763, MASP.

42. *RM* 1:282, 287.

43. Ettwein to Nathanael Seidel in Bethlehem, Feb. 19, 1765, MASP.

44. *RM* 1:324, 327, 328.

45. Ibid., 320.

46. *Vorsteher Collegium* in Bethlehem to *Aeltesten Conferenz* at Bethabara, Aug. 31, 1763, trans. Elizabeth Marx, MASP.

47. Schropp to Nathanael Seidel at Bethlehem, Oct. 5, 1766, MASP. Schropp had been asking Bethlehem to send down some carpenters and masons for at least seven months prior to this time. See letter from Conference in Bethabara to Provincial Synod in Bethlehem, April 14, 1766, trans. Kenneth G. Hamilton, MASP; F.W. Marshall in Bethlehem to *Aeltesten Conferenz* at Bethabara, June 24, 1766, trans. Kenneth G. Hamilton, MASP.

48. Schropp to Bethlehem, Nov. 20, 1766, MASP.

49. *RM* 1:387.

50. Thomas Haupert, "Apprentices in the Moravian Settlement," *Communal Societies* 9 (1989): 3; Rowan CPQS. Individual justices of the peace could witness the signing of apprentice bonds in North Carolina; see McCain, "Magistrates Courts," 29.

51. No doubt the failure of the original plan at Bethlehem is what led church officials to allow craftsmen at Bethania, a farming community, and to plan a farm directly outside of Salem and encourage the artisans in Salem to raise crops on their outlots and meadows. *RM* 1:315.

52. Gollin, *Moravians in Two Worlds*, 141, 158-59, 162-64.

53. F.W. Marshall in Bethlehem to Ettwein in Bethabara, Oct. 25, 1762, trans. Kenneth G. Hamilton, MASP.

54. *Vorsteher Collegium* in Bethlehem to Elder's Conference at Bethabara, Aug. 31, 1763, trans. Elizabeth Marx, MASP.

55. Letter of instructions from the directing board of the Unity to a company of brethren leaving for Wachovia, in Herrnhut dated Aug. 30, 1765, and in Zeyst dated Sept. 11, 1765, *RM* 2:595-96.

56. Plans for Wachovia made by the committee appointed by the Unity's *Vorsteher Collegium* in Herrnhut, July 8, 1767, *RM* 2:601.

57. *RM* 2:599.

58. Ibid., 605-6.

59. Ibid., 607.

60. Thorp, *Moravian Community*, 113-16.

61. Hooker, ed., *Carolina Backcountry*, 78.

62. Albert Matthews, ed., *Journal of William Loughton Smith, 1790-1791* (Cambridge: Cambridge Univ. Press, 1917), 73.

63. *North-Carolina Journal*, Halifax, Feb. 20, 1793, 1 (obtained from the North Carolina Research File, General Information, at the Museum of Early Southern Decorative Arts, Winston-Salem, N.C.).

64. *RM* 2:597.

65. Thorp, *Moravian Community*, 101.

66. *RM* 1:484-94.

67. Ibid., 247.

68. *Aeltesten Conferenz Protocol*, Sept. 30, 1766, MASP; Schropp to Seidel in Bethlehem, Oct. 5, 1766, MASP.

69. *Protocoll der Helfers Conferenz*, Jan. 20, 1767, MASP; *RM* 1:357.

70. Lorenz Bagge in Bethabara to Nathanael Seidel in Bethlehem, Nov. 21,1766, MASP; *RM* 2:836.

71. Bethabara Diary, Oct. 17, 1768, MASP, on loan to Old Salem, Inc.; *Aufseher Collegium*, Dec. 21, 1773, trans. Erika Huber, MASP, on loan to Old Salem, Inc.

72. *RM* 1:250; *Rowan Deed Abstracts*, 6:145, 146, 450.

73. *Aeltesten Conferenz Protocol*, Mar. 27, 1770, MASP.

74. *RM* 2:411, 413, 435, 443.

75. Gollin, *Moravians in Two Worlds*, 208; Thorp, *Moravian Community*, 203-4. The church spelled out the economic regulations governing every member of the Salem Congregation in the "Brotherly Agreement and Contract of the *Evangelische Brüder-Gemeine* at Salem" (also known as the Salem Statutes) in May 1773, trans. Elisabeth Somers, MASP.

76. *Aufseher Collegium Protocol* 1772-1775, MASP, on loan to Old Salem, Inc.; Chester S. Davis, *Hidden Seed and Harvest: A History of the Moravians* (Winston-Salem, N.C.: Wachovia Historical Society, 1973), 63.

77. Thorp, *Moravian Community*, 204.

Chapter 6. Women Artisans in Rowan County

1. Invoice from Ann Crosby to Elizabeth Steele, Steele Papers.

2. Spruill, *Women's Life and Work*, 81.

3. *Rowan Deed Abstracts*, 3:367, 368; Ramsey, *Carolina Cradle*, 35-36.

4. Russo, "Self-Sufficiency," 393.

5. Pamela Sharpe, "Literally Spinsters: A New Interpretation of Local Economy and Demography in Colyton in the Seventeenth and Eighteenth Centuries," *Economic History Review* 44.1 (1991): 60.

6. Will of Alexander Newberry, Rowan Wills. The same will identifies the decedent's sons as artisans, as well.

7. Jean B. Russo, "Chesapeake Artisans in the Aftermath of the Revolution" (paper presented to the U.S. Capitol Historical Association Meeting, 1989), 15.

8. Jones, "'That Also These children,'" 33, 35-36.

9. Ibid., 36; Fraser, "'Nobody's Children,'" 45.

10. *Rowan Court Abstracts*, 1:63 (April 16, 1755).

11. Jones, "'That Also These children,'' 70-94; Fraser, "'Nobody's Children,'" 80-95.

12. Burke Apprent.; Guilford CPQS; Randolph CPQS; Randolph Apprent.; Stokes CPQS; Surry CPQS; Surry Apprent.; Wilkes CPQS; and Wilkes Apprent.

13. Salisbury Misc.

14. For more information on the absence of spinning and weaving equipment in households, see T.H. Breen, "An Empire of Goods," in Stanley Katz, et al., eds., *Colonial America* (New York: McGraw-Hill, 1993), 384.

15. Rowan Wills. The percentage of spinning equipment in Rowan County is lower than the figures economic historian Carole Shammas calculated for a "non-plantation" rural area in the eighteenth century. See her *Pre-Industrial Consumer*, 54.

16. Will of John Owen, March 10, 1787, Rowan Wills.

17. Will of James McLaughlin, Sept. 4, 1779, Rowan Wills.

18. For more information see Laurel Thatcher Ulrich, "Hannah Ballard's Cupboard: Female Property and Identity in Eighteenth-Century New England" (paper presented at the Institute of Early American History and Culture Conference, Williamsburg, Va., Nov. 4, 1993).

19. Will of John Oliphant, Feb. 12, 1785, Rowan Wills.

20. The gender bias inherent in spinning dates to ancient Greece, when spinning was used as a form of punishment for men.

21. Paul Clemens and Lucy Simler, "Rural Labor and the Farm Household, Chester County, Pennsylvania, 1750-1820," in Stephen Innes, ed., *Work and Labor in Early America* (Chapel Hill: Univ. of North Carolina Press for the Institute of Early American History and Culture, 1988), 131; Joan M. Jensen, *Loosening the Bonds: Mid-Atlantic Farm Women, 1750-1850* (New Haven: Yale Univ. Press, 1986), 38.

22. Kulikoff, "Transition to Capitalism," 133, 137-38.

23. Sharpe, "Literally Spinsters," 55, 63.

24. Thorp, "Doing Business," 398; Thomas Dublin, "Women and Outwork in a Nineteenth-Century New England Town: Fitzwilliam, N.H., 1830-1850," in Steven Hahn and Jonathan Prude, eds., *The Countryside in the Age of Capitalist Transformation* (Chapel Hill: Univ. of North Carolina Press, 1985), 61.

25. For instance, Thorp inferred that Rowan County merchants dealt with women on a cash-only basis or posted their purchases to their husbands' accounts because they could not be sued for the recovery of debts (Thorp, "Doing Business," 398). Likewise, in his study of nineteenth-century New Hampshire, Dublin concluded that married women obtained store goods through exchange, as they never paid in cash or were extended credit (Dublin, "Women and Outwork," 57, 61). Theoretically, both men are correct. According to Marylynn Salmon in *Women and the Law of Property in Early America* (Chapel Hill: Univ. of North Carolina Press, 1986), no colony allowed married women the legal ability to act independently with regard to property (xv).

26. William Steel's Cash Account Book, 62.

27. Ibid., 24, 34, 54, 86.

28. Ibid., 46, 72, 94.

29. The actual number of spinsters in the county was undoubtedly higher because of the Moravian sisters who spun.

30. See table 3, p. 55, for the artisan profile in 1759, and table 4, p. 74, for the profile in 1770. Figures for 1790 derived from a data base of artisans working in Rowan, Surry, Wilkes, Iredell, Burke, Stokes, Rockingham, Randolph, and Guilford counties from 1753 to 1792, compiled from Rowan CPQS; Rowan Apprent.; Rowan Wills; Rowan Civ. Act.; Rowan Crim. Act.; Burke Apprent.; Guilford CPQS; Randolph CPQS; Randolph Apprent.; Stokes CPQS; Surry CPQS; Surry Apprent.; Wilkes CPQS; Wilkes Apprent.; and Museum of Early Southern Decorative Arts, *Index to Early Southern Artisans*.

31. Invoice from Ann Crosby to Elizabeth Steele; invoice from Mary King to William Steele, Aug. 12, 1772, Steele Papers.

32. Nisbet Ledger, 80.

33. *Surry Will Abstracts*, 1:56, 106a.

34. Salem Diary, Jan. 17, 1780, MASP.

35. Helen L. Sumner, *History of Women in Industry in the United States* (1910; reprint, New York: Arno Press, 1974), 42; Hirsch, *Roots of the American Working Class*, 38.

36. Will of Mary Myers, July 14, 1784, Rowan Wills.

37. William Steel's Cash Account Book, 52.

38. Will of Mary Myers, July 14, 1784, Rowan Wills.

39. William Steel's Cash Account Book, 52.

40. Florence Montgomery, *Textiles in America* (New York: Norton, 1984), 327.

41. Salem Diary, Jan. 17, 1780, MASP; *Aeltesten Conferenz*, Nov. 20, 1799, MASP; Museum of Early Southern Decorative Arts, *Index to Early Southern Artisans*.

42. Lewis, "Social and Architectural History," 126, 128, 131.

43. *Aeltesten Conferenz*, July 20, 1773, MASP.

44. Congregational Council Summary for 1786, MASP.

45. *Aufseher Collegium*, April 11, 1785, MASP; *Rowan Will Abstracts*, B:1.

46. *Aufseher Collegium*, Oct. 10, 1797.

47. Rowan Apprent.

48. Fraser, "'Nobody's Children,'" 80.

49. *Surry Will Abstracts*, 1:84; Surry CPQS, Feb. 11, 1782; 1782 Surry County Tax List, NC DAH; 1790 U.S. Census, 123.

50. Archibald Henderson, "Elizabeth Maxwell Steele," typed ms in Steele Papers; *Rowan Court Abstracts*, 2:157.

51. Henderson in Steele Papers; Brawley, *Rowan Story*, 27.

52. *Rowan Deed Abstracts*, 4:241.

53. Ramsey, *Carolina Cradle*, 169; *Rowan Deed Abstracts*, 4:763, 764; 5:307, 308, 309.

54. Ramsey, *Carolina Cradle*, 168; Henderson series in Steele Papers; *Rowan Deed Abstracts*, 6:160, 161.

55. William Steel's Cash Account Book, 2.

56. An inventory of that part of the Estate of Elizabeth Steale [*sic*] decd., May 5, 1791, Steele Papers.

57. Rowan CPQS, Aug. 9, 1781.

58. Invoice from W[illia]m Watts to the estate of Elizabeth [Steele] decd., June 19, 1792, Steele Papers.

59. Invoice to William Steal [*sic*], anonymous and undated; invoice from Ann Crosby to Mrs. Steele, n.d.; invoice from Arthur Erwin to William Steele deceas'd, Aug. 8, 1774, Steele Papers.

60. All invoices from Steele Papers.

61. Sharpe, "Literally Spinsters," 55.

62. Rowan Crim. Act.

63. Ibid.; Rowan County Summons, NC DAH; Salisbury Crim. Act.

64. Rowan Crim. Act.

65. Rowan CPQS, Aug. 6, 1772.

66. *Rowan Court Abstracts*, 2:366, 374, 412, 445, 448.

67. Rowan Civ. Act.; Rowan Crim. Act.

68. *Rowan Deed Abstracts*, 5:450, 451. Interestingly, the person to whom Granville originally granted the lot was also a woman, Ann Hellier.

69. Anonymous Lawyer's Account Book, Macay-McNeely Papers, SHC.

70. Rowan CPQS, July 13, 1765. In Feb. 1775, when he was ten years old, Isabella's

son, also named James Craige, was apprenticed to William Ireland to learn the art of a cordwainer until he was twenty-one. Rowan CPQS, Feb. 8, 1775.

71. Rowan Civ. Act.

72. Rowan Crim. Act.; Rowan CPQS, 3:23.

73. Spruill, *Women's Life and Work*, 83.

74. Mary H. Blewett, *Men, Women, and Work: Class, Gender, and Protest in the New England Shoe Industry, 1780-1910* (Urbana: Univ. of Illinois Press, 1988), xix.

75. Steffen, *Mechanics of Baltimore*, 45; Wilentz, *Chants Democratic*, 44, 45, 124; Rock, *Artisans*, 281.

76. Sumner, *History of Women*, 38, 40.

77. Hirsch, *Roots of the American Working Class*, 7.

78. Alice Kessler-Harris, *Out to Work: A History of Wage-Earning Women in the United States* (New York: Oxford Univ. Press, 1982), 14.

79. Barbara Mayer Wertheimer, *We Were There: The Story of Working Women in America* (New York: Pantheon Books, 1977), 12.

Chapter 7. Artisans, the Regulator Crisis, and Politics

1. Artisans regularly used their professions to identify themselves in legal papers, as discussed in the previous chapter.

2. Ramsey, *Carolina Cradle*, 25-28.

3. *Rowan Deed Abstracts* 1:72-74, 93-97; *Rowan Court Abstracts*, 1:7, 9-11, 15.

4. *Rowan Court Abstracts*, 1:34.

5. Ramsey, *Carolina Cradle*, 154-55; idem, "James Carter: Founder of Salisbury," *North Carolina Historical Review* 39 (1962): 131-39, quote from 132.

6. *CR* 5:175-76.

7. Ibid., 846, 1082-83.

8. *Rowan Deed Abstracts*, 3:367, 368; *Rowan Court Abstracts*, 2:147.

9. *CR* 5:846.

10. Ibid., 810, 982.

11. *Rowan Deed Abstracts*, 2:244-45.

12. *CR* 5:1092.

13. Guess, "County Government," 11, 29-31.

14. Ramsey, *Carolina Cradle*, 33, 76, 81.

15. *Rowan Court Abstracts*, 1:39.

16. Ibid., 2:58, 83, 116, 141, 169; *RM* 1:158, 160, 167-69, 172, 179, 181, 426.

17. *Rowan Court Abstracts*, 2:112, 217.

18. Ibid., 145, 157.

19. *CR* 5:1083-84.

20. The 1778 Rowan Tax List valued Jones at £2.18.10; *CR* 9:575.

21. Ramsey, *Carolina Cradle*, 119; *Rowan Deed Abstracts*, 1:103-8, 3:298-301.

22. *Rowan Deed Abstracts*, 1:103-8, 3:401-4; *Rowan Court Abstracts*, 2:144, 255, 348.

23. *Rowan Court Abstracts*, 2:538.

24. Ibid., 617.

25. Ibid., 695.

26. *CR* 8:156-57.

27. Ibid., 7:857.

28. *Rowan Court Abstracts*, 3:60.

29. Ibid., 147.

30. Ramsey, *Carolina Cradle*, 52, 62; *Rowan Court Abstracts*, 3:34.
31. *Rowan Court Abstracts*, 3:217.
32. *CR* 9:254; 23:857.
33. Ibid., 9:575.
34. *Rowan Court Abstracts*, 3:389-90.
35. *CR* 8:64.
36. *Rowan Court Abstracts*, 3:327, 329, 386. Colonel Lock died in 1796, and his military service is noted on his grave marker at Thyatira Cemetery in Salisbury. For more information on Lock, see William S. Powell, ed., *Dictionary of North Carolina Biography*, 4 (Chapel Hill: Univ. of North Carolina Press, 1991): 79-81.
37. *Rowan Court Abstracts*, 3:355; Rowan Wills, C:178.
38. "Petition of Citizens of Rowan and Orange Counties, Oct. 4, 1768" in William S. Powell, James K. Huhta, and Thomas J. Farnham, eds., *The Regulators in North Carolina: A Documentary History, 1759-1776* (Raleigh: NC DAH, 1971), 186-87.
39. Minutes from a Regulator Meeting in Rowan County, March 7, 1771, in William L. Saunders Papers, SHC.
40. Explanation and chronology of the Regulator crisis from Whittenburg, "Planters, Merchants, and Lawyers," 215-16; idem, "Backwoods Revolutionaries: Social Context and Constitutional Theories of the North Carolina Regulators, 1765-1771" (Ph.D. diss., Univ. of Georgia, 1974), v-viii; and Ekirch, *"Poor Carolina,"* 164-82.
41. Ramsey, *Carolina Cradle*, 35, 112; *Rowan Deed Abstracts*, 6:382; *Rowan Court Abstracts*, 1:15, 51.
42. *Rowan Court Abstracts*, 1:7, 9.
43. *RM* 1:165.
44. Ibid., 170.
45. Ibid., 210.
46. *CR* 5:1082-83.
47. *Rowan Court Abstracts*, 2:262; *Rowan Deed Abstracts*, 4:201-2.
48. *Rowan Court Abstracts*, 2:378.
49. Ibid., 293, 478.
50. *RM* 1:271, 287.
51. Anonymous Lawyer's Account Book, Macay-McNeely Papers, SHC.
52. *RM* 1:452-53. Ironically, outside of this incident, Hughes does not appear as a Regulator or sympathetic to the Regulators in any other records.
53. Bassett, "Regulators," 161-64.
54. Kay, "North Carolina Regulation," 71-123; Kay and Cary, "Class, Mobility, and Conflict." For a more thorough analysis and critique of the historiography of the Regulation see Whittenburg, "Planters, Merchants, and Lawyers," 216-21.
55. Ekirch, *"Poor Carolina,"* 172-75.
56. Whittenburg, "Planters, Merchants, and Lawyers," 222.
57. James P. Whittenburg, "Colonial North Carolina's 'Burnt-Over District': The Pattern of Backcountry Settlement, 1740-1770" (paper presented at the Southern Historical Association Meeting, 1986).
58. Quote from Hugh T. Lefler and William S. Powell, *Colonial North Carolina: A History* (New York: Scribner's, 1973), 220.
59. *Rowan Court Abstracts*, 3:22.
60. Data base of individuals involved in the Regulator movement compiled by James P. Whittenburg.
61. 1759 Rowan County Tax in *Rowan Will Abstracts*, 114. Unfortunately, his leadership of the Regulator militia at the Battle of Alamance led to a trial for treason in which

Merrill was found guilty and sentenced to die in a most gruesome manner. His sentence read "that you Benjamin Merrill, be carried to the place of Execution, where you are to be hanged by the Neck; that you be cut down while yet alive, that your Bowels be taken out and burned before your Face, that your Head be cut off, your Body divided into Four Quarters." *CR* 8:642-43.

62. Nash, *Urban Crucible*, xii. Other studies of urban artisans include Wilentz, *Chants Democratic*; Steffen, *Mechanics of Baltimore*; Rock, *Artisans*; and Olton, *Artisans for Independence*.

63. Guess, "County Government," 31.

64. Figures on artisans holding political office from data base of Rowan County office holders compiled from Rowan CPQS in dBase III+. Two other justices who may have been artisans were Squire Boone (weaver) and George Smith (blacksmith).

65. *Rowan Court Abstracts*, 1:17, 2:365.

66. Ramsey, *Carolina Cradle*, 60.

67. *Rowan Court Abstracts*, 1:32.

68. Ibid., 2:176, 288, 361.

69. Rowan Crim. Act.

70. *Rowan Court Abstracts*, 4:28.

71. Rowan Wills, C:12.

72. *Rowan Deed Abstracts*, 7:160, 161, 5:331, 332.

73. *Rowan Court Abstracts*, 2:487, 564.

74. *Rowan Deed Abstracts*, 6:430-32; *Rowan Court Abstracts*, 3:95, 4:21.

75. Stokes Wills, 1:67.

76. Ramsey, *Carolina Cradle*, 57, 151. The exception to this situation was the Moravians, whose knowledge of the English language and legal process was an essential tool in keeping their community separate from the remainder of the county.

77. *Rowan Deed Abstracts*, 4:512-14.

78. Ibid., 4:925-27, 5:217-18; *Rowan Court Abstracts*, 2:536, 704, 721.

79. Ramsey, *Carolina Cradle*, 191; *Rowan Court Abstracts*, 3:381, 4:10, 22.

80. Carl Hammer, Jr., *Rhinelanders on the Yadkin*, 2d ed. (Salisbury: Rowan Printing Co., 1965), 29, 31; Ramsey, *Carolina Cradle*, 191.

81. Ramsey, *Carolina Cradle*, 165; *Rowan Deed Abstracts*, 3:516-18.

82. *Rowan Deed Abstracts*, 2:156-57; *Rowan Court Abstracts*, 2:138, 217.

83. *Rowan Deed Abstracts*, 4:921-23, refers to this land, but the actual deed has not survived; *Rowan Deed Abstracts*, 4:686.

84. *Rowan Court Abstracts*, 2:201, 214, 217, 294, 311, 325; *Rowan Deed Abstracts*, 4:323, 656-59, 686, 921-23.

85. Rowan Civ. Act.; Rowan Crim. Act.

86. Anonymous Lawyer's Account Book, Macay-McNeely Papers.

87. *Rowan Deed Abstracts*, 5:208-10; 4:925-27; 5:359-60, 527-29; 6:170-72.

88. *Rowan Court Abstracts*, 2:311, 325, 585, 619; Rowan Wills, C:194; *Rowan Deed Abstracts*, 2:156, 157; 4:323-25, 686; 5:377, 378; 6:145, 146, 247, 248, 516; 7:13, 14, 458; Anonymous Lawyer's Account Book, Macay-McNeely Papers; *CR* 23:810-13; Steele Papers.

89. Invoice from Beard to Elizabeth Steele dated Nov. 3, 1773; receipt dated Feb. 24, 1774, Steele Papers.

90. Beard's Account with Mrs. Steele, Nov. 16, 1773-Nov. 17, 1774, Steele Papers.

91. Elizabeth Steele's account with Beard for 1773-1774, Steele Papers.

92. Hammer, *Rhinelanders*, 29, 31.

93. *Rowan Deed Abstracts*, 7:13-14; *Rowan Court Abstracts*, 3:58.

94. John Burgess Fisher, Dorothy Brown Koller, and Margaret Brown Anderson,

comps. and eds., *The Ancestors and Descendants of Abraham (Braun) Brown, the Miller. The Ancestors and Descendants of Jacob (Braun) Brown, the Wagonmaker* (Charlotte: Delmar Publishers and Printers, 1983), pp. iii, xxxiv.

95. *Rowan Court Abstracts,* 2:229.

96. *Rowan Deed Abstracts,* 4:253-55, 273-75.

97. *Rowan Court Abstracts,* 2:361.

98. *Rowan Deed Abstracts,* 4:727-29; *Rowan Court Abstracts,* 2:422, 508, 559.

99. Fishers, Koller, and Anderson, *Ancestors and Descendants,* xxxiv; Richard L. Brown, *A History of the Michael Brown Family of Rowan County, North Carolina* (Charlotte: Delmar Printers, 1973), 38, 187; Ramsey, *Carolina Cradle,* 89-90.

100. *CR* 7:521; *Rowan Deed Abstracts,* 7:13-14; *Rowan Court Abstracts,* 3:58, 297.

101. *Rowan Court Abstracts,* 3:46, 64, 121, 136, 238, 240, 247, 252, 256, 287, 297, 345; 4:5, 8, 18, 41; Rowan CPQS.

102. Steele Papers; Rowan Wills.

103. Ramsey, *Carolina Cradle,* 111, 129, 159-60.

104. *Rowan Deed Abstracts,* 1:143-48. Carson eventually owned three tracts of land in the Trading Settlement, and two were located directly on creeks.

105. *Rowan Court Abstracts,* 1:30, 41; 2:88, 149, 175, 226, 252, 257; *Rowan Deed Abstracts,* 2:76-77; 4:198-201; Rowan Wills, A:143.

106. *Rowan Deed Abstracts,* 1:143-48; 2:48-51; 3:537, 538; 5:359, 360; 6:187, 188; 4:493, 494, 198-201; *Rowan Court Abstracts,* 2:495, 446.

107. Rowan Civ. Act.; Salisbury Civ. Act.; Salisbury Trial; Salisbury Crown/State Superior Court Docket, 1762-1779; all court records from NC DAH.

108. Rowan Crim. Act., 1764; Salisbury Trial, 1763.

109. Rowan Crim. Act., 1760.

110. Salisbury Trial, 1763.

111. Rowan Civ. Act.

112. Salisbury Civ. Act., 1756-1763.

113. Salisbury Crim. Act.

114. Artisans' activity in political office parallels their proportion (11.5%) of the voting population as recorded by the 1759 Rowan County Tax List, *Rowan Will Abstracts,* 111-17.

Bibliography

Primary Sources

UNPUBLISHED SOURCES

Dickey, John. Account Books. Manuscripts Dept., Perkins Library, Duke Univ.

Henderson, Archibald. Collection. Steele Family Series. Southern Historical Collection. Manuscripts Dept., Wilson Library, Univ. of North Carolina at Chapel Hill.

Hogg, Robert. Account Books. Southern Historical Collection. Manuscripts Dept., Wilson Library, Univ. of North Carolina at Chapel Hill.

Lowrance, Alexander and John. Papers. Manuscripts Dept., Perkins Library, Duke Univ.

Macay-McNeely Papers. Southern Historical Collection. Manuscripts Dept.,

Wilson Library, Univ. of North Carolina at Chapel Hill.

Moravian Archives, Southern Province, Winston-Salem, N.C.

Aeltesten Conferenz Correspondence.

Aeltesten Conferenz Protocol (Minutes).

General Early Correspondence.

Letters from Bethlehem Archives (concerning Bethabara).

Letters from Spangenberg to the Brethen at Bethabara.

Memoirs.

Nisbet Collection. Southern Historical Collection. Manuscripts Dept., Wilson Library, Univ. of North Carolina at Chapel Hill.

North Carolina Court Papers. Southern Historical Collection. Manuscripts Dept., Wilson Library, Univ. of North Carolina at Chapel Hill.

North Carolina Department of Archives and History, Raleigh.

Burke County Apprentice Bonds and Records, 1784-1873.

Guilford County Court of Pleas and Quarter Sessions Minutes, 1781-1811. Microfilm.

Iredell County Court of Pleas and Quarter Sessions Minutes, 1789-1834. Microfilm.

Randolph County Apprentice Bonds and Records, 1779, 1780, 1781, 1783-1805.

Randolph County Court of Pleas and Quarter Sessions Minutes, 1779-1782, 1787-1794. Microfilm.

Rockingham County Court of Pleas and Quarter Sessions Minutes, 1786-1808. Microfilm.

Rowan County Apprentice Bonds and Records, 1777-1804.

Rowan County Civil Action Papers, 1755-1774.

Rowan County Court of Pleas and Quarter Sessions Minutes, 1753-1772, 1773-1800. Microfilm.
Rowan County Criminal Action Papers.
Rowan County Estates Records.
Rowan County Wills, 1762-1804.
Salisbury District Superior Court Civil Action Papers, 1756-1763, 1770-1773, 1778-1783.
Salisbury District Superior Court Criminal Action Papers.
Salisbury District Superior Court Crown Docket, 1767-1779.
Salisbury District Superior Court Execution Docket, 1755-1767, 1767-1769, 1770-1772.
Salisbury District Superior Court Miscellaneous Records, 1754-1807.
Salisbury District Superior Court Reference Docket, 1767-1769.
Salisbury District Superior Court Trial and Minute Docket, 1761-1776.
Salisbury District Supreme Court Trial and Minute Docket, 1776-1790.
Stokes County Court of Pleas and Quarter Sessions Minutes, 1790-1793. Microfilm.
Stokes County Wills.
Surry County Apprentice Bonds and Records, 1779-1921.
Surry County Court of Pleas and Quarter Sessions Minutes, 1779-1802. Microfilm.
Surry County Tax List, 1782.
Wilkes County Apprentice Bonds and Records, 1778-1908.
Wilkes County Court of Pleas and Quarter Sessions Minutes, March 1778-July 1790, Oct. 1790-May 1797. Microfilm.

Old Salem, Inc.
Translation of Helper's Conference Minutes Extracts (on loan from the Moravian Archives, Southern Province).
Translation of Elder's Conference Minutes Extracts (on loan from the Moravian Archives, Southern Province).

Steele, John. Papers. Southern Historical Collection. Manuscripts Dept., Wilson Library, Univ. of North Carolina at Chapel Hill.

PUBLISHED SOURCES

Absher, Mrs. W.O. *Surry County, N.C., Deed Abstracts.* Book D, *1779-1790.* North Wilkesboro, N.C.: Mrs. W.O. Absher, 1976.

———. *Stokes County, N.C., Wills. 1790-1864.* 4 vols. Easley, S.C.: Southern Historical Press, 1985.

———. *Stokes County, N.C., Deeds. 1787-1797.* 2 vols. Easley, S.C.: Southern Historical Press, 1985.

———. *Surry County, N.C., Deeds.* Books D, E, F, *1779-1797.* Easley, S.C.: Southern Historical Press, 1985.

Boyd, William G., ed. *William Byrd's Histories of the Dividing Line Betwixt Virginia and North Carolina.* New York: Dover, 1967.

Coulter, Shirley, Edie Purdy, and Lois Schneider. *Iredell County, N.C., Deed Abstracts.* Vol. 1, *1788-1797, Books A, B.* Statesville, N.C.: Abstract Publishers, 1977.

———. *Minutes of the Court of Pleas and Quarter Sessions, Iredell County, N.C., 1789-1800*. Statesville: Abstract Publishers, 1978.

Daughters of the American Revolution. *Roster of Soldiers from North Carolina in the American Revolution*. Reprint, Baltimore: Geneaological Publishing Co., 1977.

Fries, Adelaide L., Douglas LeTell Rights, Minnie J. Smith, and Kenneth G. Hamilton, trans. and eds. *The Records of the Moravians in North Carolina*. 11 vols. Raleigh: North Carolina Historical Commission, 1922-1969.

Grimes, J. Byron, ed. *Abstract of North Carolina Wills*. Raleigh: Department of Archives and History, 1910.

———, ed. *North Carolina Wills and Inventories*. Raleigh: Department of Archives and History, 1912.

Hooker, Richard J., ed. *The Carolina Backcountry on the Eve of the Revolution: The Journal and Other Writings of Charles Woodmason, Anglican Itinerant*. Chapel Hill: Univ. of North Carolina Press, 1953.

Huggins, Edith Warren. *Burke County, N.C., Land Records, 1779-1790 and Important Miscellaneous Records, 1777-1800*. 2 vols. Easley, S.C.: Southern Historical Press, 1981.

Lawson, John. *A New Voyage to Carolina*. Ed. Hugh T. Lefler. Chapel Hill: Univ. of North Carolina Press, 1967.

Linn, Jo White. *Abstracts of the Minutes of the Court of Pleas and Quarter Sessions, Rowan County, North Carolina*. Vol. 1, *1753-1762: Abstracts of Books 1-2*. Vol. 2, *1763-1772: Abstracts of Books 2-4*. Salisbury, N.C.: Mrs. Stahle Linn, Jr., 1977, 1979.

———. *Abstracts of Wills and Estates Records of Rowan County, North Carolina, 1753-1805, and Tax Lists of 1759 and 1778*. Salisbury, N.C.: Mrs. Stahle Linn, Jr. 1980.

———. "Pennsylvania-North Carolina Migrations: As Identified in the First Ten Deed Books of Rowan County, N.C." *Pennsylvania Geneaological Magazine* 34 (1985): 55-66.

———. *Rowan County, North Carolina, Deed Abstracts*. Vol. 1, *1753-1762: Abstracts of Book 1-4*. Vol. 2, *1762-1772: Abstracts of Books 5-7*. Salisbury, N.C.: Mrs. Stahle Linn, Jr., 1972.

———. *Rowan County, North Carolina, Will Abstracts, 1805-1850: Abstracts of Books G-K, 1850*. Salisbury, N.C.: Mrs. Stahle Linn, Jr., 1971.

———. *Surry County, North Carolina, Will Abstracts*. Vols. 1-3, *1771-1827*. Salisbury, N.C.: Mrs. Stahle Linn, Jr., 1974.

Matthews, Albert, ed. *Journal of William Loughton Smith, 1790-1791*. Cambridge, England: Univ. Press, 1917.

Old Salem, Inc. General Research Files.

———. Lot Past History Files.

———. Map Files.

———. Personnel Files.

———. Photography Files.

Saunders, William L., Walter Clark, and Steven B. Weeks, eds. *The Colonial and State Records of North Carolina*. 30 vols. Raleigh: Department of Archives and History, 1886-1941.

Schneider, Lois M.P. *Abstracts of Unrecorded Wills, 1788-1915 and Will Book III, 1845-1868, of Iredell County, N.C.* Statesville, N.C.: Privately published, 1983.

Seidler, Ute-Ingrid, trans. "German Wills of Rowan County." *North Carolina Genealogical Society Journal* 1 (July 1975): 136-40.

U.S. Government. *Heads of Families at the First Census of the United States Taken in the Year 1790: North Carolina*. Washington, D.C.: Government Printing Office, 1908; reprint. Baltimore: Genealogical Publishing Co., 1966.

Webster, Irene. *Rockingham County, N.C., Deed Abstracts, 1785-1800*. Madison, N.C.: Mrs. S.F. Webster, 1973.

———. *Rockingham County, N.C., Will Abstracts, 1785-1865*. Easley, S.C.: Southern Historical Press, 1984.

White, Emmett R. *Revolutionary War Soldiers of Western North Carolina: Burke County*. Vols. 1-2. Easley, S.C.: Southern Historical Press, 1984.

Secondary Sources

Africa, Philip. "Slaveholding in the Salem Community, 1771-1851." *North Carolina Historical Review* 54 (July 1977): 271-307.

Agner, Martha W., and Mary Jane Fowler, eds. *The Old Lutheran Cemetary, Salisbury, North Carolina, since 1768*. Salisbury, N.C.: Old Lutheran Cemetery Committee and Historic Salisbury, 1981.

Albright, Frank P. "The Crafts of Salem." *Antiques* (July 1965): 94-97.

Ames, Kenneth, and Gerald W.R. Ward. *Decorative Arts and Household Furnishings in America, 1650-1920*. Winterthur, Del.: Henry Francis du Pont Winterthur Museum, 1989.

Appleby, Joyce. "Commercial Farming and the 'Agrarian Myth' in the Early Republic." *Journal of American History* 68 (March 1982), 833-49.

Ashe, Samuel A. *History of North Carolina*. Greensboro: Charles L. Van Noppen, 1908.

Bailyn, Bernard. *Voyagers to the West: A Passage in the Peopling of America on the Eve of the Revolution*. New York: Knopf, 1986.

Bassett, John S. "The Regulators of North Carolina." American Historical Association, *Report for the Year 1894*, 142-212. Washington, D.C., 1895.

Bean, Eugene. *Rowan County Records: The Early Settlers*. Washington, D.C.: Carnahan Press, 1914.

Beeman, Richard R. *The Evolution of the Southern Backcountry: A Case Study of Lunenburg County, Virginia, 1746-1832*. Philadelphia: Univ. of Pennsylvania Press, 1984.

Billings, Warren, John Selby, and Thad W. Tate. *Colonial Virginia: A History*. White Plains, N.Y.: KTO Press, 1986.

Bivins, John, Jr. *The Moravian Potters in North Carolina*. Chapel Hill: Univ. of North Carolina Press, 1972.

———. *Longrifles of North Carolina*. 2d ed. York, Pa.: George Shumway, 1988.

———, and Paula Welshimer. *Moravian Decorative Arts in North Carolina: An Introduction to the Old Salem Collection*. Winston-Salem: Old Salem, Inc., 1981.

Blewett, Mary H. *Men, Women, and Work: Class, Gender, and Protest in the New England Shoe Industry, 1780-1910*. Urbana: Univ. of Illinois Press, 1988.

Brawley, James S. *Rowan County . . . A Brief History*. Raleigh: North Carolina Division of Archives and History, 1974.

———. *Old Rowan: Views and Sketches*. Salisbury, N.C.: Rowan Printing Co., 1959.

———. *The Rowan Story, 1753-1953: A Narrative History of Rowan County, North Carolina*. Salisbury, N.C.: Rowan Printing Co., 1953.

Breen, T.H. "An Empire of Goods: The Anglicization of Colonial America, 1690-1776." In Stanley Katz, John M. Murrin, and Douglas Greenberg, eds. *Colonial America: Essays in Political and Social Development*, 367-89. New York: McGraw-Hill, 1993.

Bridenbaugh, Carl. *Cities in Revolt: Urban Life in America, 1743- 1776*. New York: Oxford Univ. Press, 1953.

———. *Cities in the Wilderness: The First Century of Urban Life in America, 1625-1742*. New York: Knopf, 1955.

———. *The Colonial Craftsman*. Chicago: Univ. of Chicago Press, 1961.

———. *Myths and Realities: Societies of the Colonial South*. New York: Atheneum, 1976.

Brown, Richard L. *A History of the Michael Brown Family of Rowan County, North Carolina*. 2d ed. Charlotte: Delmar Printers, 1973.

Burgess, Fred. *Randolph County, Economic and Social*. Reprint, Randolph County Historical Society, 1969.

Butler, Lindley S. *Rockingham County: A Brief History*. Raleigh: North Carolina Department of Archives and History, 1982.

Carr, Lois Green, Philip D. Morgan, and Jean B. Russo, eds. *Colonial Chesapeake Society*. Chapel Hill: Univ. of North Carolina Press for the Institute of Early American History and Culture, 1988.

Clemens, Paul E.G. *The Atlantic Economy and Colonial Maryland's Eastern Shore: From Tobacco to Grain*. Ithaca, N.Y.: Cornell Univ. Press, 1980.

Clewell, John Henry. *History of Wachovia in North Carolina: The Unitas Fratrum or Moravian Church in North Carolina during a Century and a Half, 1752-1902*. New York: Doubleday, Page, 1902.

Corbitt, David Leroy. *The Formation of the North Carolina Counties, 1663-1943*. Raleigh: North Carolina Department of Archives and History, 1950.

Craig, James H. *The Arts and Crafts in North Carolina, 1699-1840*. Winston-Salem: Museum of Early Southern Decorative Arts, 1965.

Crittenden, Charles. *The Commerce of North Carolina 1763-1789*. New Haven: Yale Univ. Press, 1936.

Crow, Jeffrey J., and Larry E. Tise, eds. *Writing North Carolina History*. Chapel Hill: Univ. of North Carolina Press, 1979.

Cutten, George Barton. *Silversmiths of North Carolina*. Raleigh: State Department of Archives and History, 1948.

Daniels, Christine. "'WANTED: A Blacksmith who Understands Plantation Work': Artisans in Maryland, 1700-1800." *William and Mary Quarterly*, 3d ser., 50 (Oct. 1993): 743-67.

Davis, Chester S. *Hidden Seed and Harvest: A History of the Moravians*. Winston-Salem, N.C.: Wachovia Historical Society, 1973.

———. "The Moravians of Salem." *Antiques*, July 1965, 60-64.

Doerflinger, Thomas. *A Vigorous Spirit of Enterprise: Merchants and Economic Development in Revolutionary Philadelphia*. Chapel Hill: Univ. of North Carolina Press for the Institute of Early American History and Culture, 1986.

Droughton, Wallace R., and William Perry Johnson. *North Carolina Geneaological Reference*. Rev. ed. Durham: Wallace Droughton, 1966.

Dunaway, W.F. *The Scotch-Irish of Colonial Pennsylvania*. Chapel Hill: Univ. of North Carolina Press, 1944.

Earle, Carville, and Ronald Hoffman. "Staple Crops and Urban Development in the Eighteenth-Century South." *Perspectives in American History* 10 (1976): 7-78.

Ekirch, A. Roger. "'A New Government of Liberty': Hermon Husband's Vision of Backcountry North Carolina, 1755." *William and Mary Quarterly*, 3d ser., 34 (1977): 632-46.

———. *"Poor Carolina": Politics and Society in Colonial North Carolina, 1729-1776*. Chapel Hill: Univ. of North Carolina Press, 1981.

Ernst, Joseph A., and H. Roy Merrens. "'Camden's turrets pierce the skies!': The Urban Process in the Southern Colonies during the Eighteenth Century." *William and Mary Quarterly*, 3d ser., 30 (1970): 549-74.

Ervin, Samuel. *A Colonial History of Rowan County, North Carolina*. James Sprunt Studies in North Carolina History, Vol. 16 (1917): no. 1.

Fisher, David Hackett. *Albion's Seed: Four British Folkways in America*. New York: Oxford Univ. Press, 1989.

Fisher, John Burgess, Dorothy Brown Koller, and Margaret Brown Anderson, comps. and eds. *The Ancestors and Descendants of Abraham (Braun) Brown, the Miller. The Ancestors and Descendants of Jacob (Braun) Brown, the Wagonmaker.* Charlotte, N.C.: Delmar Publishers, 1983.

Fisher, Roscoe Brown. *Michael Brown of the Old Stone House: His Influence and His Descendants*. 2d ed. Charlotte, N.C.: Delmar Publishers, 1975.

Fox-Genovese, Elizabeth. *Within the Plantation Household: Black and White Women of the Old South*. Chapel Hill: Univ. of North Carolina Press, 1988.

Frantz, John B. "The Awakening of Religion among the German Settlers in the Middle Colonies." *William and Mary Quarterly*, 3d ser., 33 (1976): 266-88.

Fraser, Lynne Howard. "'Nobody's Children': The Treatment of Illegitimate Children in Three North Carolina Counties, 1760-1790." Master's thesis, College of William and Mary, 1987.

Fries, Adelaide. *The Moravians in Georgia, 1735-1740*. Winston-Salem: n.p., 1945.

———, Stuart Thurman Wright, and J. Edwin Hendricks. *Forsyth: The History of a County on the March*. Chapel Hill: Univ. of North Carolina Press, 1976.

Garvan, Beatrice B., and Charles F. Hummel. *The Pennsylvania Germans: A Celebration of Their Arts, 1683-1850*. Philadelphia: Philadelphia Museum of Art, 1982.

Gaynor, James M., and Nancy L. Hagedorn. *Tools: Working Wood in Eighteenth Century America*. Williamsburg, Va.: Colonial Williamsburg Foundation, 1993.

Gehrke, William Herman. "The German Element in Rowan and Cabarrus Counties." Master's thesis, Univ. of North Carolina at Chapel Hill, 1934.

Gill, Harold B. *Apprentices in Colonial Virginia*. Salt Lake City: Ancestry Publishing, 1990.

Gollin, Gillian L. *Moravians in Two Worlds: A Study of Changing Communities*. New York: Columbia Univ. Press, 1967.

Greene, Jack P. "Independence, Improvement, and Authority: Towards a Framework for Understanding the Histories of the Southern Backcountry during the Era of the American Revolution." In Ronald Hoffman, Thad W. Tate, and Peter

J. Albert, eds., *An Uncivil War: The Southern Backcountry during the American Revolution*, 3-36. Charlottesville: Univ. Press of Virginia for the United States Capitol Historical Society, 1985.

———. *Pursuits of Happiness: The Social Development of Early Modern British Colonies and the Formation of American Culture*. Chapel Hill: Univ. of North Carolina Press, 1988.

———, and J.R. Pole, eds. *Colonial British America*. Baltimore: Johns Hopkins Univ. Press, 1984.

Griffin, Frances. *Less Time for Meddling: A History of Salem Academy and College, 1772-1866*. Winston-Salem: Blair, 1979.

Guess, William Conrad. *County Government in Colonial North Carolina*. James Sprunt Studies in History and Political Science, Vol. 11, no. 1, 1-24.

Gusler, Wallace. *Furniture of Williamsburg and Eastern Virginia, 1710 - 1790*. Richmond: Virginia Museum, 1979.

Hahn, Steven, and Jonathan Prude, eds. *The Countryside in the Age of Capitalist Transformation: Essays in the Social History of Rural America*. Chapel Hill: Univ. of North Carolina Press, 1985.

Hamilton, Kenneth G. "The Moravians and Wachovia." *North Carolina Historical Review* 44 (1967): 144-53.

Hammer, Carl, Jr. *Rhinelanders on the Yadkin*. 2d ed. Salisbury, N.C.: Rowan Printing Co., 1965.

Hammond, Michael. *The Archaeological Investigations of the Charles Alexander Cooper House, Lot 41; An 1840's Barn, Lot 71; the John Ackerman House, Lot 91, Old Salem, N.C.*. Three manuscripts on file at Old Salem, Inc., 1984, 1986.

———. "Archives and Archaeology." In *Three Forks of Muddy Creek* 12 (1987): 28-36.

———. "Garden Archaeology at Old Salem." In William Kelso, ed. *Earth Patterns*. Charlottesville: Univ. Press of Virginia, 1990.

———. "New Light on Old Salem." *Archaeology*, Nov./Dec. 1989, 37-41.

Hanes, Ralph P. "Old Salem." *Antiques*, July 1965, 99.

Haupert, Thomas. "Apprentices in the Moravian Settlement." *Communal Societies* 9 (1989): 1-9.

Hawk, Emory Q. *Economic History of the South*. Westport, Conn.: Greenwood Press, 1973.

Hendricks, Christopher. "The Planning and Development of Two Moravian Congregation Towns: Salem, North Carolina, and Gracehill, Northern Ireland." Master's thesis, College of William and Mary, 1987.

Henretta, James A. "Families and Farms: *Mentalité* in Pre-Industrial America." *William and Mary Quarterly*, 3d ser., 35 (1978): 3-32.

Hindle, Brooke. "A Retrospective View of Science, Technology, and Material Culture in Early American History." *William and Mary Quarterly*, 3d ser., 41 (1984): 422-35.

Hirsch, Susan E. *Roots of the American Working Class: The Industrialization of Crafts in Newark, 1800-1860*. Philadelphia: Univ. of Pennsylvania Press, 1978.

Hoffman, Ronald, Thad W. Tate, and Peter J. Albert, eds. *An Uncivil War: The Southern Backcountry during the American Revolution*. Charlottesville: Univ. Press of Virginia for the United States Capitol Historical Society, 1985.

Holcomb, Brent. *Marriages of Rowan County, 1753 - 1868*. Baltimore: Geneaological Publishing Co., 1981.

Hood, David Foard. *The Architecture of Rowan County: A Catalogue and History of Surviving 18th, 19th, and Early 20th Century Structures*. Salisbury, N.C.: Rowan County Historic Properties Commission, 1983.

Horton, Frank L. "Johannes Krause, Master Joiner of Salem." *Antiques*, July 1965, 92-93.

Hutson, James H. "An Investigation of the Inarticulate: Philadelphia's White Oaks." *William and Mary Quarterly*, 3d ser., 28 (Jan. 1971): 3-26.

Innes, Stephen, ed. *Work and Labor in Early America*. Chapel Hill: Univ. of North Carolina Press for the Institute of Early American History and Culture, 1988.

Jensen, Joan M. *Loosening the Bonds: Mid-Atlantic Farm Women, 1750- 1850*. New Haven: Yale Univ. Press, 1986.

Jones, Kathi R. "'That Also These children May Become Useful People': Apprenticeships in Rowan County, North Carolina from 1753 to 1795." Master's thesis, College of William and Mary, 1984.

Kay, Marvin L. Michael. "The North Carolina Regulation, 1766-1776: A Class Conflict." In Alfred Young, ed., *The American Revolution: Explorations in the History of American Radicalism*. DeKalb, Ill.: Northern Illinois Univ. Press, 1976

———. "The Payment of Provincial and Local Taxes in North Carolina, 1748-1771." *William and Mary Quarterly*, 3d ser., 26 (1969): 218-39.

———. "Provincial Taxes in North Carolina during the Administrations of Dobbs and Tryon." *North Carolina Historical Review* 42 (1965): 440-53.

Kay, Marvin L. Michael, and Lorin Lee Cary. "Class, Mobility, and Conflict in North Carolina on the Eve of the Revolution." In Jeffrey J. Crow and Larry E. Tise, eds., *The Southern Experience in the American Revolution*. Chapel Hill: Univ. of North Carolina Press, 1978.

———, and Lorin Lee Cary. "A Demographic Analysis of Colonial North Carolina with Special Emphasis upon the Slave and Black Populations." In Jeffrey J. Crow and Flora J. Hatley, eds. *Black Americans in North Carolina and the South*. Chapel Hill: Univ. of North Carolina Press, 1984.

Kerber, Linda. "Separate Sphere, Female Worlds, Woman's Place: The Rhetoric of Women's History." *Journal of American History* 75 (1988): 9-39.

Kessler-Harris, Alice. *Out to Work: A History of Wage-Earning Women in the United States*. New York: Oxford Univ. Press, 1982.

Kindig, Joe, Jr. *Thoughts on the Kentucky Rifle in Its Golden Age*. Annotated 2d ed. York, Pa.: George Shumway, 1983.

Klees, Frederic. *The Pennsylvania Dutch*. New York: Macmillan, 1950.

Kulikoff, Allan. "The Transition to Capitalism in Rural America." *William and Mary Quarterly*, 3d ser. 46 (Jan. 1989): 120-44.

———. *The Agrarian Origins of American Capitalism*. Charlottesville: Univ. Press of Virginia, 1992.

Larson, John. "A Mill for Salem." *Three Forks of Muddy Creek* 9 (1983): 12-18.

Laurie, Bruce. *Artisans into Workers: Labor in Nineteenth-Century America*. New York: Noonday Press, 1989.

Ledgerwood, Mikle Dave. "Ethnic Groups on the Frontier in Rowan County, 1750-1778." Master's thesis, Vanderbilt Univ., 1977.

Lefler, Hugh Talmadge, and Albert Ray Newsome. *North Carolina: The History of a Southern State*. 3d ed. Chapel Hill: Univ. of North Carolina Press, 1973.

———, ed. *North Carolina History Told by Contemporaries*. 4th ed. Chapel Hill: Univ. of North Carolina Press, 1985.

———, and William S. Powell. *Colonial North Carolina: A History*. New York: Scribner's, 1973.

Lemisch, Jesse. "The American Revolution Seen from the Bottom Up." In Barton Bernstein, ed., *Towards a New Past: Dissenting Essays in American History*, 3-45. New York: Pantheon, 1968.

———, and John K. Alexander. "The White Oaks, Jack Tar, and the Concept of the 'Inarticulate,'" with a note by Simeon J. Crowther and a rebuttal by James H. Hutson. *William and Mary Quarterly*, 3d ser., 29 (Jan. 1972): 109-42.

Lemon, James T. *The Best Poor Man's Country: A Geographical Study of Early Southeastern Pennsylvania*. Baltimore: Johns Hopkins Univ. Press, 1972.

———. "Comment on James A. Henretta's 'Family and Farms: *Mentalité* in Pre-Industrial America'" (with a reply by James A. Henretta). *William and Mary Quarterly*, 3d ser., 37 (1980): 688-700.

Lewis, Johanna Miller. "The Salem Congregational Mill." *Three Forks of Muddy Creek* 13 (1988): 39-46.

———. "A Social and Architectural History of the Girls' Boarding School Building at Salem, North Carolina." *North Carolina Historical Review* 66 (April 1989): 125-48.

———. "The Use of Water Power on the Wachovia Tract of North Carolina by the Moravians during the Eighteenth Century." *Communal Societies* 9 (1989): 10-22.

Leyburn, James G. *The Scotch-Irish: A Social History*. Chapel Hill: Univ. of North Carolina Press, 1962.

Lounsbury, Carl. "The Building Process in Antebellum North Carolina." *North Carolina Historical Review* 60 (Oct. 1983): 431-56.

McCain, Paul M. "Magistrates Courts in Early North Carolina." *North Carolina Historical Review* 48 (Jan. 1971): 23-24.

McCusker, John, and Russell Menard. *The Economy of British America, 1607-1789*. Chapel Hill: Univ. of North Carolina Press for the Institute of Early American History and Culture, 1985.

Main, Jackson Turner. *The Social Structure of Revolutionary* America. Princeton, N.J.: Princeton Univ. Press, 1965.

Merrens, H. Roy. *Colonial North Carolina in the Eighteenth Century: A Study in Historical Geography*. Chapel Hill: Univ. of North Carolina Press, 1964.

Michel, Jack. "'In a Manner and Fashion Suitable to their Degree': A Preliminary Investigation of the Material Culture of Early Rural Pennsylvania." *Working Papers from the Regional Economic History Research Center* 5, no. 1 (1981).

Miller, Henry M. "Colonization and Subsistence Change on the 17th Century Chesapeake Frontier." Ph.D. diss., Michigan State Univ., 1984.

Miller, Johanna Carlson. "Mills on the Wachovia Tract, 1756-1849." Master's thesis, Wake Forest Univ., 1985.

Mitchell, Robert D. *Commercialism and Frontier: Perspectives on the Early Shenandoah Valley*. Charlottesville: Univ. Press of Virginia, 1977.

———, ed. *Appalachian Frontiers: Settlement, Society, and Development in the Preindustrial Era*. Lexington: Univ. Press of Kentucky, 1991.

Montgomery, Florence. *Textiles in America*. New York: Norton, 1984.

Morris, Francis Grave, and Phyllis Mary Morris. "Economic Conditions in North Carolina about 1780." Parts 1, 2. *North Carolina Historical Review* 16 (1939): 107-33, 296-327.

Murtaugh, William J. "The Architecture of Salem." *Antiques*, July 1965, 69-75.

———. *Moravian Architecture and Town Planning*. Chapel Hill: Univ. of North Carolina Press, 1967.

Museum of Early Southern Decorative Arts. *Index to Early Southern Artisans*. New York: Clearwater Publishing, 1985.

———. *The Museum of Early Southern Decorative Arts*. Winston-Salem: Old Salem, Inc., 1979.

————. Research File on James Gheen. Winston-Salem, N.C.

Nash, Gary B. *Class and Society in Early America*. Englewood Cliffs, N.J.: Prentice Hall, 1970.

———. "Poverty and Poor Relief in Pre-Revolutionary Philadelphia." *William and Mary Quarterly*, 3d ser., 33 (Jan. 1976): 3-20.

———. *The Urban Crucible: Social Change, Political Consciousness, and the Origins of the American Revolution*. Cambridge, Mass.: Harvard Univ. Press, 1979.

Nelson, Vernon. "The Moravian Church in America." In Mari P. Van Buijtenen, Cornelius Dekker, and Huib Leeuwenberg, eds., *Unitas Fratrum: Moravian Studies*, 145-76. Utrect: Rijksarchief, 1975.

Nobles, Gregory H. "Breaking into the Backcountry: New Approaches to the Early American Frontier, 1750-1800." *William and Mary Quarterly*, 3d ser., 46 (Oct. 1989): 641-70.

Olton, Charles S. *Artisans for Independence: Philadelphia Mechanics and the American Revolution*. Syracuse, N.Y.: Syracuse Univ. Press, 1975.

———. "Philadelphia's Mechanics in the First Decade of the Revolution, 1765-1776." *Journal of American History*, 59 (Sept. 1972): 311-26.

Powell, William S., James K. Huhta, and Thomas J. Farnham. *The Regulators in North Carolina: A Documentary History, 1759-1776*. Raleigh: State Department of Archives and History, 1971.

Powell, William S. *The North Carolina Gazetteer*. Chapel Hill: Univ. of North Carolina Press, 1968.

———, ed. *Dictionary of North Carolina Biography*. 4 vols. Chapel Hill: Univ. of North Carolina Press, 1979-1991.

Price, Jacob. "Economic Function and the Growth of American Port Towns in the Eighteenth Century." *Perspectives in American History* 7 (1974): 121-86.

Pruitt, Bettye Hobbs. "Self-Sufficiency and the Agricultural Economy of Eighteenth-Century Massachusetts." *William and Mary Quarterly*, 3d ser. 41 (1984): 333-64.

Quimby, Ian M.G., ed. *The Craftsman in Early America*. New York: W.W. Norton for the Winterthur Museum, 1984.

———, ed. *Material Culture and the Study of American Life*. New York: W.W. Norton for the Winterthur Museum, 1978.

Ramsey, Robert W. *Carolina Cradle: The Settlement of the Northwest Carolina Frontier, 1747-1762*. Chapel Hill: Univ. of North Carolina Press, 1964.

———. "James Carter: Founder of Salisbury." *North Carolina Historical Review* 39 (1962): 131-39.

Raynor, George. *Sketches of Old Rowan*. 2d ed. Salisbury, N.C.: American Association of University Women, 1963.

Reichel, Levin T. *The Moravians in North Carolina: An Authentic History*. 1857. Reprint, Baltimore: Geneaological Publishing Co., 1968.

Rock, Howard B. *Artisans of the New Republic: The Tradesmen of New York City in the Age of Jefferson*. New York: New York Univ. Press, 1984.

Roeber, A.G. "In German Ways? Problems and Potentials of Eighteenth Century German Social and Emigration History." *William and Mary Quarterly*, 3d ser., 44 (1987): 750-74.

Rubin, Cynthia Elyce, ed. *Southern Folk Art*. Birmingham, Al.: Oxmoor House, 1985.

Rumple, Jethro. *A History of Rowan County, North Carolina*. 1881. Reprint, Baltimore: Regional Publishing Co., 1978.

Russo, Jean B. "Free Workers in a Plantation Economy: Talbot County, Maryland, 1690-1759." Ph.D. diss., Johns Hopkins Univ., 1983.

———. "Chesapeake Artisans in the Aftermath of the Revolution." Paper presented at the U.S. Capitol Historical Association Meeting, 1989.

Salinger, Sharon V. "Artisans, Journeymen, and the Transformation of Labor in Late Eighteenth-Century Philadelphia." *William and Mary Quarterly*, 3d ser., 40 (Jan. 1983): 62-84.

———. "'Send No More Women': Female Servants in Late Eighteenth-Century Philadelphia." *Pennsylvania Magazine of History and Biography* 107 (Jan. 1983): 29-48.

———. *"To serve well and faithfully": Labor and Indentured Servants in Pennsylvania, 1682-1800*. New York: Cambridge Univ. Press, 1987.

Salmon, Marylynn. *Women and the Law of Property in Early America*. Chapel Hill: Univ. of North Carolina Press, 1986.

Sappington, Roger E. "Dunker Beginnings in North Carolina in the Eighteenth Century." *North Carolina Historical Review* 46 (July 1969): 214-38.

Schiffer, Margaret Berwind. *Furniture and Its Makers of Chester County, Pennsylvania*. Philadelphia: Univ. of Pennsylvania Press, 1966.

Sellers, Charles G. *The Market Revolution: Jacksonian America, 1815-1846*. New York: Oxford Univ. Press, 1991.

Sensbach, Jon. "A Separate Canaan: The Making of an Afro-Moravian World in North Carolina, 1763-1836." Ph.D. diss., Duke Univ., 1991.

Shammas, Carole. "How Self-Sufficient was Early America?" *Journal of Interdisciplinary History* 13 (Autumn 1982): 247-72.

———. *The Pre-Industrial Consumer in England and America*. Oxford: Clarendon Press, 1990.

Sharpe, Pamela. "Literally Spinsters: A New Interpretation of Local Economy and Demography in Colyton in the Seventeenth and Eighteenth Centuries." *Economic History Review* 44:1 (1991): 46-65.

Sheller, Tina H. "Artisans, Manufacturing, and the Rise of a Manufacturing Interest in Revolutionary Baltimore Town." *Maryland Historical Magazine* 83 (Spring 1988): 3-18.

Smith, Billy G. "The Material Lives of Laboring Philadelphians, 1750 to 1800." *William and Mary Quarterly*, 3d ser., 38 (April 1981): 163-202.

Spraker, Hazel Atterbury. *The Boone Family*. Rutland, Vt.: Tuttle Co., 1922.

Spruill, Julia Cherry. *Women's Life and Work in the Southern Colonies*. 1938. Reprint, New York: Norton, 1972.

Steffen, Charles G. "Changes in the Organization of Artisan Production in Baltimore, 1790 to 1820." *William and Mary Quarterly*, 3d ser., 36 (Jan. 1979): 101-17.

———. *The Mechanics of Baltimore: Workers and Politics in the Age of Revolution, 1763-1812*. Urbana: Univ. of Illinois Press, 1984.

Sumner, Helen L. *History of Women in Industry in the United States*. 1910. Reprint, New York: Arno Press, 1974.

Surrat, Jerry L. *Gottlieb Schober of Salem: Discipleship and Ecumenical Vision in an Early Moravian Town*. Macon, Ga.: Mercer Univ. Press, 1983.

———. "The Moravian as Businessman: Gottlieb Schober of Salem." *North Carolina Historical Review* 60 (1983): 1-23.

Taylor, Gwynne S. *From Frontier to Factory: An Architectural History of Forsyth County*. Raleigh: Division of Archives and History, Dept. of Cultural Resources, 1981.

Thorp, Daniel B. "Assimilation in North Carolina's Moravian Community," *Journal of Southern History* 52 (1986): 19-42.

———. "The City That Never Was: Count von Zinzendorf's Original Plan for Salem." *North Carolina Historical Review* 56 (Jan. 1984): 36-58.

———. "Doing Business in the Backcountry: Retail Trade in Colonial Rowan County, North Carolina." *William and Mary Quarterly*, 3d ser., 48 (July 1991): 387-408.

———."Moravian Colonization of Wachovia, 1753-1772: The Maintenance of Community in Late Colonial North Carolina." Ph.D. diss. Johns Hopkins Univ. 1982.

———. *The Moravian Community in Colonial North Carolina: Pluralism on the Southern Frontier*. Knoxville: Univ. of Tennessee Press, 1989.

Thyatira Memorial Association. *Inscriptions on Stones in Thyatira Cemetary*. Salisbury, N.C.: Thyatira Memorial Association, 1967.

Tillson, Albert H. "The Southern Backcountry: A Survey of Current Research." *Virginia Magazine of History and Biography* 98 (July 1990): 387-422.

Tise, Larry E. "Building and Architecture." Vol. 9 of *Winston-Salem in History*. Winston-Salem: Historic Winston, 1976.

———. *The Yadkin Melting Pot: Methodism and the Moravians in the Yadkin Valley, 1750-1850, and Mt. Tabor Church, 1845-1966*. Winston-Salem: Clay Printing Co., 1967.

Tryon, Rolla Milton. *Household Manufactures in the United States, 1640-1860*. Chicago: Univ. of Chicago Press, 1917; reprint, Johnson Reprint Corp., 1966.

Ulrich, Laurel Thatcher. "Hannah Ballard's Cupboard: Female Property and Identity in Eighteenth-Century New England." Paper presented at the Institute of Early American History and Culture Conference, Williamsburg, Va., Nov. 4, 1993.

Weekley, Carolyn. "James Gheen, Piedmont North Carolina Cabinetmaker." *Antiques*, May 1973.

Wellenreuther, Hermann. "Urbanization in the Colonial South: A Critique," with a letter from Fred Siegel and a reply from Joseph A. Ernst and H. Roy Merrens. *William and Mary Quarterly*, 3d ser., 31 (1974): 653-71.

Wertenbaker, Thomas W. *The Old South: The Foundation of American Civilization*. 1942. Reprint, New York: Cooper Square, 1963.

Wertheimer, Barbara Mayer. *We Were There: The Story of Working Women in America*. New York: Pantheon, 1977.

Whatley, L. McKay. "The Mount Shepard Pottery: Correlating Archaeology with History." *Journal of Early Southern Decorative Arts* 6 (May 1980), 21-57.

Whittenburg, James P. "Backwoods Revolutionaries: Social Context and Constitutional Theories of the North Carolina Regulators, 1765-1771." Ph.D. diss., Univ. of Georgia, 1974.

———. "Colonial North Carolina's 'Burnt-Over District': The Pattern of Backcountry Settlement, 1740-1770." Paper presented at the Southern Historical Association Conference, 1986.

———. "'The Common Farmer (Number 2)': Herman Husband's Plan for Peace between the United States and the Indians, 1792." *William and Mary Quarterly*, 3d ser., 34 (1977): 647-50.

———. "Planters, Merchants, and Lawyers: Social Change and the Origins of the North Carolina Regulation." *William and Mary Quarterly*, 3d ser., 34 (1977): 215-38.

Wilentz, Sean B. *Chants Democratic: New York City and the Rise of the American Working Class, 1788-1850*. New York: Oxford Univ. Press, 1984.

Winston-Salem Section, North Carolina, American Institute of Architects. *Architectural Guide, Winston-Salem, Forsyth County*. Winston-Salem, 1978.

Zea, Philip. "Rural Craftsmen and Design." In Brock Jobe and Myrna Kaye, *New England Furniture*, 47-72. Boston: Houghton Mifflin, 1984.

Zug, Charles G., III. *Turners and Burners: The Folk Potters of North Carolina*. Chapel Hill: Univ. of North Carolina Press, 1986.

Index